Irish Education:
Its History and Structure

For my wife Mary

Irish Education:
Its History and Structure

John Coolahan

Institute of Public Administration
Dublin

Published by the
Institute of Public Administration
57-61 Lansdowne Road
Dublin 4
Ireland

First Published 1981
Reprinted 1983
Reprinted 1985
Reprinted 1987
Reprinted 1991
Reprinted 2000
Reprinted 2002
Reprinted 2004
Reprinted 2005
Reprinted 2007
Reprinted 2009
Reprinted 2011
Reprinted 2012

British Library Cataloguing in Publication Data
Coolahan, John
Irish education
1. Education - Ireland - History
I. Title
370' .9415 LA641

ISBN 0-906980-119
ISBN - 13: 978-0-906980-11-8

Typeset by Lagamage Company Limited

Printed in Ireland by Gemini International

Contents

v

List of Tables

Preface

This book provides a short history of education in Ireland since the early nineteenth century and a guide to the structure of the Irish education system today. Not since the publication of T.J. McElligott's *Education in Ireland* (Institute of Public Administration, 1966) has there been a book with a somewhat similar scope. That book has long been out of print and in the meantime Irish education has undergone fundamental policy and institutional changes.

Among the small number of books on Irish education there are some historical works which treat of various aspects of the system. These include D.H. Akenson's *The Irish education experiment* (1970), a study of the national school system in the nineteenth century. That author has also published *A mirror to Kathleen's face* (1975), a study of first and second-level schooling from 1922 to 1960. Norman Atkinson's *Irish education: a history of educational institutions* (1969) was a general study of education in Ireland from Celtic times to the early 1960s. P.J. Dowling's *History of Irish education* (1971) also covered ancient Irish education up to about 1900. *Catholic education* (1971), Volume V in the *History of Irish Catholicism*, contained three sections on primary, secondary and university education up to 1960. There have been two recent publications, Stan McHugh's *The school survival kit* (1980) and Christina Murphy's *School report* (1980), which were primarily designed as guides to the system for parents.

The present book attempts to fulfil the need for a single work which provides a general history of education at all levels from the early nineteenth century up to the 1980s and which also treats of contemporary institutions, policies and trends in the light of their evolving historical context. In this way the formative influences on the system are related to current developments: as well as knowing about the education system there is a need to understand why it is

ix

as it is and the parameters within which change and reform operate. As such it is hoped that *Irish education: its history and structure* will be valuable to a wide range of readers. In a particular way it may meet the needs of trainee teachers/students of education who have frequently expressed frustration at the lack of a work giving an overall perspective on modern Irish education. Many teachers, parents and school administrators have also felt the need for a guide which places today's complex education system within its formative context, gives a general understanding of the dynamics of the system and facilitates coherent future development.

The education budget today, at about £700 million, is the second biggest element of government spending. The system employs over 40,000 teachers and affects the lives of all citizens in significant ways. About one in every three members of the population is involved in formal educational activities. With wider community involvement in education and a growing stress on cost-effectiveness in government expenditure, debate on education questions has become a central public concern. Apart from those directly involved — pupils, parents, teachers and administrators — informed awareness of the system and of educational issues is important for politicians, the public service and general taxpayers. Decisions on education tend to have long-term effects and it behoves Irish society to ensure that the policy decisions taken in the last two decades of this century are those that will best serve our increasing youth population and the needs of our society generally. The book may contribute to the debate and decisions by acting as a reference work and data resource.

The book, then, was planned with the needs of a varied readership in mind. It is structured to allow the user to locate particular items of information quickly and to sustain the overall perspectives within which particular items are understood. Part I comprises four chapters on primary, secondary, technical and university education up to 1960. Each chapter begins with a general introduction highlighting the main issues involved. The main lines of development of each sector are identified together with the political, social and educational influences which shaped them. Clarity and conciseness are aimed for and the reader requiring more detail is guided by means of date charts, references and bibliography to relevant source material. Part II covers the period from 1960 to the present, a major transitional one for Irish society and for education as well. The pace and extent of educational change in the past two decades has given rise to considerable confusion. This part describes the present structure of the system, outlines the institutional, legal, economic and social environments in which it exists and examines the changes occurring. It treats of issues such as curriculum and examination policies, management boards, types of school, third-level policy, adult education, special education and the teaching profession. The implications for future policy arising from the *White paper on educational development* published in 1980 are taken into account.

I wish to thank Rev Dr Donal Cregan, Dr Seán Ó Mathúna, Dr Pádraig Hogan, Áine Hyland and John Nolan who read a draft of the book and made helpful suggestions. I am grateful to Jim O'Donnell of the Institute of Public Administration for inviting me to write the book and for his cordial assistance at all times. My thanks are also offered to the editorial staff of the Institute and, in particular, to Brigid Pike. Of course I myself am responsible for any defects which remain in the book.

John Coolahan
University College, Dublin
Spring 1981

Part I: Irish Education 1800-1960

Chapter One

Primary Education

Overview

The late eighteenth and early nineteenth centuries saw a new and quickening pulse of concern on the part of many individuals, groups and the state itself in several European countries in relation to education. European society was undergoing profound political, social, economic and demographic change: it was experiencing the effects of events such as the industrial revolution, rising population and increasing urbanisation. These, as well as political and social values released by the French revolution and changing conceptions of childhood linked to the romantic movement, were among the forces which shaped the emergence of modern society. In the area of education the great new challenge was the provision of mass popular education and the significant new departure was the involvement of the state as the agency providing such an education. The role of the state in this area increased enormously as the decades progressed.

Countries such as Switzerland, Holland, Prussia, France, Spain, Greece, Italy, Denmark, Sweden and Norway all experienced significant initiatives in the state's involvement in educational provision in these decades. England, influenced by its prevailing political philosophy of laissez-faire, was much slower to involve the state directly in education. A privy council on education was set up in 1839 but it was the Education Act of 1870 which gave the state a more shaping influence on education. The Act of Union of 1800, which brought Ireland under the direct control of the government and parliament at Westminster, sought to bind Ireland more closely to Britain through a policy of cultural assimilation. Interestingly, however, Ireland was frequently used as a social laboratory where various policy initiatives were tried out which might be less acceptable in England. Ireland, which had a long-established tradition of British government financial support for

3

various education agencies, got a state-supported primary school system under the control of a state board of commissioners in 1831. At first sight Ireland would not seem to have been a likely place for such an intervention by the state. Factors which in other countries acted as a propelling force, such as the industrial revolution and growing urbanisation, were not significant issues in the Irish context. Ireland was also a difficult case in that strong animosities and suspicions existed between the denominations. The Established Church, though the church of the minority, thought it had a special position and a right to government support in promoting Protestantism. The Catholic Church, emerging from a period of suppression, felt that it was being very unfairly treated in not getting financial support for its massive job of educating the Catholic populace. The Presbyterians, who had also suffered under penal legislation, sought state support for schools of their own tradition.

On closer examination, however, there were many reasons which favoured the state action of 1831. There had been a long tradition of state legislation relating to education in Ireland. The work of various commissions, as well as focusing debate on educational issues, had also indicated a path forward for state action for which, at least at official level, there was general agreement. There had been a strong and well-recognised tradition of active interest in education evident among the general Irish population. In the context of post-Union politics the government felt that the schools could serve politicising and socialising goals, cultivating attitudes of political loyalty and cultural assimilation. The danger of separate school systems operating without official supervision needed to be countered. Further, theorists such as Adam Smith had urged that the state should promote literacy and numeracy at elementary level as an essential factor for industrial progress. Ireland, as a colony, could be used as an experimental milieu for social legislation which might not be tolerated in England where laissez-faire politico-economic policies were more rigid and doctrinaire. Thus, education was one of a series of social policies such as an organised police force, improved health services, a Board of Works, which were introduced in Ireland in the 1830s.

The achievement of Catholic emancipation in 1829 was a practical demonstration that Catholic demands for fair treatment could not be suppressed any longer and the national school system under state control seemed to the government the best way of directing educational provision. Further, a number of influential, informed and respected Irish members of parliament, such as Daniel O'Connell, Thomas Spring-Rice, Thomas Wyse, kept up the pressure for action. Members of the new Whig government of 1830, such as Lord Anglesey, the Lord Lieutenant, and Lord Stanley, the Chief Secretary, judged the time to be ripe for action and so this highly significant government initiative was undertaken.

It was the state's intention to operate a non-denominational primary education system wherein children of all denominations would be educated together in secular subjects and separate arrangements would be made for doctrinal instruction according to different denominational tenets. This effort to draw a distinction between secular and religious instruction was to prove a most contentious one: each of the denominations disputed it, seeing the whole schooling process as an extension of pastoral care with religion interpenetrating all facets of education. Moreover, in the context of strong denominational animosities and a live tradition of proselytism, the concept of a mixed education system would prove difficult to realise. The churches were anxious to benefit from state finance in support of schooling but each denomination strove to shape the national school system towards its denominational requirements.

This conflict between state and church on the control of schooling pursued a tortuous and labyrinthine path resulting in the state's retaining the concept of a de jure mixed system which, from mid-century onwards, became increasingly denominational in fact.

A related area of conflict for the Commissioners of National Education was the question of teacher training for the national school system. The Commissioners saw teacher training as their prerogative: they set up model schools and a training college in Marlborough Street in Dublin in the 1830s and from the late 1840s they followed this up with a scheme of district model schools throughout the country. These schools were pioneering ones in that they were the first schools in the United Kingdom which were established and fully financed by the state. They were schools with boarding facilities for the pupil teachers, completely under the management of the National Board and run strictly on the multi-denominational principle. As ordinary schools they were objectionable to the churches but as centres for the formation of the future teachers they were regarded as intolerable. The campaign for state support for denominational teacher training gathered momentum from about 1860. In its efforts to pressurise the government, the Catholic hierarchy banned Catholic attendance at the model schools and the central training college. Although only about one-third of teachers were receiving formal training, the state did not give state support for denominational training colleges until 1883, by which time the model schools had become white elephants.

The mode of financing the national school system was also to prove a matter of recurrent dispute. It was intended that the system should be financed jointly from central funds and local sources but, even from early days, the local sources never matched the sums envisaged. Central funds were given under a parliamentary vote which was monitored by the Treasury. From the middle of the century, with the hardening climate of financial accountability and stringency in public expenditure, the Treasury became increasingly dissatisfied with the heavy reliance on central funding. From 1870 onwards several efforts were made to secure higher levels of local funding either through voluntary effort or by levying a local rate. Linked to this was a desire to involve the local communities more in the management of schools rather than to rely on a single clergyman which had become the norm. This formed part of a general dissatisfaction on the part of the government with the mode of administration of Irish education which became more evident in the period 1900 to 1920. No success was achieved and the Treasury's reaction during this period was to limit expenditure from the exchequer on Irish education with serious consequences for the quality of the system. The wealthy classes in Ireland were infamous for their lack of support for and interest in the promotion of education. Apart from centralising control within a department of education under the control of a minister in 1924, little change took place in the administration and financing of national education in independent Ireland. Though Article 40 of the Constitution of 1937 emphatically acknowledged the priority of parents in the education of their children, a notable tradition in Irish education up to recent times has been the lack of direct involvement by parents and the general laity in the policies and administration of schools.

The state, through the National Board and, after independence, through the Department of Education, maintained control over the curriculum of national schools. Further, the Board published most of the textbooks used in the schools and retained the right of sanction on any other books proposed. The books tended to endorse the prevailing political and social orthodoxy and value system while being careful to avoid hurting denominational sensitivities. They also included a great deal of factual and 'useful' information along utilitarian lines. Until late in the century the books avoided specific reference to Irish contexts, thus helping to promote the cultural assimilation process which had been signalled by the Act of Union. The main aim of education policy was literacy and numeracy and the century witnessed the virtual elimination of illiteracy. Official census figures showed a decline in the numbers of people over five years of age unable to read or write from 53 per cent in 1841 to 14 per cent by 1901. Of course, the illiteracy figures referred to the English language, as the national schools carried on the hedge-school tradition of concentrating on English, the language needed for commerce in the money economy and for emigration, to the neglect of and disregard for the Irish language. This continued a decline which had set in prior to the establishment of national schools. There were three main policy initiatives with regard to the curriculum. One was in 1872 with the introduction of the payment-by-results system in an attempt to accelerate the drive towards the 3 Rs and to make teachers more accountable for children's progress. The new century saw the introduction of an altogether new programme based on child-centred educational thought. In 1922 there was a further radical change with the introduction of a programme inspired by the ideology of cultural nationalism. What was attempted following independence was a cultural revolution with the schools acting as the agents of change.

Throughout the nineteenth century the education pursued was predominantly bookish. It is true that the National Board conceived ambitious plans for agricultural education. They set up a farm training institute at Glasnevin and by 1870 the Board administered a scheme of nineteen model agricultural schools and recognised eighteen others which were under local management and eighty-three national schools had school farms and gardens attached. The schemes for agricultural education had their biggest impact in the middle of the century. During the last third of the century, owing to the failure to realise expectations and the more rigid Treasury attitudes, this education rapidly faded from the scene, existing largely as a book subject under the payment-by-results system. Industrial concerns took little interest in the national school programme though the late nineteenth century saw increasing criticism of its non-practical character. Such criticism was a factor which led to subjects such as drawing and elementary science and manual training being introduced in 1900. These were abandoned as obligatory subjects in the post-1922 epoch when the programme again was primarily based on the 3 Rs, with Irish being given priority in the life of the schools.

The state-supported national school system intended largely for the education of the poorer classes grew at an impressive rate. In 1835 there were 1,106 national schools with 107,042 pupils on the rolls, by 1850 this had increased to 4,547 schools with 511,239 pupils and by 1900 the number of schools was 8,684 with 745,861 pupils enrolled. Despite the great controversies which occurred at official level focusing usually on denominational issues, the parents, teachers, pupils, inspectors and managers at local level went on with the basic business of schooling, implementing with various degrees of enthusiasm the programmes and regulations of the system. National schools were not, however, the only form of primary schooling. Hedge schools continued as a dwindling system until about 1870 and schools such as those conducted by the Church Education Society and the Irish Christian Brothers operated outside the national system. Yet the national school became a landmark institution in the life of the Irish countryside, so much so that by 1900 every parish and many townlands could boast of having their own national school.

The school situation in the early nineteenth century

The history of education in nineteenth-century Ireland provides a most interesting study of the evolution of mass schooling and education during the modern epoch. Ireland had long had an honourable tradition of concern and regard for education perhaps most notably reflected in the great monastic schools which served as 'lights of the north' during Europe's dark ages, and the bardic schools which helped to preserve and transmit much of the cultural heritage of the people. From the early days of the Tudor conquest, English policy aimed through legislation and encouragement to promote schooling as an agency of conquest with a view to spreading the use of the English language and the Protestant faith. Legislation designated various types of school such as parish, diocesan, royal and charter schools to achieve these aims but no concerted and sustained campaign resulted and their influence failed to reach the mass of the people.[1] A different approach was adopted through a series of penal laws begun in the late seventeenth century which forbade catholics to send their children abroad to be educated, to set up school in Ireland or to teach Catholic children. Despite such harsh proscription Irish Catholics felt the need to retain some form of education as a vital agent in their cultural survival. Accordingly they developed a wide-ranging, if rather haphazard, system of unofficial schools which became known as hedge schools.[2] These hedge schools were very popular, many of the teachers being poets or ex-students of the priesthood. Some offered a wide range of subjects and achieved high standards, going beyond primary education. The government authorities were suspicious of these schools fearing their potential for political subversion and alleging immoral content in books used in hedge schools. Many hundreds of Irish youths from more wealthy Catholic families succeeded in emigrating to 'Irish Colleges' on the European mainland for higher education and for the priesthood. This pattern was established from the late sixteenth century.[3]

Except for the prohibition of Catholic endowments the rest of the penal legislation against Catholics was repealed by relief acts of 1782, 1792 and 1793. However, this period saw increased activity by many voluntary religious groups in the field of education. Protestant societies such as the Association for Discountenancing Vice, the London Hibernian Society, the Baptist Society for Promoting the Gospel in Ireland, the Sunday School Society for Ireland, were avowedly proselytising in intent and the fact that some of them got grants from public funds was a cause of increased concern to Catholic opinion.[4] On the Catholic side various religious orders became increasingly active in these decades in educational endeavour. Groups such as the Ursuline Sisters, the Presentation Sisters, the Christian Brothers, the Sisters of Mercy, the Loreto Sisters were laying the foundations of an educational apostolate which was to grow considerably as the nineteenth century progressed.[5]

Thus, at the outset of the nineteenth century there was much educational activity in Ireland and many and varied schools were provided by individuals and voluntary societies. By the year 1824 an official commission calculated that there were about 11,000 schools in Ireland catering for upwards of half a million children and staffed by about 12,000 teachers. By far the largest category of schools was the 'pay' schools, most of them corresponding to hedge schools, which numbered about 9,000 and catered for almost 400,000 children. The number of pupils enrolled in all schools, but whose attendance could often be sporadic and short-lived, has been calculated as amounting to two out of every five children of school-going age at that time.[6]

Emergence of the national school plan

The existence of such a level of schooling, most of it with no state support, might be viewed as admirable from one point of view. However, by now the government, the churches and many educational commentators had come to realise that the ability to read, write and do basic arithmetic was highly desirable for the general population. A range of motives from altruism to exploitation was behind the new interest in education, with literacy, in particular, being regarded as the great channel to wider knowledge. It was clear that a majority of the children were not benefiting from any formal schooling. Further, some government commissions held that much of the existing schooling was haphazard in character, lacked organisation and method, varied greatly in quality and was potentially subversive.

A number of commissions were set up to advise on education in Ireland, most notably those of 1791, 1806-12 and 1824-27.[7] Even in the report of 1791 one detects a prefiguring of the scheme adopted as the national education system in 1831.[8] It suggested a scheme of parish schools, managed by a lay and clerical committee of mixed denomination, schools to be open to children of all denominations, and clergy of all denominations to have access to give religious instruction. The overall supervision of the system was to be entrusted to a state board of control. The commission of 1806-12 also agreed with the idea of a system supervised by a permanent body of education commissioners. These would administer parliamentary grants in support of existing approved schools as well as establish new schools. This commission proposed a most significant principle which should guide the system. They felt that it should 'be explicitly avowed, and clearly understood, as its leading principle, that no attempt shall be made to influence or disturb the peculiar religious tenets of any sect or description of Christians'.[9] To aid the carrying into practice of this principle pupils were to be combined for literary and moral instruction while children would attend the separate religious instruction of their own denomination. This concept of a distinction between secular and religious instruction remained a cornerstone of a state policy but was opposed by the churches. This opposition hardened in the mid-nineteenth century with the churches fearing the growth of secularism.

The state did not see fit to put the proposals of this 1806-12 commission into effect but it did give parliamentary support to some of the voluntary societies engaged in education. Catholics were opposed to and highly suspicious of these societies because of their proselytising activities. There was one society, however, the Society for Promoting the Education of the Poor of Ireland, set up in 1811, which set out to be religiously neutral, 'divested of all sectarian distinctions in Christianity'. In the schools of this society, better known as the Kildare Place Society, the bible would be read without note or comment, hoping thereby that controversial doctrinal issues might be avoided. This approach seemed to come close to the principle proposed by the commission of 1806-12 and when the society sought government financial support in 1816 this was readily forthcoming. It received annual grants of varying amounts ranging from £6,000 in 1816 to £30,000 in 1831, the last year in which it got parliamentary support.[10]

In its early years the Kildare Place Society got the support of Catholics. As an educational society it showed great activity: by 1831 it had 1,621 schools associated with it, in which 137,639 pupils were enrolled. The Society adopted the Lancastrian monitorial teaching method, a scheme which had been designed to teach large numbers of children basic literacy and numeracy with a small teaching force and the use of the older children as monitors. The Society issued a series of textbooks and supplementary library books for its schools and operated male and female model schools to help train teachers for the schools. The Society also broke new ground in establishing an efficient inspectoral system.

From about 1820 Catholic attitudes to the Society changed. They were uneasy about the fact that the majority of the committee were Protestants; they declared that the rule of the Society which called for bible reading without note or comment was discriminatory against Catholics, for whom the Catholic Church required authoritative interpretation of scripture. It also became clear that some funds of the Society were finding their way to support overtly proselytising groups. Daniel O'Connell led the Catholic opposition to the Society, which refused to alter its rules in response to Catholic demands. Thus, it became clear that the most hopeful initiative for action through a voluntary society was not going to meet the requirements of the largest and poorest section of the population, the Catholics. The government agreed to set up an investigative commission into Irish education in 1824, which continued in existence until 1827.

This commission's report endorsed the earlier proposal of a government board to superintend a state-supported school system.[11] The channelling of public funds through voluntary societies was rejected as an unsatisfactory mode of operation. The commission favoured combined literary instruction for children of different denominations with separate religious instruction. These general principles were again put forward by a parliamentary committee in 1828.[12] Finally, the government took a direct initiative and, in 1831 through the agency of Lord Stanley, Chief Secretary for Ireland, the Irish national school system was established.

Administrative structure of the national school system
It is worth noting that in announcing to parliament in 1831 that parliamentary funds in support of education would henceforth not be channelled through voluntary societies but through a board of commissioners appointed by the government, Lord Stanley did not seek to establish a new statute. The political climate of the time did not favour such a procedure and, further, the lack of legislative prescription allowed more flexibility to monitor the success or failure of the scheme. The ideals and structure of the national system were set out in a letter from Lord Stanley to the Duke of Leinster inviting him to become chairman of the new Board of Commissioners for National Education.[13] The following were the chief points in this foundation document of the national school system. Opening with a historical review of proposals of earlier commissions Stanley rejected the mode of applying state funds for education through voluntary societies such as the Kildare Place Society. Instead he proposed a government-appointed mixed denominational board comprised of men of high personal character, including individuals of exalted station in the church. This board was to exercise complete control over schools erected under its control. A main aim of the system was to unite the children of different denominations and so applications for aid from mixed denominational groups were to be especially favoured. Local funds

had to be forthcoming for the aid of teacher salaries, the cost of furniture and maintenance, while the school site and one-third of the building costs should also be provided by local sources. Schools were to be open for four or five days each week for literary instruction while separate religious instruction could take place on the remaining one or two days. The Board was to have complete control over textbooks used and, by means of inspection, ensure that regulations were enforced. Funds approved by parliament were to be disbursed by the Board for such things as aid for building schools, payment of inspectors, gratuities to teachers, providing a model school for teacher training and publishing textbooks for schools.

The strategem of employing an unpaid board of commissioners for education had many precedents and continued to be employed in many areas of administration in the nineteenth century.[14] An obvious advantage of the board of unpaid members, chosen to represent the different sectors of the community, was that it would command a greater degree of public confidence than a department controlled directly by the government. It was also felt that the pooling of their knowledge and experience would be beneficial. Members of the Board were appointed by the Lord Lieutenant who also had the right (never exercised) to dismiss any member. In 1831 a board of seven Commissioners of National Education was established with a denominational representational balance of three Established Church, two Catholics and two Presbyterians. The Duke of Leinster, a liberal Protestant, was appointed chairman. At an early stage a Resident Commissioner was appointed. This was a full-time paid position, analogous to that of the permanent head of a department. With the aid of sub-committees the Resident Commissioner had responsibility for a great deal of the Board's work and prepared briefs for the final decision of the Board on important matters.

The control structure of the national school system reflected an interesting division of power between central and local bodies. At the top of the pyramid was parliament which retained final authority and voted annual grants. The Lord Lieutenant, assisted by the Chief Secretary, appointed Commissioners, approved rules and liaised with the government. The Commissioners of National Education held the important powers of distributing funds and approving schemes, of setting out rules and regulations, of controlling the curriculum, of publishing and sanctioning textbooks, of suspending teachers and removing managers. The inspectors acted as agents of the Commissioners to ensure that regulations were carried out. The legal titles to schools were vested in trustees and although originally it was hoped that buildings aided by the Board would be vested in the Board in reality many of them became vested in local trustees approved by the Board, or they retained a non-vested status. The patron was the individual who took the local initiative in having a school established and was usually the bishop or ecclesiastical authority of the area in question. The patron could act as manager or appoint a manager who, in most cases, was the local clergyman. The school manager had the right to hire and dismiss teachers, to distribute teacher salaries, to arrange the timetable, to oversee the general work of the school and he was also responsible for the general maintenance and equipment of the school. From this division of powers it can be seen that the most important powers remained with the central authority though at local level the manager had considerable power over the teachers.

Denominational reactions
It was a fundamental tenet of the national school scheme that it was to be a multi-denominational or mixed system. It was clearly intended that children of different religious beliefs should undergo their literary and moral education together and engage in doctrinal religious instruction peculiar to their own denomination on separate occasions. However, in a climate of hostility and suspicion between the churches and with fears of proselytism rife, Ireland presented a difficult arena for the success of multi-denominational schooling and, in fact, the early decades of the system saw much conflict and controversy on the issue of mixed education. The result was that by the middle of the nineteenth century the system had become increasingly denominational though the theory of its being a mixed system continued to apply. In the political hope of merging children of different traditions the state tried to establish a distinction between secular and religious instruction, a distinction which the various churches refused to accept. Further, the state did not want to budge from the principle of 'no state support' for purely denominational education. Thus, the stage was set for what turned out to be a long-running clash between the state and the churches.

In sketching an outline of the developments which led to the increasing denominationalism it is not possible to do justice to the complexities of the various viewpoints. The Commissioners, themselves, in the first instance, helped to put the trend in motion by not pressing Stanley's call for fostering and promoting mixed applications for aid. It seems likely that in their anxiety to get the system off the ground they were not inclined to be too probing on the mixed aspect of applications received.

Of the three main denominations the Presbyterians were the first to force significant changes in the rules in order to make the system more acceptable to them. Under the leadership of Dr Cooke, a forceful but illiberal man, the Synod of Ulster quickly opposed the national system.[15] Their reasons included the mixed nature of the Board's composition, the powers retained by the Board particularly over textbooks and teachers, the separation of religious from literary instruction, the removal of the bible as the central focus of all education and the right of clergymen of different denominations to attend the school premises for separate religious instruction. From 1832 to 1840 the synod carried out a strong campaign of negotiation, lobbying and intimidation which eventually, by 1840, achieved changes in the regulations which satisfied them and allowed them to accept the much-needed public money for their schools. The key changes were the right that non-vested schools (schools built without the aid of the Commissioners) should be entitled to funds from the Board, provided the rules by which they were conducted were approved by the Board, though not the actual rules and regulations of the Board itself. Clergymen of different faiths did not have the right to attend the schools in an ex officio capacity, but they could visit as general members of the public. A separate day no longer had to be set aside for religious instruction; this could now be given at any time provided advance notice was given. Hitherto there had been an onus on the manager or teacher to exclude children of a different denomination from religious instruction other than their own. This responsibility was now changed and such children need only be excluded if their parents specifically intervened to request such exclusion. These concessions represented a large departure from the original non-denominational plan but the Presbyterians were satisfied and from 1840 gave their support to the system.

The Church of Ireland, or as it was called, the Established Church, also opposed the national school system from the beginning, seeing it as a Whig measure which weakened the Established Church's position in Irish society. As the 'Established Church' it felt that it had a special prerogative in the area of education and it was opposed to sharing control of educational institutions with any other groups. It was opposed to the separation of secular and religious instruction and regarded the bible in its original form, as distinct from scriptural extracts, as central to all education. The Established Church was also opposed to allowing Catholic clergy the right to use school premises for promulgating 'popery'.

Expressing their opposition to the national school system the Church of Ireland made many petitions to parliament and endeavoured to convert politicians to their way of thinking. Outside parliament, agitation was orchestrated by means of mass meetings both in Ireland and England. Having failed to persuade the government, the Established Church set up its own school system – the Church Education Society – in 1839, in opposition to the national system. The schools of this society were initially well financed. They were open to children of all faiths and while only Church of Ireland children need attend specific catechetical instruction, all pupils were to be present at scripture readings from the authorised version of the bible. Some expectations were entertained that the return of a Tory government in the 1840s might lead to a restructuring of the national school system. However, by 1842 Prime Minister Peel made it clear that he favoured the mixed education principle for Irish circumstances. The existence of an alternative Church of Ireland school system, although not exclusively confined to Church of Ireland children but accommodating most of them, particularly through the south of Ireland, was ensuring that many of the national schools were attended by Catholics only. This emphasised the de facto denominational aspect of the school system. As time went on, the Church of Ireland found it more difficult to finance its separate school system and through the 1850s it became clear that some of their schools were no longer in a thriving condition. In 1860 the Lord Primate Beresford urged parishes which were in financial difficulty to make some accommodation with the national school system. This resulted in a bitter split but gradually many members of the Church of Ireland came to accept participation within the national school system. The Disestablishment Act of 1869 was a further propelling force and the numbers of pupils of the Established Church faith in national schools increased from 70,000 in 1868 to 86,000 in 1873. By 1880 such pupils formed 10 per cent of the total of national school pupils. Parallel to this the number of Church Education Society schools fell from 1,141 with 38,159 pupils in 1871 to 500 with 14,970 pupils by 1881.[16]

The Catholic church represented the majority of the population but had in the past suffered much suppression. It too would have preferred a system whereby state financial support would underpin a school system directly under its control. Realising the political unreality of such a prospect in the early 1830s, the Catholic church authorities, with notable exceptions such as Bishop John MacHale, tolerated the national school system. They saw it as a considerable advance from, and protection against, the traditional proselytising efforts of the societies whose activities had previously been supported by public funds. Bishop Doyle (J.K.L), who wrote extensively and in a liberal vein on education, saw many advantages in the mixed system for Irish circumstances.[17] Thus, aid was sought by Catholic clergy for large numbers of schools which were attended in the main by Catholic children.

However, it was not long before considerable disagreement emerged within the Irish hierarchy about the system. The first period of agitation was between 1838 and 1841 when Dr Murray, Archbishop of Dublin and member of the Board of Commissioners for National Education, led the group in favour of the system and Dr MacHale, Archbishop of Tuam, led the opposition which consisted of a sizable minority of the hierarchy.[18] There was public controversy and appeal was made to Rome for a statement on the question of the national schools. In January 1841 the Irish bishops received the papal view which said 'that no judgement should be definitely pronounced in this matter, and that this kind of education should be left to the prudent discretion of each individual bishop'.[19]

Catholic unease, which had been alerted by the changes in rules introduced in response to the Presbyterian campaigns up to 1840, was further aggravated by some developments in the mid-1840s. The Board was given statutory existence by a charter of 1844 and in 1845 it declared that in future any schools which benefited from Board building grants must be vested in the Board who would act as trustees. Further, the Board was now in a better financial position to move ahead on its scheme of district model schools which would be mixed denominational schools and have boarding facilities for trainee teachers, directly under the management of the Board itself. And in 1847 the responsibility of the parents for excluding children from denominational instruction other than their own was now extended to include vested as well as non-vested schools.

The arrival from Rome of Dr Paul Cullen as Archbishop of Armagh in 1849 heralded the start of a strongly-led Catholic attack against the national school system.[20] Attitudes in Rome had hardened against mixed education and the Catholic church had become more suspicious of the state's involvement in education. Pope Pius IX feared the increasing trend towards secularisation and liberalism in European society.[21] The synod of Thurles in 1850, presided over by Dr Cullen, issued several decrees warning about dangers in the national school system and stated clearly that 'the separate education of Catholic youth is, in every way, to be preferred to it'. Direct clashes occurred in the following years on such things as the compulsory use of scripture books in model schools and a restatement by the Board of its rules in 1855 which brought issues of dispute and unease to the surface.[22]

The Christian Brothers initially put a few of their schools under the National Board but withdrew them in 1836 regarding the Board's regulations as undermining their educational ideals. The Christian Brothers' schools were run on the basis of religion inter-penetrating the whole pattern of the daily life of the school and they also gave a more Irish orientation to the content of their textbooks than did the National Board. Several unsuccessful efforts were made, notably in the 1890s, to establish a rapprochement between the Brothers' schools and the National Board. It was not until after political independence, in 1925, that the Christian Brothers became part of the national school structure.

There was a significant change in the attitude of the Catholic hierarchy in the 1850s and 1860s, compared with that of thirty years previously.[23] A more self-confident church now demanded separate, state-supported education for Catholics as a right. Dr Cullen, who succeeded Dr Murray as Archbishop of Dublin in 1852, refused to accept Murray's seat on the National Board. Relations between the Catholic hierarchy and the Commissioners became more stern and aggressive. The church was determined to delimit as far as possible the mixed education system at primary level and firmly to oppose state plans to extend it to secondary and higher education. Pressure by the Catholics won them the right of having ten Catholic members on a Board of twenty commissioners in 1859 but such a concession was too little to stop the demands. In 1863 the bishops condemned the attendance of Catholics at any of the twenty-eight model schools which had been established. By 1866 there were strong indications of a more conciliatory line by the government which resulted in several concessions and which eventually led to the setting up in 1868 of a Royal Commission to investigate the whole national school system and to make recommendations for reform.

Growth of the system, 1831-70

With so much debate and controversy concentrated on the issues of control and rules, one might wonder if the system itself was making any progress. In fact considerable progress was being made and the basis of a wide infrastructure was being laid all the time that more ideological debate was going on at a higher level.[24] Table 1 gives a general picture of the expansion during the first forty years of the system.

Table 1: **Growth of the national school system, 1831-70**

Year	Parliamentary grant (£)	Number of schools associated with Board	Number of pupils on rolls
1833	25,000	789	107,042
1840	50,000	1,978	232,560
1850	125,000	4,547	511,239
1860	294,000	5,632	804,000

Source: *Annual Reports of the Commissioners of National Education.*

The growth of parliamentary expenditure on the system was impressive by contemporary standards and was one of the factors which led to the Royal Commission of Inquiry of 1868, as there was unease about whether the system was yielding value for money expended. A further cause of financial unease was that the extent of local funding envisaged by Lord Stanley had not materialised and central government was assuming the preponderant role in financing the system. Unlike England there was no tradition among the Irish landowning classes of public service towards education. Philanthropists such as Vere Foster, who provided much equipment, furnishings and books for national schools in the mid-nineteenth century, were the exception rather than the rule.[25]

Of the schools operating in association with the Board some had already been in existence before 1831 and had become affiliated to and absorbed into the national system. Some schools had received support for building and other non-vested schools benefited from the grants for teacher salaries and textbooks. The number of pupils on rolls seems very impressive at first sight but one needs to note that average daily attendance never corresponded to the total enrolled. For instance, in 1870 it was calculated that the percentage of those enrolled who were in daily attendance amounted to only 30 per cent. Further, the number of years spent at school varied considerably in the absence of compulsory attendance legislation: a study of census returns indicates that the early decades of the national school system did not witness a dramatic transformation of school attendance patterns. Further, many primary schools remained unassociated with the National Board; in 1871 there were 2,661 such schools with 125,182 pupils.

The scheme of textbooks envisaged in the Stanley letter proved a considerable success. The Commissioners published a set of reading books for five different grades which quickly established a high reputation for themselves in Ireland, and they even enjoyed a considerable export demand in England and some of its colonies. The books were not obligatory for schools but their cheap price as well as grants of books free to schools encouraged their use on a wide scale. As well as reading-books, texts on arithmetic, geography and agriculture were also published under the auspices of the Board. The reading-books contained a great deal of factual material rather than imaginative fiction, and lessons on English grammar, natural history, political economy, geographical material and biblical stories were featured. There was a strong moralistic and socialising aura to the books urging acceptance of the prevailing social, economic and political value system.[26] The books were well bound but tended to be long, the dense pages of text being occasionally lightened by half-page, black-and-white line drawings. The level of vocabulary was pitched at a high standard and in the senior books was far higher than would be deemed appropriate for the senior classes of a primary school today. A pupil's progression through the school was commonly denoted by the 'book' he/she was on. The Irish language was not acknowledged as a national school subject, even in areas where the living and sole vernacular of the people was Irish. Indeed for much of the century the books contained very little material relating to a distinctively Irish environment and were geared towards the British cultural assimilation policy of the time. It was the scripture lessons published by the Board which gave rise to most discussion and led to a serious crisis in 1853 with the resignation from the Board of the Church of Ireland Archbishop Whately when the Board refused to prescribe some of his scripture texts for compulsory use in model schools.

The neglect of the Irish language and of Irish culture was an important charge made against the national school system from the late nineteenth century onwards. It had already been made by some early opponents of the system such as Dr MacHale. (In this regard it might be noted that the term 'national' school referred to its nationwide role and not to any cultural connotations as regards national or ethnic culture.) The fact that the decline of the Irish language was already in evidence before 1831 and that the majority of parents favoured English, seeing it as a language of prestige linked to economic and social position, does not exonerate the Board from blame for its neglect of Irish.[27] Both by the omission of an Irish dimension to the school courses and by the assumptions conveyed through the content of the programmes, the system weakened the sense of cultural identity of the pupils and teachers. The particular plight of Irish-speaking children who did not know English was well highlighted, for instance, in detailed reports by Patrick Keenan as an inspector in the 1850s, but the Board refused to take action. In 1879 permission to teach Irish for fees outside school hours was given and, from 1883, Irish could be used as a medium of instruction in Gaeltacht areas 'as an aid to the elucidation of English'. Even at the turn of the century the bitterness of several Board members against the Irish language postponed the introduction of a bilingual programme until 1904. The national school system was one important factor in the decline of the Irish language in nineteenth-century Ireland. The policies adopted were in line with the cultural assimilation policies typically pursued by colonial powers.

The style of teaching which was most usual in the hedge schools was the 'individual instruction' method whereby the master dealt with individual pupils in sequence. It was a wasteful method from the point of view of maximising the use of the teacher's time, but it had the respect of parents who felt the teacher was giving direct attention to their child. In the early nineteenth century a teaching method known as the monitorial system or 'mutual instruction' system became very popular throughout Europe, America and places in Asia.[28] It was a system whereby very large groups of pupils could be taught by a small teaching force. The teacher himself did not engage in teaching directly but oversaw the work of monitors (senior pupils) as they taught their slightly younger peers along set, well-drilled lines. The children were divided into classes which were sub-divided into 'drafts' of between ten and twenty pupils who were placed under monitors. At a time when many countries were facing the challenge of mass education it was a system which recommended itself because of its cheapness and apparent efficiency in achieving rudimentary standards of education. The monitorial system was the one adopted by the Kildare Place Society in Ireland and in turn the National Board favoured the system for a while. As the number of teachers increased, however, a transition to a third method, 'the simultaneous method', took place. Now it was the teacher himself who taught the class group and monitors acted as teacher aides in the school. From the 1840s the simultaneous method was the one most favoured, though practitioners of the two older methods could still be found in Irish schools.[29] The simultaneous method, or class group method, remained the predominant approach right up to 1970 when there was more emphasis placed on small group and individual instruction to supplement class teaching.

In devising its school inspection system the National Board took the efficient scheme which had been pioneered by the Kildare Place Society as a model. In 1832 four inspectors were selected, one for each province. As the system expanded the inspectorate grew apace so that by 1838 there were twenty-five inspectors, by 1849 forty and sixty-six by 1858. The inspectorate was organised into head inspectors and district inspectors with two chief inspectors who had overall authority. The district inspectors had districts allotted to them, each covering about 100 schools. They were instructed to make their visits unexpectedly and their duties were extensive, involving a considerable amount of bureaucratic checking and report writing.[30] In this way the inspector acted as a vital linkman between the Board and the growing network of schools throughout the country.

Following Stanley's direction about a model school for training teachers, the Board opened a training school in Dublin for male students in Marlborough Street in 1838. In 1835 the Board had devised a plan for a system of district model schools to serve various regions throughout the country, some of whose senior pupils would go on to the central training establishment in Marlborough Street for a two-year course of training. Money was not forthcoming for such a grandiose scheme and it was only in 1846 that action began to be taken. The first district model school opened in 1848 and between then and 1867 twenty-five others were established. These were some of the earliest public schools fully financed by the state in any country. Many of the model schools were very elaborate buildings and the Board held high expectations for their future role. They were completely funded and managed by the National Board, contained boarding facilities for pupil teachers and were strictly conducted on the mixed denominational principle. The Catholic church authorities were opposed to this principle and were apprehensive about the formative influence which the experience of mixed denominational education might have on future teachers. In 1863 the hierarchy declared an outright ban on Catholics attending the model schools. The future of these schools and the question of state support for denominational teacher training were central questions for investigation by the Royal Commission of Inquiry into Primary Education (Powis Commission) which was set up in 1868 and reported in 1870.

A further example of the ambitious outlook of the National Board in its early years was its plans for agricultural education in Ireland.[31] Though not specifically referred to in Lord Stanley's letter the Board shared the contemporary widespread interest in scientific agriculture and the expectations of its potential contribution to improving practical farming. In 1838 the Commissioners of National Education opened their model farm at Glasnevin which, linked to the teacher training establishment in Marlborough Street, was intended to give agricultural training to national teachers. In 1840 an agricultural sub-committee of the Board was set up and devised a plan for twenty-five model agricultural schools. By 1847 seven such institutions had been established. The ravages of the Famine added urgency to implementing these plans so that by 1858 thirty-six model agricultural schools were operating as well as about sixty ordinary national schools with school farms attached.

However, the financial outlay was considerable and in a growing climate of accountability for public expenditure as well as official assertions of laissez-faire ideology, strong criticism emerged of the state's being involved in this type of educational provision. The agricultural schools did not live up to their early expectations and disillusionment set in. In line with these trends the Powis Commission in 1870 opposed the continuation of the agricultural model schools though it allowed agriculture as a textbook subject under the payment-by-results system. This was further endorsed by a Treasury committee report of 1874 which led to the disposing of the Board's agricultural model schools with the exception of the Albert College, Glasnevin and the Munster Institute in Cork. Agricultural education went into decline until the end of the century.

The Royal Commission of Inquiry into Primary Education 1868-70 (Powis)

While several groups in Ireland were pressing for a re-appraisal of the national school system, notably the Catholic Church authorities, the English Treasury was also anxious for a review. During the 1850s public expenditure on education had risen sharply: in 1851 the expenditure in England was £150,000, while in Ireland it was £125,000; by 1859 the figures for education had reached £837,000 in England and £294,000 in Ireland. In a political climate of control and accountability for public expenditure questions were raised about the increasing costs of education and the returns. As a result, the Newcastle Commission was set up in England in 1858, the Argyll Commission for Scottish Education in 1864 and the Powis Commission of Inquiry into Primary Education in Ireland in 1868. The Powis Commission carried out a thorough investigation into many aspects of the system and its voluminous report gives a fascinating insight into the working of the system about 1870.[32] It is desirable to take note of some of the Report's findings before proceeding to their recommendations for reform.

Although there were 6,520 schools registered by roll-number with the National Board in 1867, the number of schoolhouses was less and so the report dealt with information on 5,547 national schools. There were about 2,600 other schools providing elementary education though not supported by the National Board.

The report showed that the majority of the national schoolhouses

(77 per cent) were non-vested. Although vested schools were regarded as being better provided for, it was found that teachers kept one-fifth of all the schoolhouses in repair themselves. Only two-thirds of the schools were held to have 'good' roofs, floors and windows and less than half had playgrounds and enclosing walls. Over a third of the schools lacked toilets. About 400 schools were reported as 'deficient' in desks, lighting, ventilation and heating. More than half the schools had no pictorial charts and maps were deficient in about 700 schools; what maps and wall-charts there were, were usually provided at the teacher's own expense. Schools which lacked the basic amenities must have been unattractive to pupils and must have provided many impediments to the teacher's work.

The teaching force, of which 34 per cent had received formal training, was 57 per cent male and 43 per cent female. Teachers were graded into three classes with internal sub-divisions: 9 per cent were listed in first class, 25 per cent in second class and 49 per cent in third class, and 17 per cent were listed as probationers. The average annual salary of male principal teachers was £42, with female principals receiving £34. Assistant male teachers earned £22 p.a. and assistant females £19 p.a. By comparison the average wage of a labourer in 1870 varied from £16 to £23, if he was fortunate to get work throughout the year. There was considerable outward mobility from teaching at the time and within the period 1863 to 1867 the Powis Report calculated that 2,594 teachers either resigned for other jobs, emigrated or were dismissed.

The Commission was seriously disturbed at the standard reached by pupils attending the primary schools, concluding that 'the progress of the children in the national schools of Ireland is very much less than it ought to be [and] that, in Church Education Society schools, non-national convent schools, and Christian Brothers' schools, the result is not very different'.[33] Of the pupils examined by inspectors in 1866 it was shown that 45 per cent were at book 1 level and only 23 per cent were at book 3 level or higher. Many other aspects of the system such as poor attendance rates, quality of management, meagre extent of local aid and unsatisfactory teacher training arrangements aroused the concern of the Commission.

The Report of the Powis Commission listed 129 conclusions and recommendations, the chief of which were as follows:

— A payment-by-results scheme in addition to a fixed class salary for teachers should be introduced.

— The categories of teachers should be reduced to three and all teachers should have a contract of employment with a notice of dismissal clause.
— Local funding should amount to one-third of the Board's grant and should help provide more teacher residences.
— All state-aided schools should have management committees.
— In districts where two or more schools had been operating under Catholic and Protestant management for at least three years, with not less than twenty-five pupils on the roll, such schools should be adopted by the Board, subject only to the operation of a conscience clause.
— In localities where only one school existed, religious instruction should be at fixed hours and be confined to pupils of particular denominations.
— All teachers should have a formal pre-service training of twelve months duration.
— State aid should be extended to training institutions of religious societies under certain conditions, while the existing district model schools should be gradually discontinued.
— The National Board should discontinue the publication of textbooks but retain the right of sanctioning such books.
— School attendance in rural areas should not be compulsory, but provision should be made in urban areas for all children not at work.

The Powis recommendations entailed fundamental readjustments in the national school system. In particular, the Report tended to endorse the denominational trend, through easier recognition of denominational schools, accepting the principle of state aid for denominational teacher training and urging the discontinuance of the model schools. The financing and management of the system was to be on a new basis. Teacher employment conditions were to be altered and a change in curricular policy was to be initiated. The setting up of the Commission in the first place had been interpreted by the Presbyterians as a yielding to Catholic pressure. Now its proposals, particularly those touching on denominational aspects of the system, were seen as confirming this view and in the contemporary climate of anti-Catholic feeling in Britain it was politically inopportune to act on them. In the event the government was selective in its adoption of the recommendations: some were given immediate attention while others were acted on in a piecemeal and gradual manner but by the end of the century many of them had been given practical effect. The ones which were given immediate attention were those relating to payment-by-results, the teacher employment agreement, local funding and management committees and these last two became rather closely intertwined in the early 1870s.

The payment-by-results approach to primary education had already been put into practice in England in 1862 following the report of the Newcastle Commission of 1861, and it had also been suggested for Scotland by the Argyll Commission. This was one of a number of policy initiatives prompted by the prevailing utilitarians and classical economic theorists who, while allowing for state intervention at elementary level, were very anxious to ensure that the monies expended were economically and efficiently employed.[34] The belief was that the school system was not producing satisfactory results to justify the growing public expenditure. The remedy suggested was very simple and direct, namely, to restrict payment to those instances where results were clearly demonstrated through individual examination of pupils by inspectors in the three Rs mainly.

This crude and simplistic mechanism appealed to many in mid-Victorian society and it was no surprise that the Powis Commission looked to it for a remedy for the poor standards of attainment and attendance which it detected among Irish school-children. The full rigour of the English system was modified for Irish teachers in that the payments on the basis of their pupils' results were in addition to a basic (albeit inadequate) class-salary. The scheme was implemented on a country-wide basis in 1872 but teachers who looked for their reward had to wait for their money. In an endeavour to exert pressure on managers to grant employment contract agreements to teachers, the government withheld payments for the scheme until the teachers had been given a signed contract. After much politicising a compromise was reached in February 1873 whereby an alternative to the Board's form of agreement was allowed and so teachers got the benefit of a contract of employment as well as their results fees for the previous year.

The British government also used the introduction of payment-for-results as a lever in another direction. It only authorised payments on a temporary basis for a three-year period until such time as local funding or rates for education were levied to combine with educational funding from the central exchequer. Thus 1875 was to be a year of decision with teachers again being used as pawns in the political jockeying between church and state. The Treasury was anxious to have local rates for education accompanied by boards of management for schools; the church authorities were loath to relinquish the position of control they had obtained in the schools; and local authorities were not anxious to increase rates. Teachers badly needed increased incomes regardless of the source of the money. In the event a weak Act, the National School Teachers' (Ireland) Act, was passed in 1875 which allowed local Boards of Poor Law Guardians to levy a rate for education, which amounts would be matched by the Exchequer for results fees to teachers. The Boards evinced little enthusiasm in accepting their new privilege and less than half the boards, at the best, ever raised such local levies. In practice this scheme of local funding for Irish primary education petered out and no management boards for schools were established. The amounts made available from central funds continued to rise from £394,209 in 1870, to £722,366 in 1880, to £734,467 in 1890 and reached £1,145,721 in 1900.[35]

The payment-by-results era 1872-99

The payment-by-results scheme as devised and operated within the Irish national school system repays close examination and provides a good insight into the content and method of Irish schooling during the last thirty years of the nineteenth century.[36] As a system of accountability for teachers it laid down precise programmes, regular examinations, and encouraged a narrow and mechanical approach to teaching. Specific programmes were laid down in each subject for each grade in the school from infants to sixth grade. The obligatory subjects were reading, writing, spelling and arithmetic for all grades, while grammar, geography, needlework (for girls) and agriculture (for boys) were taken from third grade upwards. Provided success was achieved in the three Rs two extra optional subjects could be taken in the senior classes from a long optional list.

Irish was accepted as one of the extra subjects for which fees could be paid from 1879. As a spur to improve attendance a minimum of ninety (raised in 1875 to 100) days' attendance per annum per pupil was required to qualify for the examination and certain age regulations were enforced which encouraged more movement from the lower to the higher grades. A scale of fees was devised for each subject in each grade and a pupil at sixth grade, who was successful in all subjects including two extra subjects, could earn about eighteen shillings for the teacher. Regrettably, the average teacher, particularly in small rural schools, had few such pupils.

Each school had its own school year, as it were, dating from the time when its annual examination took place. This examination was conducted by the inspector who examined and tabulated the success of each individual pupil in each subject, using his own ingenuity in devising the tests. Samples of writing could be taken; spelling tests could be dictated to groups; pre-prepared arithmetic cards could be used to speed up the process; the reading tended to be somewhat of a rigmarole with parrot-like repetition. The system of examining did not encourage probing for comprehension or grasp of principles, and mechanical proficiency sufficed for passing and payment purposes.

On a statistical level it would seem that significant improvements were brought about under the results system. The percentage success rates in all the obligatory subjects showed impressive increases over the period, in all probability owing to genuinely higher standards, but also influenced by the growing familiarity of teachers and pupils with the unchanged courses and the nature of the obstacles to be surmounted. The level of promotion from junior to more senior grades accelerated so that while in 1866 only 23 per cent reached Book 3 or higher, by 1899 48 per cent of pupils were in Class 3 or higher, which, even allowing for a reduction in the course demands, was a more satisfactory balance between junior and senior. Illiteracy had also declined as revealed in the decennial censuses. In 1871 the percentage of people over five years of age unable to read and write was 33 per cent and this was reduced to 14 per cent by 1901, though this percentage rate was flattering as the illiteracy figures were not obtained in a rigorous manner. Bad pupil attendance had also been a cause of concern: in 1871 the average daily attendance of those on rolls was about 37 per cent but by 1899 it had increased to 65 per cent. The Commissioners on a number of occasions drew attention to the fact that the percentage of passes for reading and writing was higher in Ireland than in England or Scotland, though Scotland got the palm for arithmetic in the results exams.

Despite various caveats which can be made about these statistics, evidence of significant improvements in literacy and numeracy was recorded during this period. However, the system took a serious toll of various other aspects of schooling. Educationally speaking the evaluation of the quality of a school system by such a crude evaluation scheme was unsatisfactory. The system fostered a narrow focus both in content and method — course content became stereotyped with mechanical rote learning being applied. All sizes of schools in every type of location and children of weak as well as of high ability faced the same courses. The absence of a satisfactory attendance Act, even in towns, created difficulties for teachers. Further, the predominantly rural, agricultural community with the demand for child labour to do seasonal work — apart altogether from epidemics, weather, inadequate clothing — made sporadic attendance the norm. The role of examiner and clerk generally adopted by inspectors tended to foster bad relationships between inspectors and teachers. Many of the qualitative aspects of teaching such as introducing lesson topics, questioning techniques, establishing rapport with pupils tended to go unacknowledged. At a time when countries on the European mainland were aligning their curricula with evolving educational thought and societal needs, the Irish programme adopted a mechanistic system, divorced from the realities of life and work outside the school. It is probable that the undeveloped state of the Irish school system around 1870 benefited from the formally structured payment-by-results system but it was carried on too long and in too unvaried a manner. The end result was that it caused serious defects in Irish schooling at the time and there were few who lamented the abolition of the system in 1900.

The position of teachers
The teacher held a rather peculiar position within the national school system. At local level he benefited from the older tradition of the hedge schoolmaster, which held the teacher — the man with knowledge and learning — in a position of relatively high status. On the other hand, by the world of officialdom he was treated in a rather perfunctory manner and pains were taken to impress upon him that he ought not to have ideas above his station, which was the giving of elementary education to the children of the common poor. His main function was seen as cultivating approved moral qualities among his pupils and inculcating necessary levels of literacy and numeracy. It was believed that a little knowledge ahead of his senior pupils might suffice for the teacher. For many this involved a thorough grounding in the content of the Board's

lesson books as their main preparation.

The Commissioners laid down a detailed set of rules and regulations for the ordering of the teacher's work and behaviour.[37] These remained largely unchanged throughout the century and a brief account of them indicates a good deal about the role and status of the teacher. The persons preferred for teaching were to be people of Christian sentiment, of calm temper and discretion and they should be imbued with a spirit of peace, of obedience to the law, and of loyalty to their sovereign. Teachers were forbidden to take part in any occupation which might impair their usefulness as teachers and they were specifically forbidden to keep public houses or to take lodgings therein. They were also forbidden to attend meetings, fairs, markets and meetings for political purposes or to participate in elections other than by voting. In the execution of their duties 'the great rule of regularity and order — a time and a place for everything and everything in its proper time and place' was enjoined as a basic guideline. They were expected to be very accurate in their completion of attendance books, report books and registers. They were to teach according to the approved methods included in the officially sanctioned manuals of method and organisation. In endeavouring to promote the virtues of cleanliness, neatness and decency teachers were not alone to give good example themselves but to carry out personal inspections every morning of children's faces, hair and clothes. Other duties were many and varied ranging from looking after school requisites to sweeping, ventilating and white-washing the school apartments. Such attitudes towards and demands made of teachers were by no means unique to Ireland; most state systems conceived the elementary teacher's role in a similar way. Many interest groups placed demands on the teacher — the national board, the inspectors, the managers, the parents and, of course, the pupils.

In return for all the demands and duties, teachers, particularly from the 1860s onwards, felt that they were getting very inadequate rewards in terms of salary or recognition. In an effort to secure redress of their grievances teachers began to combine in associations and eventually these associations came together in 1868 to form the Irish National Teachers' Association (later Organisation). This was the period in which the Powis Commission was established and in which payment by results was in the offing, so the INTO was early called upon to exercise skill in negotiation and political manoeuvring and, despite some internal traumas, it succeeded in doing so.[38]

Although not successful in preventing the payment-by-results system, the INTO nevertheless ensured that from 1875 onwards any further improvements would be by means of class-salary rather than results grants. It campaigned strongly for security of tenure for teachers and its efforts contributed to the winning of teacher contracts in 1873. The establishment of a pension scheme for retired teachers was a further campaign which led to a successful outcome in 1879. The appointment of a new Resident Commissioner, Patrick Keenan, in 1871 led to more cordial contact between the Board and teacher representatives. As a result teachers influenced the changes in textbook standards which were introduced in 1873. It took considerable agitation over the decades before teachers secured the right in 1917 of being paid directly from the Board and on a monthly basis.

The question of teacher training was an issue around which much controversy had centred. The Powis Report expressed dissatisfaction with the small percentage (34 per cent) of teachers who had received formal training but it was also critical of the quality and duration of the courses provided. The Report urged that students attending the Marlborough Street College be allowed to reside in boarding houses under denominational supervision and it also took the important step of recommending state aid for denominational training colleges under certain conditions. Despite the seriousness of the situation these proposals were not quickly adopted and the situation was allowed to deteriorate further. In the 1870s the Catholic Archbishop of Dublin supported the establishment of two colleges for Catholic student-teachers, one for males under the Vincentian Fathers in Drumcondra in 1875 and the other for females under the Sisters of Mercy in Baggot Street, Dublin in 1877. Eventually, after considerable pressure from Church of Ireland and Catholic sources, the government relented in 1883 and agreed to give state support to denominational training colleges.[39] Courses were reformed and extended to two years for new entrants to teaching. At this stage only 34 per cent of all certified teachers receiving salaries from the Board had received formal training, Catholic teachers being in a particularly bad plight. The situation gradually improved so that by 1900 almost 50 per cent of national teachers had been trained. The number of training colleges had also increased so that by 1903 the

following training colleges were in operation:
— Central Training Establishment, Marlborough Street, Dublin
— St Patrick's College, Drumcondra, Dublin
— Our Lady of Mercy College, Carysfort, Dublin
— De La Salle College, Waterford
— Church of Ireland College, Dublin
— St Mary's College, Belfast
— Mary Immaculate College, Limerick

A new approach to national education 1900-22
As the nineteenth century drew to a close, dissatisfaction with the content, nature and method of education provided by national schools was being voiced from many quarters. A combination of factors and developments abroad and at home in Ireland contributed to this. A number of movements in educational thought, notably the 'practical educationists' and the 'child-centred educationists', were challenging traditional approaches to elementary schooling in these islands.[40] The one group felt education was too artificial, too bookish and narrow and they sought a wider curriculum with more scope for practical and manual subjects linked more obviously to everyday life. The child-centred movement inspired by the writings and works of Rousseau, Pestalozzi and Froebel felt that child-nature was being ignored in much of the schooling and sought a basic change of emphasis wherein the nature, interests and needs of the child would provide the central focus round which school courses would be framed. A new and much needed concern was being expressed for the education of very young children and the kindergarten system was influencing approaches to early education. Payment by results was fully abolished in England and Scotland by 1897 and moves were afoot to abolish it in Ireland too.

Sir Patrick Keenan, who had been a keen champion of the system, had died in 1894 and by 1896 the voices of inspectors were joined to the persistent demands of the teachers for the serious reform of the system. The 1890s saw several initiatives in Irish society directed towards improving the industrial and agricultural aspects of the economy. The Congested Districts Board had been established in 1891 to promote local crafts and trades along the western seaboard. The Irish Agricultural Aid Organisation founded in 1894 aimed at co-ordination and improvement in agricultural trading. The Recess Committee's report of 1896 urged educational reform. In 1899 the establishment of the Department of Agriculture and Technical Instruction was a clear indication of the widely felt need for a new direction and promotion along these lines. In this context many commentators felt that the national school system was too academic and not aligned to the needs of the society nor did it equip children with skills in many areas which would be needed as a foundation for further technical education and for improving Ireland's agricultural and industrial performance.

Thus, it was not surprising to find a commission entitled the Commission on Practical and Manual Instruction set up in January 1897. This Commission, more commonly known as the Belmore Commission, carried out wide-ranging inquiries into contemporary educational trends in Britain, Europe and America. It concluded that the Irish system, with its narrow concentration on a three Rs-type curriculum, was out of date and needed fundamental reform. Its general report incorporated much of the thinking and attitudes of the child-centred movement. It recommended a much wider curriculum range, a new emphasis on kindergarten education, the abolition of payment by results for the new subjects, more practical content in subjects and, in general, the Report envisaged the school as a humane and interesting place for young children.[41] The Report was adopted by the National Board and the new Resident Commissioner, Dr Starkie, quickly set about preparing a school programme which became operational for schools in September 1900, as the *Revised Programme for National Schools.*[42]

The programme went further and faster than the Report had suggested. Payment by results was abolished in 1899. Among the key features of the radically changed programme were the adoption of wide programmes which included, as well as the three Rs, kindergarten, manual instruction, drawing, singing, object lessons, elementary science, physical education, cookery and laundry as obligatory subjects. Subjects were not to be taught in a compartmentalised manner — where possible, lines of integration were to be pursued. The importance of infant education was especially emphasised and for all pupils it was urged that school should be seen as a pleasant, interesting environment. The content of subjects such as arithmetic should deal with problems based on everyday experience. Another new emphasis was that teachers were encouraged to adapt the general programme to suit local environments. This local dimension was also urged by means of pupil visits to sites of local historical interest, and also nature trips to observe flora and fauna in their natural habitats and the collection of local geological and botanical specimens. In the *Notes for Teachers* teachers were urged to adopt heuristic, discovery-type teaching methods.

Thus the new century saw the introduction of a dramatically different programme and a modern approach to national school education. Indeed the revolutionary nature of the changes was to prove a problem for a school system which in many ways was still undeveloped: there were significant problems of implementation. Some of the problems were the fault of the formulators of the new scheme, for instance there was a noteworthy lack of public relations in enlisting support, particularly from groups whose endeavour was vital for the success of the programme. Inspectors felt a sense of grievance at this time owing to the manner in which the programme was introduced, and also because of a restructuring of the inspectorate carried out by Starkie, which caused considerable tension. Teachers were pleased at the abolition of payments by results but felt that the demands of the new programme were impractical under the prevailing circumstances.[43] Many teachers were also aggrieved at new salary arrangements and at the high level of dismissals during this period. Managers were bitterly alienated by remarks by Starkie during a speech in Belfast in 1902 in which he castigated them for their alleged lack of interest in maintaining and equipping schools.[44] A report by an English inspector, Mr F.H. Dale, on Irish primary schools in 1904 bore out the fact that many schools were not in good condition and were deficient in teaching aids.[45]

An underlying difficulty lay in the lack of sufficient funding to back the new programme. The Treasury was not prepared to increase significantly the parliamentary grants to cover all the costs and voiced yet again its complaint about the small local contribution to educational expenditure. Ambitious new plans for the design and furnishing of national schools stood no chance of success. Neither was there a satisfactory resolution of the pupil attendance issue. The average daily attendance of those on rolls was put at about 63 per cent in 1900, improving to 69 per cent by 1919 but still leaving Ireland behind many European countries. Plans for continuation education and evening schools met with little success, though the expansion of local libraries through the Carnegie Trust in these years provided some facilities for self-education. New, expanded programmes were introduced for student teachers in the training colleges and special demonstration courses were given for in-service teachers by skilled practitioners. However, as only about half the teachers were trained, even under the old programme, the difficulties facing the majority of teachers were still very great indeed.

In 1904 a number of changes occurred: specimen programmes were devised as guidelines for different sizes of school; manual instruction was dropped from the curriculum; and bilingual programmes were permitted for Gaeltacht regions. Indeed these years saw striking efforts by the now well-established Gaelic League (founded 1893) to help give teachers a knowledge of Irish through the League's many activities, as well as through special summer courses provided in colleges devised for this purpose. The Gaelic League expanded impressively from fifty-eight branches in 1898 to 600 in 1904 and engaged in a wide educational programme outside the school system involving Irish language, dances, music, history and folklore.[46]

Despite the various difficulties which existed for the national school programme, significant progress was recorded in many aspects of the new scheme. Considerable progress was made in the area of infant education which hitherto had been a neglected aspect of Irish schooling. In a short time the new subjects such as singing, drawing, physical education and object lessons were being taught in almost all schools and in a fairly satisfactory manner. Other subjects which required more equipment and facilities, such as elementary science, cookery and laundry, were not so widely available and the standard of handling them was uneven.[47] School life for many children became more varied and interesting. There was less of the drudgery accompanying the older programme and new coloured teaching charts of fauna and flora and of societies in faraway places brightened the school walls. Although teachers had big demands placed on them, it seems likely that they too benefited from the greater variety of school work and the less rigid and bureaucratic form of inspection which was introduced.

Problems of finance and control, 1900-20

The sharing of responsibility for financing the school system by central and local bodies set out by Lord Stanley in 1831 and as envisaged by the Powis Report of 1870, was never satisfactorily resolved from the British Treasury's point of view. This dissatisfaction had surfaced periodically and was a particularly live issue in the post-1900 period. By this time the vast bulk of expenditure was coming from central sources while the system had become increasingly denominational with the great majority of schools being managed by individual clergymen. In fact the Catholic hierarchy declared in 1900 that the national system of education 'in a great part of Ireland is now, in fact, whatever it is in name, as denominational almost as we could desire'.[48] Possibly influenced by contemporary events, such as the setting up of county councils in Ireland in 1898 and the passing in 1902 of Balfour's Education Act in England, which set up local education authorities, Chief Secretary Wyndham gave notice in 1904 that he intended to restructure the whole Irish education system.[49] Two central planks of this policy were to be the introduction of local rate aid for education and the establishment of management boards for national schools. Such intentions were strongly and successfully opposed by the Catholic Church and Irish MPs. Further attempts at changing the financing and administration of Irish education included in the Irish Councils Bill of 1907 were lost in the rejection of that measure. Uneasy tension continued to prevail as Irish schooling interests were highly suspicious of increased involvement by the state, or arms of the state, in the control of education and the government responded with a parsimonious policy of funding which had serious consequences for the nature and quality of both primary and intermediate education during these decades.

The outbreak of World War I served to intensify the problems of Irish education in that any hopes of increased expenditure were dimmed and, on the other hand, teachers were feeling the effects of rising prices and inadequate salaries. Yet one effect of the war as it drew to its close was a vision of a brighter and more egalitarian education system with some aspects of social legislation attached. The Fisher Education Act of 1918 in England was a good example of the new type of thinking which was making an impact.

In Ireland two committees were established in 1918, one, popularly known as the Killanin Committee, on primary education and the other, the Molony Committee, to consider the problems in the intermediate sector. The key proposals of the Killanin Committee included the idea of levying a local education rate for education and the establishment of local education committees which would have responsibility for the upkeep of schools, the organisation of medical and dental services for schools, the provision of school meals and a school-books scheme. Restrictions were to be enforced on the employment of children of school-going age and compulsory attendance was to be introduced for all between the ages of six and fourteen. The Report urged the amalgamation of many small schools. Teachers were encouraged by proposals for significant improvement in their salary structure.[50]

Many of the proposals of both the Killanin and Molony Reports were incorporated in the so-called MacPherson Education Bill of 1919 which sought a radical administrative reform of the Irish school system. In circumstances which will be discussed later this bill never passed into law and, although some improvements took place in teacher salaries, no co-ordinated reform package was implemented for Irish education prior to the political events which led to the setting up of two states in Ireland – Northern Ireland and the Irish Free State.

Curricular policy in independent Ireland, 1922-60

A programme of administrative and structural reform of the Irish educational system had been proposed in the years prior to independence, as outlined above. Another very potent force, however, concentrated on the need for curricular reform, in particular the allotting of a much more central role to the Irish language with an Irish emphasis in courses in history, geography, music etc.[51] Inspired by the ideology of cultural nationalism it was held that the schools ought to be the prime agents in the revival of the Irish language and native tradition which it was held were the hallmarks of nationhood and the basis for independent statehood. Many people held that the schools in the nineteenth century had been a prime cause of the decline of the Irish language; under a native Irish government the process would have to be reversed.

The awakening of interest in the Irish language, literature, history, mythology, games, music and dancing, which manifested itself towards the end of the nineteenth century and which spread widely in the early years of the new century, was bound to lead to demands for their prominent inclusion in school courses. The rediscovery of the Gaelic heritage gave rise to feelings of excitement and enthusiasm and for many nationalists the main purpose of education in a free Ireland was the re-establishment of Gaelic civilisation. The concepts of nation, national culture and the role of the school as contained in nationalist ideology had formed a dynamic element-in the movement for independence from Britain. The years leading up to 1922, particularly after the Sinn Féin election victory of 1918, formed a period of heightened patriotic fervour and idealism and it was an accepted element of nationalist belief that, in laying the foundations for a new state, the schools would be geared to promote the revival and extension of the Irish language and Gaelic culture. This fervour lent an urgent zeal to policy changes but such a zeal can frequently do injury to educational systems which respond in a complex way to sudden changes of direction.

On the establishment of the Irish Free State it was the curriculum reform movement rather than the movement seeking administrative restructuring which got government support and attention. Energies were harnessed for a cultural revolution based on the schools. Apart from establishing a Department of Education in 1924 to co-ordinate primary, secondary and technical education branches under the one Minister for Education, the inherited pattern of administration, financing and control remained very much as it had been under the British regime. No commission was officially established to investigate the whole system of education and no effort was made to introduce comprehensive legislation for education.

Even prior to the establishment of the Irish Free State, the INTO took the initiative of convening a conference in order 'to frame a programme, or series of programmes, in accordance with Irish ideals and conditions — due regard being given to local needs and views'.[52] Invitations to participate in the conference were sent to a number of individuals and organisations and were accepted by the following: Aireacht na Gaeilge (Dáil Éireann's Ministry for Irish), the General Council of County Councils, the Gaelic League, the National Labour Executive and the Association of Secondary Teachers. Representatives of these bodies and the INTO met to form the national programme conference; the conference was rather unrepresentative as many groups and individuals did not see fit to attend. The Report of the Conference made a special mention of the advice tendered by Rev Professor Corcoran, Professor of Education in University College, Dublin, and he had an important influence on its deliberations. The conference met on 6 January 1921 and agreed on fairly wide terms of reference.

When the report of the conference was agreed and signed on 28 January 1922, however, on the eve of the transfer of powers to the Provisional Government, it was a slim document, primarily concerned with laying down attitudes and programmes for each class in each subject in the national schools. Very little attention was given to setting out the theoretical framework or curricular philosophy which was to guide the new programmes. The terms of reference concerning educational administration and school conditions received only the scantiest treatment. The report confined itself to proposing adjustments which would answer what were held to be the two main objections to the existing system: the allegedly overcrowded curriculum and the general feeling that the programme was 'out of harmony with national ideals and requirements, particularly with regard to the subordinate position held by the Irish language'.

To ameliorate the first problem the report recommended the elimination of drawing, elementary science, hygiene, nature study and needlework (for lower standards) as obligatory subjects. There were modifications in the programme requirements for history and geography, as well as in singing and drill. With regard to the second objection — the subordinate position of Irish — the status of the Irish language, both as a school subject and an instrument of instruction, was to be raised. Irish was made an obligatory subject for at least one hour per day in all standards in all national schools from 17 March 1922. Bearing political considerations in mind, a clause was added which stated: 'In the case of schools where the majority of the parents of the children object to having Irish or English taught as an obligatory subject, their wishes should be complied with'. Not alone was Irish to assume a new place of prominence in the course but as far as possible it was to be used as the medium of teaching. The programme for infants was to cause the most controversy: the report stated that 'the work of the infant school is to be entirely in Irish'; no teaching of English as a school subject was to be permitted in the infant school. For senior schools Irish was to be the medium of instruction for history, geography, drill and singing, and all songs in the singing class were to be Irish language songs. History was to be exclusively concerned with the history of Ireland and the chief aim here 'should be to develop the best traits of the national character and to inculcate national pride and self-respect'.

The programme was a radical departure from that which existed prior to independence and it became clear that the most important function of the school programme was the promotion of a knowledge of Irish. Teachers were presented with a particularly daunting challenge: in April 1922 of the 12,000 lay teachers in national schools only about 1,100 had bilingual certificates and a further 2,800 had 'ordinary certificates' which were not regarded as satisfactory indicators of proficiency in Irish.[53]

When Pádraig Ó Brolcháin, the new chief executive officer for education, informed the Commissioners of National Education of the intention to disband them on the eve of the transfer of powers, he stated the following new direction for education policy:

> In the administration of Irish education, it is the intention of the new government to work with all its might for the strengthening of the national fibre by giving the language, history, music and tradition of Ireland, their natural place in the life of Irish schools.[54]

This statement was accepted as embodying the new government's view in regard to national school education policy. The report of the national programme conference was accepted by the government of the Irish Free State and became operational for all national schools on 1 April 1922.

This programme set the general pattern and tone of Irish national education for a period of almost fifty years. There were, however, two other evolutionary stages in the early years of the state before the programme became fixed. Owing in large part to the difficulties in implementing the programme being encountered by teachers, a second programme conference was convened in 1925 under the auspices of the Minister for Education, Eoin MacNeill. The membership of this conference was more representative and it also received submissions and suggestions from a wide range of interest groups. The report of the conference was signed by all members on 5 March 1926 but it contained a significant note of reservation by the INTO representatives, seeking a limitation of the compulsory subjects to Irish, English and mathematics.[55]

The report of 1926 endorsed the policy of the programme of 1922 and it was not intended to diverge from it in any fundamental sense. What it set out to do was to indicate the steps by which the ideal of the earlier programme might be realised through a more gradual approach. Among its specific proposals was the acceptance of the principle of teaching the infant classes through the medium of Irish, though it modified the position slightly by allowing English to be used prior to 10.30 am. A higher and a lower course in the two languages were devised, the higher course to be taken in the predominant language of the school. This was a transitional measure until such time as all schools would be in a position to take the higher course in Irish and so adopt the lower course in English. Although the official policy was still to encourage the teaching of ordinary school subjects through the medium of Irish, yet an allowance was made for teachers who were not sufficiently competent to do so. Departmental circulars urged teachers 'to address themselves earnestly and courageously to the accomplishment of this important duty of extending instruction through the medium of Irish'. The other proposals of the report related to a lightening of requirements in mathematics, history and geography, and rural science was added for certain sizes of school as a compulsory subject. This report was accepted as the official departmental policy in May 1926.

The third stage in the planning of a programme for national schools occurred in 1934, subsequent to Fianna Fáil's becoming the government in 1932. The new Minister for Education, Thomas Derrig, announced at an early stage that he was committed to school programmes in which the Irish language and history would combine to foster a patriotic and Gaelic outlook. He stressed that the major responsibility for the revival of the language rested with the schools and he said he was prepared to lighten other aspects of the programme in order to advance the teaching of Irish and its use as a medium of instruction. Impatience with the rate of progress in the promotion of Irish in the schools led the Minister to issue a *Revised programme of primary instruction* to be implemented from 1 October 1934.[56]

The introduction to the revised programme contained no discussion of the reasons for change. The main changes were a reversion to an all-Irish day for an infant school and the adoption of a higher course in Irish as set out in the 1926 programme, for all schools. No programme for English was laid down for first class, and in the other classes the lower course in English was to be taken, which meant a drop in standard of approximately one year's school work. Rural science was dropped as a compulsory subject and mathematics courses were further lightened. The number of all-Irish primary schools increased from 228 in 1931 to 704 by 1939 but this formed the peak and by 1951 the number had fallen to 523.[57]

The policy devised in 1934 was to remain, with slight alteration, the policy for Irish national education up to 1971. An alteration in 1948 allowed managers to arrange English teaching for a half an hour a day in infant classes. The general programme offered a narrow subject-range, the stress was on handing on a cultural heritage in the 'Gaelic' tradition. All schools great and small, urban and rural, followed a common curriculum. Mastery of the Irish language was the primary goal of education policy.

A further policy change after 1922 was the announcement by Eoin MacNeill in 1925 that he intended to introduce a certificate examination to be taken by pupils at the end of the sixth standard course in primary schools. This proposal was endorsed by a report on school inspection in 1927 and by a report on technical education in the same year.[58] The Primary Certificate examination was introduced as an optional examination in June 1929 and covered Irish, English, mathematics, history and geography and needlework for girls. Interestingly the examination included written, oral and practical elements. However, the examination did not have a wide appeal and only about 25 per cent of eligible pupils ever sat for it and the vast majority of these were from large city national schools. In the early 1940s the government re-addressed itself to the issue and Eamon de Valera, Minister for Education at the time, announced the intention of making the examination compulsory. In tones reminiscent of those heard at the introduction of payment by results, he argued the need for accountability in teaching to justify public expenditure and the desirability of concentrating on the three Rs. As regards the opposition of teachers he remarked 'I do not care what teachers are offended by it . . . I am less interested in the teacher's method of teaching than I am in the results he achieves, and the test I would apply would be the test of an examination'.[59] The Primary Certificate examination became compulsory for pupils in sixth standard in 1943 but it now became a more limited examination, consisting of three written papers in Irish, English and arithmetic. This strengthened the tendency of stressing written rather than oral Irish. Despite the sustained opposition of the teachers it remained in this form until its abolition in 1967. With its narrow range and emphasis on written work, the examination tended to limit the work of senior primary level. This was intensified with some of the brighter pupils also preparing for the written county council scholarship examinations. Success rates in the primary certificate ranged from 70 to 80 per cent but many pupils who entered the sixth standard never sat for the examination.

Serious questioning of prevailing curriculum policy occurred on a few occasions. The INTO published in 1941 the results of an inquiry among its members on teaching through the medium of Irish which reflected considerable dissatisfaction, but the report got a frosty official reception.[60] The Commission on Vocational Organisation in 1944 urged the inclusion of drawing and rural science in all national schools.[61] Towards the end of World War II new planning for education was occurring in England as represented by the Butler Act of 1944, and in Northern Ireland as seen in the 1947 Education Act. In 1945 a departmental committee was set up within the Department of Education in Dublin with wide-ranging terms of reference to report on the needs of the education system. It should be borne in mind that at this stage many students remained on at national school after the age of fourteen years. For instance, in 1944 there were about 20,800 pupils in the age range fourteen to sixteen enrolled in national schools, about 4,000 of them in 'secondary tops' which were national schools offering the secondary school curriculum. Of the same age range only 16,400 were in secondary schools. The report of the departmental committee, presented to the Minister for Education in 1947, urged the restructuring of the school system so that the national schools would in future cater only for pupils up to twelve years of age. The pupils would then be transferred to a new institution — senior schools — which would offer a free literary and practical education. This restructuring would be linked to a raising of the compulsory attendance age to fifteen and later to sixteen years of age. Interestingly, it was proposed that the curriculum of the national schools was to be enlarged to include physical education, drawing and nature study as obligatory subjects. This report was not published or adopted as official policy and no significant educational policy changes took place at the time.

In the same year, 1947, the INTO published *A plan for education*.[62] Among its wide-ranging proposals for educational reform was one for a more child-centred focus for the school programme and a much wider subject range embracing literary, aesthetic, practical and physical education subjects. The proposals were not adopted and the relationships between government and teachers were very strained at the time. The new inter-party government elected in 1948 did adopt one of the INTO's proposals which had also been called for by the Vocational Organisation Commission in its 1944 report, and a Council of Education was set up in 1950. As its first assignment the Council was asked to report to the Minister on the function and the curriculum of the primary school. When the Council published its report in 1954 it called for no fundamental or radical changes though it did urge the inclusion of drawing, nature study and physical education as compulsory subjects, and it called for a more generous scheme of scholarships for pupil participation in secondary education.[63] Even these modest proposals got little backing and curricular policy remained much as it had been. Thus, the calls of the departmental committee, of the INTO, of the Commission on Vocational Organisation and of the Council of Education for changes in the national school curriculum gave rise to no changes in curricular policy.

Some aspects of administrative policy

There was no fundamental re-appraisal carried out in the early years of the Irish Free State of the leading characteristics of the school system which it had inherited; many of the assumptions underlying the existing system went unexamined. In January 1923 the Minister for Education, Eoin MacNeill, rejected calls for the setting up of a commission of inquiry into Irish education.[64] The school systems were reliant to a large degree, particularly the national school sector, on state funding and the new government made no effort to increase its control over the national or secondary schools, or to involve local authorities in their administration. Faith was still retained in the value of public written examinations for secondary schools though the more unacceptable elements of the results payments were dropped in 1924. There was no examination of the roles which teachers and parents might play in a reformed education system. The tradition of single-sex, single denomination schools carried on and became a more pronounced feature of the system. Social aspects of educational provision such as accessibility to secondary education, the provision of free books, organisation of free meals and school medical services, and the provision of special education received but scant attention. Harsh economic and social circumstances no doubt hindered the adoption of education as a priority area for administrative reform but underlying it also was the social conservatism of the body politic and of the churches at that period.

In the Irish Free State the de facto denominational status of the school system was recognised and no efforts were made to interfere with it. Successive ministers for education adopted the view that the state had a subsidiary role, aiding agencies such as the churches in the provision of educational facilities.[65] The new state had inherited a proliferation of small schools, badly equipped and badly attended.[66] Of approximately 5,700 national schools 80 per cent were one- or two-teacher schools. At this time many of the early national schools were badly in need of replacement or considerable renovation. Between 1922 and 1933, 343 new schools were built but in the latter year official returns stated that 325 new schools were urgently required and a further 750 schools needed reconstruction. The Killanin Report of 1919 had recommended the amalgamation of many of the small national schools. This proposal was frowned upon by the Catholic bishops who in 1926 held that 'mixed education in public schools is very undesirable, especially among older children'.[67] Ministers for education were also wary of the issue, yet gradually several hundred small boys' and girls' schools were amalgamated.[68] The physical condition of many national schools was a continual source of dissatisfaction and the improvements made always fell short of the needs of the time. As well as the replacement of ageing structures, the maintenance of schools had to be attended to and this also fell into decline in some parishes. Maintenance was the responsibility of the local manager and some were unable to discharge the duty satisfactorily. Despite this, however, church authorities firmly opposed proposals by the INTO to put the total cost of building and equipping schools as a charge on the state and to put maintenance as a responsibility on the local public health authority. Such proposals in their view would infringe their managerial rights.[69] The issue remained a continual source of friction. The first state grant for maintenance of national schools was not made until 1962. In 1964 the Investment in Education team found that the Board of Works had declared 22 per cent of national schools 'obsolete' and 40 per cent 'non-effective'.[70]

Pupil attendance at Irish schools had for long been a source of dissatisfaction. The new state introduced compulsory attendance legislation for children from six to fourteen years of age, which became operative from 1 January 1927. This led to an improvement in average daily attendance, reaching about 83 per cent by 1935. The further raising of the compulsory attendance age was provided for in this legislation and also in the Vocational Education

Act of 1930 and it was discussed on a number of occasions. A departmental committee reported on the issue in 1935 and urged against it, except in a few experimental areas. A committee on youth unemployment favoured the extension in an interim report of 1944 as did the departmental committee and the INTO in 1947. However, the upper age limit remained at fourteen years until 1972 when it was raised to fifteen. It was calculated in 1945 that about 41 per cent of the age range fourteen to sixteen years were in some kind of full-time schooling while 12 per cent of the sixteen- to eighteen-year-olds were in full-time education. Only a small proportion of pupils at national schools progressed to secondary education. For instance, in 1924-5 there were 493,382 pupils on the rolls of national schools but only 22,897 on the rolls of secondary schools. Of this number only 471 were in receipt of scholarships awarded by county councils. By 1935-6 the number on secondary school rolls increased to 35,111 of whom 1,098 held scholarships but, as this amounted to only about 3 per cent, it was not an impressive scholarship provision. By 1960-1 the proportion had not changed and of the 76,843 pupils now enrolled in secondary schools, only 2,609 held county council scholarships, or slightly over 3 per cent. It is worth noting, however, that the fees charged by some secondary schools were low and in some cases poor pupils of ability were taken free of charge.

The state took very little initiative in educational provision for the handicapped. The facilities available were very limited and were mainly provided by voluntary or religious societies, some of which got state support. The Department of Education gave some specific consideration to the matter in the late 1930s but no significant action followed. It is also true that for most of the period under review public opinion focused very little on this aspect of the education system and it was only from the late 1950s that there was greater concern, and this aspect is discussed in Part Two of this book.

Teachers and teacher training

The national schools suffered from an insufficiency of trained teachers. After independence the non-denominational training establishment in Marlborough Street was closed which was taken as an unkind move by Northern interests. The training of teachers in the Irish Free State was carried out in denominational boarding training colleges, supported by the state. In 1925 recruitment through the monitorial system was terminated as it was regarded as an out-dated system.

In the context of the curricular policies then operating there was an acute shortage of teachers with a fluent or competent knowledge of Irish, and making up this shortage was an urgent goal of the teacher training colleges. Although making Irish a compulsory subject in training colleges and the fostering of Irish as a teaching medium in the colleges would produce results in the long run, the immediate problem was how to equip existing teachers with a competence in the language. In 1922 there were about 12,000 lay teachers in Ireland and of those about 1,100 had bilingual certificates, which reflected a competence to teach through Irish or English, and a further 2,800 held ordinary certificates in Irish. As has been noted, this latter was not regarded as a satisfactory qualification for teaching through the medium of Irish so the task in hand was of great proportions. Attendance at expanded summer courses as well as vacations in Gaeltacht regions were undertaken by many teachers to develop competence in the language around which the school day was centred. Teachers had an important incentive to become proficient in Irish in that inspectors' grading of their work as 'efficient' or 'highly efficient' required good performance in Irish teaching, and such grades were coveted by teachers, and important for their career prospects.

A significant step towards remedying the shortage of student teachers with a fluent knowledge of Irish was the establishment of preparatory colleges — the first four of six colleges were established in 1926. These were residential, second-level colleges in which candidates for a teaching career would 'get a thoroughly sound secondary education, combined with the advantages of a collective school life lived in an atmosphere of Gaelic speech and tradition'.[71] Half the vacancies in each college were to be reserved for candidates who obtained not less than 85 per cent for oral Irish at the entrance test and 50 per cent of these in turn were reserved for native speakers of Irish who otherwise fulfilled the conditions for entrance. These colleges were established and funded by the state and placed under the control of Catholic religious orders or the Church of Ireland authorities. Most of them were based in or near Gaeltacht regions and helped to fill a shortage in the number of second-level schools there, a shortage highlighted by the Gaeltacht Commission of 1926. The preparatory colleges continued until it was decided to terminate the five

Catholic ones in 1961, after which they became ordinary secondary schools. In 1931 teachers were required to pass the bilingual diploma. Also from 1931, instead of the Easter scholarship examination, open competition candidates for teaching were recruited on the results of the Leaving Certificate and some oral examinations undertaken at Easter. This remained unchanged until personal suitability interviews for candidates were added in 1959.

National teachers had been very pleased with salary arrangements won in 1920. However, they were not to enjoy these for long and for several decades teachers were very aggrieved at their treatment under native governments. In line with public spending cutbacks, teacher salaries were reduced by 10 per cent in 1923. They were further reduced by 10 per cent in 1933 and 1934 and, although one of these latter cuts was restored later and the other was linked to new pension arrangements, teachers pressed without success for a restoration of the position they had enjoyed at the birth of the state. Relations between inspectors and teachers were lacking in cordiality and co-operation. Teachers pressed for an official enquiry into inspection which reported in 1927 that 'the tendency of the present system is to stress the disciplinary, assessing and controlling rather than the directive and helpful functions of inspection'.[72] This report, however, did not resolve the tensions.

Bad planning of the teacher supply in the 1930s and 1940s led to great problems for young teachers in getting permanent employment. From 1 October 1933 a ban was imposed on the continued employment of female teachers and this was not removed until 1958. The surplus of teachers was not used to reduce teacher-pupil ratios in large schools. The regulations for employment remained linked to average daily attendance rather than school enrolments until 1948. Some teachers at certain times of the year were teaching groups of up to eighty or ninety pupils. Overall there was a decline in the child population – the number of pupils dropped from 513,349 in 1933 to 472,145 in 1940. Student numbers in training colleges were drastically reduced and some colleges were actually closed for periods in the 1940s.

The over-supply of teachers, in a context of the government retaining existing quota patterns, was a factor in the depression of teacher salaries. However, the increased cost of living of the war years added an acute dimension to teacher dissatisfaction. Finally in 1946 the INTO called a strike employing the strategy of withdrawing labour from Dublin schools. After a long and bitter seven-month dispute the government refused to yield and at the request of the Archbishop of Dublin the teachers resumed duty.[73] Relationships with the interparty government elected in 1948 were more cordial and the setting up of the Council of Education as well as a scheme of conciliation and arbitration for teacher salaries reflected a somewhat more eased climate but no dramatic changes took place in teacher salary. The rating 'highly efficient' was abolished in 1949 and ten years later, in 1959, the rating system of inspection was dropped altogether and relations between teachers and inspectors improved.

Events and reports relating to national education (1800-1954)

1800	Act of Union
1806-12	Reports from the Commissioners of the Board of Education, particularly 14th Report, H.C. 1813-14 (47) V
1824-27	Reports of the Commissioners of Irish Education Inquiry, particularly 9th Report, H.C. 1826-27 (516), XIII, 999
1828	Report from the Select Committee on Education in Ireland H.C. 1828 (80) IV, 223
1829	Catholic emancipation
1831	Establishment of National School System (Stanley Letter in H.C. 1831-32 (196) XXIX, 751)
1837	Report of Select Committee on Foundation Schools etc, H.C. 1837 (701) VII, 345 (Wyse)
1844	National board's charter of incorporation
1850	Synod of Thurles
1859	Re-constitution of National Board giving Catholics half of representation
1863	Catholic ban on model schools
1868-70	Reports of Commission of Inquiry (Powis) — Report, H.C. 1870 (C.6) XXVIII
1872	Payment by results made nationwide
1873	Teacher contracts of employment
1879	Teacher superannuation scheme
1883	State support for denominational training colleges
1898	Report of Commission on manual and practical instructions (Belmore) — Final Report, H.C. 1898 (C. 8923), XLIII, 405
1900	Revised programme for primary schools

1904	Bilingual programme
1904	Dale Report, H.C. 1904 (Cd. 1981), XX, 947
1913	Report of Vice-Regal Committee of Inquiry into Primary Education (Dill) — Final Report, H.C. 1914 (Cd. 7235) XXVIII, 1081
1919	Report of Vice-Regal Committee of Inquiry (Killanin), H.C. 1919 (Cmd. 60) XXI, 741
1921-22	Report of National Programme Conference
1922	New national school programme
1924	Department of Education set up
1925-26	Report and Programme of National Conference
1926	Compulsory attendance legislation
1926	Founding of the preparatory colleges
1929	Primary Certificate (Optional)
1934	Revised programme for national schools
1943	Primary Certificate examination made compulsory
1947	INTO's *Plan of Education*
1954	Report of Council of Education on Function and Curriculum of the Primary School (Pr. 2583)

Chapter Two

Secondary (Intermediate) Education

Overview

Secondary education in Ireland in the post-reformation era was very much affected by the political and religious policies of the neighbouring colonial power. As a result of legislation or state patronage a number of secondary schools were established which were used as an *instrumentum regni* to foster the English language and behaviour as well as Protestant belief. Prohibitions were placed on Catholic secondary schooling and these were intensified from the end of the seventeenth century during the penal law era. With the relaxation of the penal laws in the 1780s Catholic religious orders began founding secondary schools without public endowment. For three quarters of the nineteenth century a dual system of secondary schools existed — Protestant schools, many of them benefiting from older public endowment, and Catholic schools operating with no support from public funds. The state-endowed schools were not, however, under the management of the state.

Laissez-faire economic theory drew a sharp distinction between state support for basic or elementary education, regarding this as of central importance to the state, and support for secondary education. In the class-structured view of education which prevailed secondary education was seen as a concern for the middle classes who, if they saw fit, should buy it as a commodity just like any other personal goods. Irish circumstances, however, were unusual and two special reports in 1838 and 1858 urged state support for secondary education but on the basis of the extension of the mixed denominational schooling principle which had been established for the national school system in 1831. The churches were opposed to such an extension of integrated education and practical difficulties were obvious, particularly in the context of boarding schools. Catholic diocesan schools, for instance, were seen as formative schools for future clergy, though they also educated others, and so it was preferred to conduct schools on a private basis unless the state was prepared to fund denominational secondary schools.

A compromise was arrived at whereby the Intermediate Education Act of 1878 permitted the state to give indirect funding to denominational secondary schools by establishing an examination board which disbursed funds to school managers on the basis of the success rates of their students at the public examinations. During the first two decades of the twentieth century the state was anxious to get a more direct role in the planning and operation of secondary schools but its efforts were fended off, schools struggling on in an unreformed state and suffering from gross inadequacy of funds. Ideas for educational reform were voiced from time to time but they were stifled by the economic and political power play.

Following the establishment of the Irish Free State in 1922 the mode of state financing was altered to capitation grants for pupils in 'recognised' schools and incremental salaries for 'recognised' secondary school teachers. However, the schools continued as purely private denominational institutions which were free to conduct their own affairs once they complied with the rules for recognised status. The state established no ordinary secondary schools and the initiative was left purely in voluntary hands. It was not until 1964 that the first state grant was given for capital expenditure on secondary schools. There was perennial opposition on the part of the churches in Ireland to state encroachment on secondary school management. Thus, provision for state support for secondary school buildings and for an inspection system were dropped from the draft documentation of the 1878 Intermediate Act and, although a circumscribed mode of inspection was eventually tolerated, the suspicions continued.[1] The state for its part was loath to devote public funds for private buildings without accountability or representation on management of the schools.

The curricular pattern of Irish secondary schools was firmly fixed within the humanist grammar-school tradition. Language and literary studies predominated with the classics and English getting pride of place though many pupils got some acquaintance with French. Mathematics was also offered and science was sometimes taught, but mainly through a non-experimental methodology. School prospectuses sometimes offered elaborate subject ranges but the reality did not always live up to the promises. Several commissions criticised the range and methodology pursued in the endowed schools, notably the commission of 1838 which sought to bring new utilitarian and practical subjects into the curriculum which would relate more closely to the economic needs of the community. However, the examination structure introduced by the Act of 1878 copperfastened the grammar-school approach by allotting greater marks and rewards to the core subjects of that tradition. Efforts made in 1902-3 to set up alternative courses grouped under the headings classical, modern, mathematical and scientific, failed to alter the prevailing trend. The courses pursued were linked to requirements of traditional university study, careers in the church and in the professions but did little to orient students towards careers in agriculture, industry or commerce. This coincided with a wider social trend among the middle classes to aspire to careers for their children in the professions or public service, with their promise of status, security and comfort, rather than in commerce and industry.[2] While reforms took place in the public examinations following independence, the written examinations continued to dominate secondary schooling. The main curricular change was the greater concentration on the Irish language and Irish history. Very little change occurred in later decades. A tradition of non-specialised general education prevailed. In its report on the secondary school curriculum in 1960, the Council of Education identified and endorsed the curriculum as 'a grammar-school type' — humanistic and intellectual in character.[3]

Unlike national school teachers, who had achieved structured salary scales, contracts of employment, pension rights, as well as facilities for teacher training and, in some instances, school residences by 1880, secondary teaching remained very much an amateur and unattractive occupation in the nineteenth century. Operating in private institutions many of the assistant teachers were clerics, intending clerics, ex-clerics or laymen from varying backgrounds. No regulations existed concerning teacher qualifications, no formal training was available or demanded of teachers, no inspection system was operated, no set salary scales existed and there was no security of tenure or pension rights. No chair of education existed in an Irish university. There can be no doubt but that such defects had a bearing on the quality of the education provided and reflected society's lack of concern about secondary education. Lay people did operate a number of academies, commercial schools and classical schools in various towns, conducted as private businesses and frequently geared to the examinations which proliferated in the second half of the nineteenth century.

It was only gradually, however, in the twentieth century that professional status was won. A registration council came into operation in 1918 and its regulations called for graduates with teacher training; in 1924-25 incremental salary scales paid by the state were conceded; in 1929 a superannuation scheme was implemented; and in 1937 a contract of employment with right of appeal was conceded to secondary teachers. The lay teacher's role in Catholic secondary schools, which were predominantly clerically owned, was usually a limited one; he was never able to aspire to being principal and he was rarely involved in the policy-making of the school.[4]

Secondary schooling conducted in private, fee-paying institutions was seen as very much a middle-class concern. It was the professional and merchant classes of the towns and established tenant farmers who aimed at giving their children the benefit and prestige of a secondary education; for most parents survival or an emigrant ticket were the main concerns. Schooling was not viewed as a means of achieving greater social equality; rather the poor and the working classes were largely seen by leaders of church and state as a self-perpetuating sector of society for whom a limited education in literacy and numeracy was deemed sufficient. Secondary school buildings varied enomously, from fine boarding schools in splendid parkland settings of old estates to ramshackle schoolrooms in converted dwelling houses. Access to the schools remained limited to a small proportion of the age range thirteen to nineteen. In 1871 the census showed that about 22,000 pupils were attending 'superior' schools, that is schools which taught a foreign language. By 1911 this had increased to 40,840, but this figure only amounted to 6 per cent of the school-going population. The vast majority of those who went to secondary school dropped out before completing the senior course.

The Dale and Stephens Report of 1905 calculated that only about one in ten of those who entered the preparatory grade completed the senior grade.[5] This also meant a considerable wastage of time because the level of competence in, say, classical languages which could be attained by those who left early was minimal, leading neither to enjoyment nor profit. Girls as well as boys benefited from prizes and results fees though the competitive regulations were different. Many schools, particularly convent schools, did not favour subjecting the 'maidenly modesty' of girls to the rigours of the examination system. Yet the percentage of candidates who were girls rose between 1879 and 1921 from 24 per cent to 43 per cent in junior grade, from 23 per cent to 39 per cent in middle grade and from 16 per cent to 36 per cent in senior grade. Overall, the number of examination candidates more than trebled from 3,954 in 1879 to 12,419 in 1921. Chance and circumstance, rather than any pre-conceived plan, frequently dictated the siting of schools. There was a geographical imbalance in the distribution of schools and the boarding school tradition became strongly established. As late as 1944 almost half the schools were boarding schools and they catered for one-third of secondary school pupils. There was also a strong tradition of single-sex schools.

A problem frequently touched on by the Intermediate Board set up under the Intermediate Act of 1878, was the lack of transfer arrangements whereby children could change from the national schools at young enough age levels to fit in with secondary programmes. One reason for this was that the various education boards were independent of each other and conducted their affairs with little liaison between them. Another reason was that national schools from 1892 onwards were free and were closer to the people in geographical location and ethos so that children sometimes stayed on well into their teens. National schools were excluded from the terms of the 1878 Act; later some national schools called 'secondary tops' offered the secondary school programme. The tradition of staying on in national schools survived after independence; for instance in 1944 there were more pupils between the ages of fourteen and sixteen in the national schools than in secondary schools. The idea of a meritocracy ladder whereby bright working-class pupils could be supported by scholarships, which became current in England at the turn of the century, did not get wide support in Ireland before or after independence. In 1924 there were 278 secondary schools with 22,847 pupils; by 1960 these had increased to 526 schools and 76,843 pupils, the greatest increase occurring during the 1950s. However, even in 1960 only about 3 per cent of the enrolled pupils held county council scholarships.

Before the Intermediate Education Act, 1878
Secondary education was not attended with the high level of conflict and controversy which focused on national education in nineteenth-century Ireland. It was the concern of a small minority of the population and, faithful to the canons of laissez-faire

ideology, the state was slow to assume a direct responsibility for its provision. Secondary education, usually termed 'intermediate education' at the time, was provided through a wide range of institutions which varied enormously in quality. There was no co-ordinating agency to lay down standards. The schools largely followed the denominational divisions of the community.

Church of Ireland schools were more favourably placed as some of them benefited from endowments which penal legislation had forbidden to Catholics, and generally Protestants were the better-off section of the community. Some of the schools were old foundations such as the diocesan free schools for which legislation was passed under Elizabeth I in 1570, the royal free schools, originating in 1608 during James I's reign, and the Erasmus Smith schools which owed their origin to benefactions of a Cromwellian settler, Erasmus Smith. However, these and other privately founded schools were never numerous.

The Commission of Irish Education Inquiry of 1791 found that a large proportion of endowed funds 'had been grossly misapplied'.[6] The majority of the schools were adjudged to be inefficient both in their educational endeavour and in their management. In an effort to improve the management of endowed schools the Board of Commissioners of Education in Ireland was set up in 1813 with authority over most of these schools. However, this unpaid body showed no great zeal in carrying out its functions and gave little close attention to remedying defects in the quality and range of education provided by the schools under its care.

Secondary education for Catholics was seriously hindered by the operation of the penal laws. Some of the hedge schools provided higher level education including the classics but these fell into rapid decline following the establishment of the national school system in 1831. During penal times Catholic students journeyed to Irish colleges which had been established at earlier periods in continental centres of learning, such as Paris (1578), Salamanca (1592), Douai (c.1600), Louvain (1624) and Rome (1625). Towards the end of the eighteenth century conditions became more favourable for promoting Catholic secondary schools in Ireland itself. The Relief Acts of 1782, 1792 and 1793 removed many of the penal disabilities against Catholic education and developments in Europe following the French Revolution tended to make Europe a less attractive destination for Irish students. Religious orders began to found secondary schools, seeing Catholic education as a vital area for an active apostolate. The Ursulines were introduced by Nano Nagle in 1771 and she went on to found the Presentation Sisters in 1782. The Loreto nuns were established in Ireland in 1822, followed shortly afterwards by the Sisters of Mercy in 1827. The founding of Maynooth College in 1795 removed the necessity for many aspirants to the priesthood to go abroad. St Patrick's College, Carlow and St Kieran's College, Kilkenny were founded in 1793 and heralded an era which saw seven more such colleges established before 1820. Clongowes Wood and Tullabeg were two Jesuit colleges which were set up in 1814 and 1816 respectively. The Christian Brothers were founded by Ignatius Rice in 1802 and, although their schools mainly provided elementary education for the poor, education of a secondary character was also provided for advanced pupils. There were also private schools and academies of various kinds which made secondary schooling available, albeit of an uncoordinated nature.

The establishment of the national school system in 1831 was followed in 1835 by the setting up of a select committee to inquire into 'the existing condition of the endowed schools and to suggest plans for their improvement and the advancement of education'. To some it seemed as if action on secondary education in Ireland similar to that which had been taken for elementary education was in the offing. This committee was chaired by Thomas Wyse 'the education MP' who had already played a central part in planning the national system. The Committee's report appeared in 1838 and, as well as containing proposals for a wide-ranging curriculum in the national schools, it projected a radical plan for secondary and higher education.[7] It urged the re-organisation of the endowed schools as well as their enlargement and expansion so as to become academies providing day secondary schooling. The report sought the extension of the mixed education principle of the national system into secondary education, financing of the new scheme to be a joint effort of local and state funding. The curriculum was to be a wide and balanced one, similar to what nowadays is termed a 'comprehensive curriculum'. It envisaged training for teachers who would also benefit from a salary structure and pension rights, and the efficiency of the system was to be monitored by 'systematic inspection'. The report suggested that provincial colleges should be provided in each of the four provinces offering higher level studies and also based on the mixed education principle, and four agricultural colleges were also called for.

This elaborate and, for its time, very radical plan did not stand much chance of being adopted and successfully implemented. The zeal of the committee was not matched by the many interested parties. Prevailing political attitudes tended to regard secondary education as a matter for the middle-classes to provide for themselves without state support. Further, the late 1830s saw much opposition among the three denominations to the concept of inter-denominational education and no desire to see it extended into more advanced schooling. The structure and condition of secondary schooling was so weak and undeveloped at this period that it would have been extremely difficult to adjust to the reforms proposed. The report was shelved and the system carried on in an unreformed and under-financed state. The idea of the provincial colleges, however, did have an influence on the emergence of the plan of 1845 for Queen's Colleges.

The Royal Commission on Endowed Schools presented a report in 1858 which found many faults with the existing schools and also supported the expansion and curricular reform of state-supported intermediate education, on the basis of the mixed education principle. The report urged that a general system of intermediate education should 'embrace instruction not only in the Classics and Mathematics, but in the English language and literature, foreign languages and the experimental and natural sciences'.[8] Schools should also offer book-keeping mensuration, drawing and singing. The government gave some indications of moving on intermediate education in 1859 but by this time the Catholic church had become much more firmly opposed to the extension of mixed education beyond the national school level. The expansion of Catholic intermediate schools under direct church control continued during these years with twenty-seven new schools being founded between 1850 and 1867, no mean feat in post-Famine Ireland. Public debate centred more on the national and university sectors and it was only in the 1870s that positive moves were put into action to make public funds available in support of intermediate education.

The census of 1871 gives an indication of the intermediate education available in Ireland at that time.[9] The censuses employed the term 'superior' schools for schools which taught a foreign language and in turn regarded this as indicating intermediate-type education. In 1871 there were 574 superior schools — 252 male, 162 female and 160 mixed sex — and there were 21,225 pupils in attendance. Although Catholics formed 77 per cent of the total population of 5,412,377 in Ireland in 1871, only 50 per cent of pupils in superior schools were Catholic. The quality of education provided was questionable for some at least, in that 1,389 of the pupils were under seven years of age, with a further 13,838 between the ages of seven and sixteen years. The census listed eighteen Catholic diocesan schools, twenty-four schools under male religious orders, seventy-five convent and monastic schools and sixty-nine Protestant endowed schools. The majority of schools were 'private' and they catered for 50 per cent of the pupils. There was also a tradition at the time among wealthy parents of sending children to intermediate schools in England. Apart from English the main subjects studied were Latin (9,440 pupils), Greek (6,605 pupils), modern languages, mainly French (13,205 pupils), and 8,595 pupils were studying mathematics with one or more of the foregoing subjects. The census report urged caution in interpreting the numbers for modern languages where they were taken more as an 'accomplishment' with the depth of study 'very limited indeed'.

The total of 574 schools in 1871 was a peak not subsequently reached again and, viewed from one perspective, it shows a live interest in such schooling prior to the state's direct involvement. The prospectuses of some of the larger schools of the time such as St Kieran's in Kilkenny, Clongowes Wood in Kildare, Blackrock College and St Columba's in Dublin, indicate a wide subject range.[10] Irish students were also known to perform creditably in the various public competitive examinations which became available from the middle of the nineteenth century. However, it would seem that the type of intermediate education available to the small proportion of the overall population who participated in the system suffered from many shortcomings. The various commissions of inquiry on endowed schools (Wyse Committee 1855-7; Kildare Commission 1857-8; the Rosse Commission 1881) were all critical of the quality of education and curriculum as well as of the administration of the schools they examined. It was not until the Endowed Schools Commission, which was set up in 1885 and continued its work until 1894, that the terms of old endowments were examined and reformed schemes devised.

Unendowed schools depended on fees and on any local contributions which might be forthcoming for the provision of buildings, teaching equipment and payment of teachers. Some of these unendowed schools did very creditable work and their pupils achieved positions of eminence. Yet contemporary criticisms of the work of some Catholic intermediate schools by Catholics such as Patrick Keenan and Professor O'Sullivan, President of the Queen's College in Cork, paint a rather dismal picture of the quality of the education provided.[11]

There is little reason to believe, however, that the education provided in the many private schools which existed excelled the others in quality. The Census Report of 1871 puts the position very forcibly when it remarks: 'By some means or other the higher intellect of the country is plainly being dwarfed; nor is there, we venture to submit, a moment to be lost before those upon whom the care lies should apply their faculties to the infusion of blood and spirit into the dry bones of public instruction in Ireland.'[12] In the 1870s it was clear to many that there was an urgent need to set intermediate education in Ireland on a more satisfactory footing – only small numbers being catered for, the financial support was inadequate and the standard of education provided was uneven or generally low.

The Intermediate Education Act, 1878

From the mid-nineteenth century in England open competitive examinations had assumed a position of great importance, being the means of entry into the civil service and the armed forces. The universities had set up examining boards for intermediate students and several other bodies such as the College of Preceptors and the Science and Art Department conducted public competitive examinations on a large scale. Irish students participated in such competitive examinations with considerable success. In 1860 the Queen's University established a system of examinations in Ireland which died out with the Queen's University in 1879. By 1874 there were thirty-seven Irish schools affiliated to the Catholic University, which had been established in 1854, and it paid prizes and burses to schools. Thus, the tradition of public competitive examination was well established prior to the Intermediate Education Act of 1878.

The problem in financing intermediate education in Ireland was finding the mechanism whereby the admitted needs of such education might be met without at the same time giving assistance from public funds directly to denominational education. In the context of the time it was not surprising that the resolution of the difficulty was formulated around a system of competitive examinations. In the 1860s a number of proposals had been made for a system of payment by results in intermediate education.[13] Patrick Keenan, as a special commissioner, introduced such a system in Trinidad in 1869. One of the colleges which benefited from the system there was St Mary's College which was run by the Holy Ghost Fathers, which congregation had founded the 'French College' at Blackrock, County Dublin in 1860. In 1871 Edward Howley, a barrister who had taught in the French College, was encouraged by Fr Leman, the President of the College, to write a pamphlet urging the introduction of a results system for Irish schools.[14] The establishment of payment by results in national schools in 1872 ensured that public awareness of such schemes was at a high level. Irish MPs such as The O'Conor Don and William Monsell gave their support to the scheme through which public funds could be channelled to intermediate education via competitive examinations. Sir Michael Hicks-Beach, Chief Secretary for Ireland, asked Patrick Keenan to prepare a scheme. As might be anticipated Keenan's plan went along the lines of a payment-by-results policy. Hicks-Beach accepted the principles and nearly all the details of Keenan's scheme and soundings were taken as to the probable reaction of interested parties.[15]

The Intermediate Education (Ireland) Bill was introduced into the House of Lords on 21 June 1878 and received the royal assent on 16 August 1878, having encountered little opposition in its passage through parliament.[16] Two significant amendments were added to the bill in that its provisions were extended to include girls 'as far as conveniently may be' and Celtic language and literature were added to the list of approved subjects. Despite misgivings by Keenan about its suitability, the administrative strategy of the unpaid mixed denominational board was again employed. By the terms of the Act an unpaid board of seven commissioners was to be appointed and aided by two full-time assistant commissioners. The board was to institute and administer a system of public examinations in secular subjects on the results of which fees would be paid to school managers who fulfilled the board's regulations, while prizes, exhibitions and certificates would be made available to successful pupils. The board had a million pounds allocated to it, not directly from Treasury funds but from the funds of the disestablished church, and it was the annual interest arising from this sum which was to finance the operation of the results examinations. The Act was a significant break in the laissez-faire ideology and preceded by a quarter century the formal acceptance of the principle of secondary education supported from public funds incorporated in the English Education Act of 1902.

The first examinations under the Intermediate Board took place in June 1879 with boys and girls in separate centres. At first there were three grades of examination — junior, middle and senior — and a preparatory grade was added from 1892 to 1913. The subjects were arranged in seven divisions as follows: Greek, Latin, English, modern languages, mathematics, natural sciences, music and drawing. The subjects were not treated equally, however, because subjects such as the classics and English received more favourable mark weighting and higher results fees. This gave a 'grammar school' or academic-type bias to the programme which persisted until the end of the results era, despite later efforts to redress the trend.

Ostensibly the Act was non-denominational and gave no direct support to denominational education as such; schools were required to exercise a conscience clause whereby pupils whose parents objected to the form of religious instruction in the school were to be excluded from such instruction. In reality, however, the Act did support denominational secondary education. Once schools fulfilled the examination requirements and presented students who passed the examinations, then managers and pupils were entitled to their rewards with no further investigation of how the schools managed their affairs.

The Act had many limitations as an educational measure. It made no effort to re-organise existing endowments and make them more generally available for intermediate education. The board's functions were limited to devising programmes, conducting the examinations and paying awards. The Act took no cognisance of the need to support, equip or found schools. The Act made no mention of teachers and laid down no conditions for teacher competence or remuneration, nor did it support any schemes for teacher training. As the board was quickly to discover the financial arrangements under the Act were to prove very inadequate for the limited functions assigned to it and the board's greatest and perennial problem was how to balance its books. The passage of time served only to highlight the many deficiencies in Irish intermediate education which the Act failed to resolve.

The board exercised a great influence on the content and method of intermediate education throughout the country, through its control of the examinations. Schools had to respond to any changes in the programmes of the examinations, if they were to receive public money; programmes became increasingly defined and itemised in the years prior to 1900 and, when coupled with examiners' reports issued from 1888, they dictated a great deal of what was being done in schools. The outcome of the examinations, particularly in the early years, was awaited with extraordinary interest, the public seeing them as contests not alone between pupils but between types of school. The unhealthy rivalry was fanned by the publication of results setting forth the names of successful pupils and the schools they attended.

The inadequate funds at the disposal of the board, amounting to about only £32,000 per annum, caused immediate problems. About £12,000 went on administration and about £8,000 on pupil prizes, leaving about £12,000 for distribution to school managers. The board employed various stratagems to stretch the small sum available to cover demands, such as the reduction of the results fees originally envisaged, changes in the rules for passing, and the recalibration of the examination successes so that the expenditure involved would match the original budgeted figure. An extra grant became available under the Local Taxation Act of 1890 and this eased the financial strain for a period but it re-asserted itself and the fundamental weakness caused by lack of funds continued to haunt Irish intermediate education for decades to come.

The finance available was a more significant factor in determining the examination results awards than pupils' abilities. The graph showing the success rates for pupils over the years is not impressive. It reached an all-time high in 1880 with 72 per cent success but for most of the 1880s it was in the low 60 per cent range, dropping below 60 per cent for most of the following decade. During the last eighteen years of the system it topped 60 per cent on only four occasions and, strange to relate, it fell below 50 per cent for three years. A further cause of disquiet was that the vast preponderance of the pupils being presented were examined at the junior levels. In 1880 the percentage examined at senior grade amounted to 9.5 per cent of the total examined and by 1898 this had dropped to 4.4 per cent, while in the same year about 83 per cent of pupils were at preparatory or junior grade.[17] This would suggest that the vast majority benefited only from the early stages of intermediate education. There were also many pupils in the schools who were not presented for examination at all and for whom, of course, no results fees were available. The education of academically weak pupils suffered because of the highly competitive examination structure which prevailed.

The main increase in the number of pupils in superior schools took place in the decade 1891 to 1901, when the number rose from 24,271 to 35,306. The introduction of the preparatory grade in 1892 would seem to have been a key factor in the increase which was also matched by an increase in Christian Brother pupils from 2,837 to 10,160. By 1901 Catholics formed 68 per cent of the pupils in superior schools and, although male and female numbers had been close to equal in 1871, the ratio of male to female had increased to 2:1 by 1901. Despite the extra marks and results fees favouring Greek, it had gone into decline, with only 3,727 pupils studying it, and Irish on the other hand had become very popular.[18]

The Commission on Intermediate Education, 1898 (Palles)

After twenty years' experience of the system established under the Intermediate Education Act, the Commissioners 'felt satisfied that there are many defects in the system', and called on the lord lieutenant to establish a commission of inquiry into its operation and the effects of existing legislation. The lord lieutenant, Lord Cadogan, appointed the Intermediate Board itself to act as the special commission and its report became available in August 1899.[19] Whatever about its composition, the setting up of the commission provided a valuable opportunity for appraisal of the system and the evidence submitted to the commission contained revealing insights into the attitudes of those closely involved in intermediate education.

Many witnesses praised the increased financial support for intermediate education which had resulted from the 1878 Act and pointed to increased student numbers getting intermediate-type education. The number of pupils in 'superior schools' rose from about 22,000 in 1871 to about 35,000 by 1901, and the number of candidates for the board's examinations had increased from 3,954 in 1879 to 9,073 in 1898. The system was also praised for the impartiality with which the examinations were conducted and some felt that the examinations gave a valuable stimulus to the work of teachers and pupils. However, many defects were also emphasised. These included the cramming tendencies, the unbalanced nature of the curriculum, the heavy stress on memory work, unhealthy rivalry and competition, bad effects on teaching, many schools being driven into a set groove, neglect of weak pupils and, one fundamental defect, the narrow basis on which very limited public money was made available in support of intermediate education in Ireland.

The report of the commission seemed to point to a root and branch reform when it remarked that the system 'should be subjected to a thorough and public examination, not only as to its practical working, but also as to the principles upon which it was based'. However, its recommendations amounted only to modifications of the existing system, many of which turned out to be impracticable. The Intermediate Education (Ireland) Amendment Act was passed in 1900. This Act allowed the board to frame rules for the distribution of its funds provided the approval of the lord lieutenant and parliament was secured, whereas hitherto it had been bound by the schedule of the 1878 Act. The board membership was raised from seven to twelve members and it was given the power to appoint inspectors.

New regulations were drawn up which came into operation in 1902. In an effort to reduce competitiveness for the average student a special honours examination for prizes was taken by students aspiring to such awards at the end of the pass examination in all grades except preparatory. In an effort to adjust curricular imbalance, all subjects were awarded equal marks and students could opt for a grammar school course or a modern course (extended in 1903 to include classical, modern, mathematical and scientific courses). Results fees on individual performances were exchanged for capitation fees for all pupils in the schools, based on the proportion of pupils on the school roll who presented for and passed the examinations. Six temporary inspectors were employed to report on schools. Payments to schools were to be calculated on a triennial average.

Most of this rather cumbersome mechanism, which was aimed at modifying the results system within the general framework of the existing scheme, foundered. One result of the experiments was the need to 'doctor' the dramatic failure rate in the 1902 examinations and within two years there was a reversion to the main features of the old examination results fees pattern. The temporary inspectors ceased to operate and the question of an inspectorate became a bitter issue between the various bodies involved. The government wanted the inspectorate to replace examinations, while many schools were suspicious of the powers of an inspectorate, acting as an agent of the state, to inquire into private institutions. Eventually in 1909, following a threat of resignation by the board, approval was given for the appointment of permanent inspectors. These operated in conjunction with the examinations, although the preparatory grade examination was dropped in 1913 and payments were made on a capitation basis for pupils at this level on the reports of the inspectors.

As regards the moves towards diversification of courses the material condition of many schools, small student numbers, insufficient qualified staff, poor equipment and resources all combined to make it difficult for schools to offer varied courses catering for different student aptitudes and aspirations. The intervention of headmasters' associations in 1903 further weakened the possibility of the group subject scheme.

Some improvements did survive the changes of 1902 including the more even distribution of marks to various subjects, more freedom in the use of textbooks was allowed to schools because courses were not so narrowly specified, the names of successful pupils were no longer published or identified with named schools, science and drawing came under the aegis of the newly established (1899) Department of Agriculture and Technical Instruction. This department used an inspection system for giving capitation awards to schools and under the new arrangements these subjects got a much needed injection of support and greatly increased numbers studied these subjects. Science also benefited from the Intermediate Board grants for laboratory equipment which became available from 1902.

Report of Dale and Stephens, 1905

By 1904 the intermediate education system had, to a large extent, relapsed into the state of ill-health which had led to the setting up of the commission of 1898 and considerable dissatisfaction attended the affairs of the board. In 1904 the government appointed two English inspectors, Messrs Dale and Stephens, with wide terms of reference, to make a thorough survey of the intermediate education system in Ireland and to make recommendations. Their report of 1905 was a valuable analysis of existing defects and it made clear and unambiguous suggestions for reform.[20] It found 'grave educational defects in the results fees system' and condemned it unhesitatingly. It found conclusive evidence 'that the group system has not produced a proper differentiation of curricula in schools'. The distribution of schools in Ireland was very uneven, Connacht being particularly badly served with only 728 pupils in intermediate schools. The material condition of many schools hindered satisfactory work. The small proportion of graduates on school staffs and the absence of formal teacher training were further hindrances. The report noted the lack of pupil progression in the schools, only one out of every ten who sat for preparatory grade proceeding to senior grade.

The main recommendations of the Dale and Stephens report can be summarised as follows. They called for the setting up of a central authority to co-ordinate education at different levels of schooling. An inspection system should be instituted which, among other duties, would testify whether schools reached the 'recognised' status of the central authority in terms of premises, staff, school fees and educational endeavour. There should be block capitation grants to each 'recognised school'. The abolition of examination results fees was urged and their replacement by non-monetary junior and senior certificate examinations, to be taken by pupils about the ages of sixteen and eighteen years. Schools should formulate their own curricula with guidance from the central authority and subject to its approval. Proposals for a teacher registration council were set out.

These recommendations were a blueprint for an intermediate education system in Ireland altogether different from that adopted in 1878. However, the recommendations of Dale and Stephens were not adopted. One important reason for this was a suspicion by school authorities of the extension of state involvement in intermediate education which the proposals implied. Plans for reorganisation of Irish education as announced by Chief Secretary Wyndham in 1904 were being firmly opposed. In the absence of remedial measures the Intermediate Board continued to juggle with its regulations and passing rates so as to stretch its finances to meet the demands. This called for considerable ingenuity, 1910 being a particularly bad year when, after other expenses were paid, the board had only £18,200 for distribution to schools. In 1911 the varying amounts accruing from the Local Taxation Act (1890) were fixed at £46,566 which helped to reduce the financial buffeting somewhat. The introduction of an inspectorate in 1909, the modification of the modern course in 1908, the dropping of the science course (though not science as a subject) in 1910, the dropping of the preparatory grade in 1913 and greater emphasis on commercial subjects in 1914 and the re-establishment of a written examination in science by the Board in 1915, represented the main changes in the operation of the intermediate system until the reforms of 1924.

Padraig Pearse, who trenchantly castigated the intermediate system in *The murder machine*, set up his own secondary school, St Enda's, Cullenswood Avenue, Dublin in 1908 as an exemplar of a more noble conception of education. Both the formal and informal curriculum of this school were very impressive in their range, and the teacher-pupil relationships were integrative and humane.[21] However, it too was seriously affected by the prevailing problems of inadequate financial support.

The position of secondary teachers

Irish secondary teachers were faced with a protracted campaign to win professional status reflected in salary, tenure, training and superannuation rights. Apart from providing some financial support to school managers which might enable them to pay teachers better, the Intermediate Education Act of 1878 did nothing to change the precarious living available to most intermediate teachers in the nineteenth century. Members of religious communities could view their educational work as part of their religious commitment but for the average lay teacher the remuneration and conditions of employment were very unsatisfactory. One commentator wrote of intermediate teachers in 1878 that 'at present the service of public instruction in Ireland is about the worst mode of obtaining a livelihood open to a man of intelligence and education'.[22] Unfortunately, later decades saw no alleviation of the miserable lot of most intermediate school teachers: in terms of salary, security of tenure and pension rights their position remained unenviable so that over thirty years later, in 1911, Dr Starkie, chairman of the Intermediate Board, could comment in a similar vein that 'at present, any man or woman, no matter how incompetent, may be appointed to a position in a secondary school. Although many teach for a year or two while they are preparing for other work, no layman wilfully takes up teaching as a permanent occupation.'[23]

It was left to managers and teachers to agree their own terms concerning conditions of employment and remuneration. The state of poverty of many schools did not favour generous settlements. The first time the government showed concern for the position of intermediate teachers was in 1904 when it included the question of establishing a profession of intermediate teachers in the terms of reference issued to Dale and Stephens. Dale and Stephens found the staffing of schools very unsatisfactory, involving a large number of inexperienced assistant teachers. They declared that all their evidence indicated that 'no Irish graduate, save in exceptional circumstances, will enter the teaching profession if any other career presents itself to him'.[24] As a reflection of this they pointed out that only 11.5 per cent of male Catholic teachers and only 8 per cent female Catholic teachers were university graduates. Protestant schools were more favourably circumstanced in that 55.8 per cent of male teachers and 30 per cent of female teachers were graduates. At the turn of the century the opportunities for the training of intermediate teachers were few. The appointment of a professor of education at Trinity College in 1905 and in colleges of the National University following its establishment under the Act of 1908, led to more formal courses and structures for professional training. It was not obligatory to undergo a training course and there was no direct reward for Irish teachers to take on such a course, though registration requirements after 1918 were an incentive.

In the early years of the century intermediate teachers began co-ordinating their efforts to seek redress of their grievances. In 1909 the Association of Secondary Teachers of Ireland (ASTI) was formed and served notice that they were pushing seriously for action.[25] Chief Secretary Augustine Birrell expressed sympathy for them in 1911, commenting that the life of an ordinary assistant master in Ireland was detestable, the remuneration miserably inadequate and that the assistant master had no tenure of office at all. In 1912 Birrell attempted to follow up his words of sympathy with action, but his scheme was opposed by the Catholic authorities. He introduced a milder measure, however, in 1914 and this was more successful.[26] This included provision for an annual grant of £40,000 for lay teachers' salaries — the first direct Treasury grant for intermediate education. About this period there were 940 full-time lay assistant teachers and 343 part-time. The full-time assistants who were clergy numbered 809 with another forty part-time. This Act of 1914 also included provision for a registration council which, after protracted negotiations, was constituted in 1916. The regulations drawn up by the registration council did not, however, come into force until 31 July 1918. The total number of teachers admitted to the register between that date and 31 July 1925 was 3,130. Admission to the register required the holding of a university degree, a training diploma and probationary teaching experience, with a seven-year period allowed to existing teachers for transition.[27]

An extra grant of £50,000 from parliament in 1918 did little to alleviate the grievances of teachers and in 1919 the Report of the Vice-Regal Committee declared that the position of teachers 'must be raised altogether above its present level by the removal of many disabilities under which it laboured'.[28] With regard to all registered teachers, male and female, it was recommended that their initial salaries should not be less than £180 per annum rising in incremental stages to £450 per annum. At this time only 8 per cent of lay teachers had salaries of more than £200 per annum and 30 per cent received less than £100 per annum. The report also called for employment contracts and superannuation schemes for teachers.[29]

To the dismay of hard-pressed teachers the defeat of the 1920 education bill, which was to be accompanied with improved salary scales and employment conditions, and the impending change of government meant that no significant reliefs were forthcoming. In June 1922 the Free State government gave interim grants in support of teacher salaries until the establishment in 1924 of the incremental salary grant. Henceforth, the teachers would receive an incremental salary from the state, as well as a basic salary from the school employers. Teachers were also to be given a contract of employment but it took until 1937 for the ASTI to negotiate satisfactory contracts. The introduction of a contributory state-aided superannuation scheme in 1929 was a further gain for the secondary school teachers.

Report of the Vice-Regal Committee, 1919 (Molony) and the Education Bill 1919-20

As World War I drew to a close the unsatisfactory condition of intermediate education in Ireland was drawing criticism from many quarters, not least from the Intermediate Board itself. Moves towards educational reform were taking place in other countries such as England and in Ireland the campaigns conducted by national and intermediate teachers led to the setting up of the Killanin and Molony Committees in August 1918. These committees were primarily concerned with the remuneration and conditions of employment of teachers but they also included recommendations of a wider character. Many of the general proposals in the Report of the Vice-Regal Committee (Molony Committee) echoed those of Dale and Stephens in 1905, and included the following:[30] the setting up of a central departmental authority for education; the establishment of an advisory council on education, representative of various interests; the levying of a national education rate to supplement central funding; the abolition of payment by results, regarding this 'as an essential preliminary to reform'; the establishment of intermediate and leaving certificate examinations; a full inspection system; capitation grants for pupils in recognised schools; more freedom for schools to plan curricula; the setting up of a scholarship scheme for participation in intermediate education; proposals for teachers' salary.

Thus a wide-ranging reform package was intended for intermediate education; the committee stating that 'piecemeal reform is not sufficient. What is required is that the whole system should be reconstructed'. Some of the recommendations of the Molony Committee as well as those of Killanin were included in the MacPherson Education Bill of 1919/20 and suffered the fate of that defeated bill.[31] This bill included provision for the following: a department of education comprising a president, vice-president and a permanent member; an advisory council on education; local education committees which would aid, maintain and equip schools; provision for free school meals, books and school requisites; provision for scholarships and care for afflicted children. It also included clauses on compulsory attendance, evening and continuation schools, provision of an education rate to be added to departmental funds, abolition of payment by results and superannuation schemes for all teachers.

In view of its provisions it was clear that the bill would prove very controversial. The Catholic hierarchy denounced the bill at an early stage and carried on a strong campaign against it. They were followed by the Central Council of County Councils. Sinn Féin who had recently won a landslide general election victory remained officially silent on the measure, not wishing to upset the rapprochement which had been forged with the Catholic Church. The Protestant house of bishops gave approval to the bill, as did the general assembly of the Presbyterian church and the Schoolmasters' Association, representing Protestant schools. The press followed predictable party lines. To a large extent opinion on the bill formed along denominational and political lines expressive of the division within the Irish community, with Protestants and those of Unionist sympathies in favour of the bill and the Catholic Church authorities firmly opposed to it. Interestingly, the INTO came out in support of the bill. The Irish nationalist party used delaying tactics against the bill, and Edward Carson held that the nature of the opposition to the bill demonstrated the correctness of the anti-home rule stance. The education bill was eventually withdrawn in December 1920. It was the last effort at educational legislation for the whole island. An undoubted factor ranged against the success of the bill was the imminence of some form of home rule legislation and the idea that a large-scale recasting of the educational system should be left to the new administration.

The defeat of the education bill of 1919/20 left intermediate education in its chronic condition. Meanwhile the machine had to be kept running and board, managers, teachers, and pupils still faced their many problems. The strains and desperation to which the situation was giving rise can be gleaned from quotations such as the following from the Intermediate Board in its report for the year 1919: 'The position is in our opinion extremely critical and threatens a very serious breakdown throughout the country if ameliorative steps are not immediately taken. . . . Matters have been getting steadily worse in the schools, and a complete collapse seems to be not far distant'.[32] Thus it was a rickety and run-down intermediate education machine which the new independent Irish Free State inherited at the transfer of powers in February 1922.

Secondary education in independent Ireland, 1922-60

The government of the new state had no ideological objection to greater public funding of privately-run denominational secondary schools. It increased the finance for secondary schooling and changed the mode of disbursement. By this stage Irish politicians had learned the lesson that the church viewed the control of schooling as its prerogative.[33] Later, the Constitution of 1937 was formally to recognise the role of the state as subsidiary 'to private and corporate initiative'. Even if any of the new leaders had other ideas it was very prudent in the context of an Ireland divided by civil war not to antagonise such a powerful entity as the Catholic Church. In the event there evolved a great relaxation in church-state contacts on educational affairs with no conflicts on policy issues. The government was committed ideologically to curricular policy changes in education, re-establishing through the schools what was understood to be the true Irish, that is the Gaelic, cultural heritage, primarily reflected in the Irish language. It was understandable but regrettable that little generosity of attitude was shown to other Irish cultural traditions. There was little concern about structural or administrative reform in education, the social aspects of educational provision were neglected and education, as distinct from language, was not a priority feature of government policy.

The administration of the educational services was taken over by the Provisional Government of the Irish Free State on 1 February 1922. On 8 June 1923 the Board of Commissioners of Intermediate Education was dissolved and it was replaced by two Intermediate Education Commissioners, Seosamh Ó Néill and Proinnsias Ó Dubhthaigh. On the establishment of the Department of Education on 1 June 1924 secondary education came under its administration. The Report of the Department of Education for 1924-5 acknowledged the limits of state influence on the secondary schools when it remarked:

> The state at present inspects these schools regularly and exercises a certain amount of supervision through its powers to make grants to schools as a result of these inspections, but it neither founds secondary schools, nor finances the building of them, nor appoints teachers, or managers, nor exercises any power or veto over the appointment or dismissal of such teachers or the management of schools.[34]

The influence which the state could exert was through the programmes for public examinations, through regulations concerning the granting of recognised status to schools which were to be allocated financial aid and through regulations concerning the qualifications of teachers who would receive state salary awards. The result was that while the control was limited and indirect, nevertheless, it could affect a great deal of what went on in the schools which sought state support. Although the Department of Education claimed that the changes brought about in secondary education under its authority were revolutionary they can be more accurately seen as a selective implementation of proposals which had long been made under the previous regime. The methods whereby the state made financial aid available to the schools changed in fundamental ways. Grants were no longer to be payable on examination results but were to be paid on a capitation basis for pupils who fóllowed an approved course of study and made 130 attendances per annum. Managers of schools were required to hold entrance examinations at the beginning of each school year which pupils had to pass in order to be eligible for capitation grants. These entrance tests were conducted in Irish, arithmetic and one other subject, almost always English, and they were tests of a very basic standard of attainment.

As was the case with national education the changes in the secondary sector focused on the curriculum and examination regulations rather than on the control or administration of the system. Under the authority of Dáil Éireann a conference on intermediate education was held on 22 August 1921. It made a number of recommendations, chief of which were: that all examination papers be available bilingually except for English, mathematics and science; that the history and geography papers should be such as to allow a student to obtain full marks on questions relating to Ireland; that the modern literary group should have Irish a compulsory with English an optional subject.[35] The Minister for Education of the Provisional Government had the Intermediate Board issue a circular early in 1922 to schools along these lines, though Irish was not yet a compulsory subject. The Northern Ireland Minister of Education was dissatisfied with these changes and established separate intermediate examinations in June 1922 for Northern Ireland.

To prepare for more fundamental changes Dáil Éireann set up a commission on secondary education which held its first meeting on 24 September 1921. Its terms of reference were: 'to draft a programme which would meet the national requirements, while allotting its due place to the Irish language'. The report of this commission was never published but following the completion of its deliberations on 7 December 1922 it was forwarded to the Minister of the Dáil as a series of subject committee reports 'regarding which there is substantial agreement'.[36] Though some of the proposals such as oral examinations in Irish, obligatory courses in basic science, appreciation courses in the fine arts, a more central place for manual instruction, were ignored, other recommendations formed the basis of the programme for secondary schools which came into operation on 1 August 1924.

In June 1924 the Intermediate Education (Amendment) Act was passed and this allowed changes in the examination system and the programmes of instruction. Under the new system the three grades of results examination were abolished and they were replaced by two certificate examinations — the Intermediate and Leaving Certificates — which have continued since then as the examination framework for secondary education. To obtain a pass in the Intermediate Certificate examination a pupil had to pass five subjects which had to include the following categories: (1) Irish or English, (2) a language other than that taken at (1), (3) mathematics or (for girls only) arithmetic with any one of science, domestic science, drawing or music, (4) history and geography. To obtain a pass in the Leaving Certificate a pupil had to pass five subjects which must include either Irish or English. Irish was declared an obligatory subject for the award of the Intermediate Certificate from 1928 onwards, and for the Leaving Certificate from 1934. This requirement remained in force until 1973 and was controversial, some holding that it was counter-productive by fostering unfavourable attitudes to Irish. At the time of its introduction many Protestants regarded it as a discriminatory measure.[37] From the school year 1927/8 Irish became an obligatory subject for the approved courses of recognised secondary schools and from 1932 all recognised pupils had to study Irish. As was the case for national teachers, Irish summer courses were arranged to help secondary teachers achieve a competence in Irish and from 1926 a test in oral Irish became a requirement for registration as a secondary teacher. A notable feature of the new programmes for secondary schools was the introduction of 'open courses' whereby the Department prescribed the general content for each subject but each school was free to submit for approval the courses and textbooks which it intended to use.

To encourage secondary schools to give a more prominent place to Irish than just provide it as a school subject, the rules and programme of 1924 recognised three types of secondary schools — Grade A, Grade B (which became sub-divided into B1 and B2) and Grade C. Irish was to be the official language in the Grade A schools and all subjects other than English were to be taught through the medium of Irish. Irish was also to be the official language of the Grade B schools and was to be used as the medium of instruction for some subjects. In the Grade C schools Irish was just taught as a school subject. There was an extra grant of 25 per cent based on capitation paid to Grade A schools, and Grade B schools got an extra financial incentive, the amounts of which varied according to the extent of teaching through the medium of Irish. Considerable progress was recorded in the classification of schools as Grade A or B, so that by 1935 these schools formed 56 per cent of the total number of secondary schools. This progress was not sustained and by 1956 they only formed 48 per cent of the total, and only 17 per cent of them were 'A' schools. An incentive to pupils to use Irish when answering examination papers came in the form of bonus marks. A student who answered papers, other than mathematics and art, through the medium of Irish was given a bonus of 10 per cent, and an extra five per cent could be obtained in the mathematics papers. By 1935 36 per cent of all public examination papers were answered through the medium of Irish though there is reason to believe that the standard of Irish used was not impressive. One of the problems affecting the use of Irish as a medium of instruction in secondary schools was the scarcity of suitable textbooks in Irish. With a view to ameliorating this deficiency a government-sponsored publishing company, An Gúm, was established in 1926 with the purpose of encouraging and publishing books in the Irish language, particularly textbooks for use in secondary schools. With regard to Irish in the university an Act was passed in 1929 which selected University College Galway as a college where many courses would be provided through the medium of Irish and so allow students the opportunity of pursuing their full education through Irish.

Although the abolition of the results fees had removed a distasteful pressure, the public examinations nevertheless continued to exercise a huge influence on secondary education and vestiges of the attitudes engendered by results fees continued to influence the system. Further, the Department published each student's results under his examination number but named the schools at the top of the lists of numbers. The unhealthy rivalry was further fanned by many schools publishing the success rates of their named pupils, as advertisements in the public press. Apart from the changed status of Irish the main lines of the curriculum continued as they had been, though there was a decline in the study of modern continental languages. Higher and Lower courses were introduced in the early 1930s for several subjects and mark allotments varied between grades and subjects. These mark ratings were important for winning state intermediate scholarships or for careers where the aggregate of marks came into account for recruitment purposes. Modern languages, science, commerce, drawing, manual instruction all scored lower than other subjects and Irish got more marks than English. The tendency for a predominantly literary curriculum with Latin as the predominant 'extra' language continued. Referring to the school year of 1962 the Investment in Education team concluded 'the curriculum in a great many schools is limited and is of a classical grammar-school type. Small schools in particular appear to have difficulty in providing a varied course'.[38] Thus, there had been no re-organisation of the curriculum to bring it more into harmony with industrial, agricultural or commercial needs of the new state.

Following 1924 a number of scholarships, tenable for two years, were awarded by the state on the results of the Intermediate Certificate. These numbered seventy-five and had an annual value of £40. An amendment to the scheme in 1929 which increased the number of scholarships to 112 and provided separate schemes for boys and girls was the only significant change made until the 1960s. Account was not even taken of the declining value of the money originally made available. One factor here may have been the feeling that some schools were pressurising pupils for scholarship success. The main scholarship schemes for university studies, based on the results of the Leaving Certificate, were those offered by local authorities, and a limited number offered by the state to students who were prepared to follow their university courses through the medium of Irish. The local authority scholarships included the application of a means test and the number made available was never large, amounting to only 214 in 1962/3. As was the case with scholarships from national to secondary school the provision was niggardly and went very little distance in fulfilling the need of aiding the many thousands of interested and intelligent children whose families could not afford to send them on for secondary and third-level education. The fees of many of the schools were small in direct money terms; the average tuition fee for a day pupil in 1960 was as low as £13 per annum and £78 for a boarder in small schools and £102 in boarding schools with more than 200 pupils.[39] Being average figures, of course, many pupils paid less. For large families even modest fees were a problem, however, particularly when coupled with ancillary expenses for school books, school attire and transport as well as the loss of the earning power of teenagers.

In 1947 a report of a special departmental committee set up in 1945 urged a restructuring of post-primary education. This included the extension of the compulsory leaving age to sixteen years for most pupils, with free education provided. Pupils were to be transferred from primary schools at the age of twelve plus — some to secondary schools, some to vocational schools and some to a new type of institution termed 'senior school'. These senior schools would offer a blend of practical and academic studies for pupils up to sixteen years of age and be 'subject to ecclesiastical sanction'. This unpublished report also recommended state loans at favourable interest rates for new secondary school buildings and extensions and 'a greatly increased number of scholarships of adequate value'. Such plans had similarities with contemporary developments in England and Northern Ireland but with the economic difficulties of the time and a change of government they seem to have been buried to emerge in a somewhat altered form in the 1960s.

Despite the inadequacy of a public initiative on secondary schooling the number of secondary schools nearly doubled and the enrolled pupils more than trebled from 1924 to 1960 as is indicated in Table 2. In the period under consideration, the decade 1950 to 1960 saw the most considerable expansion in both numbers of schools and pupils in attendance. However, even in 1960 the pupils in secondary schools represented only about 16 per cent of those enrolled in national schools. Many secondary schools were small, as late as 1961/62 about 65 per cent of them had less than 150 pupils.[40] This affected the range of subjects, facilities and the levels of staff competency which could be offered, although staff worked hard and long to fill the need. The vast majority of the schools were single-sex schools. The schools tended to be run on very formal lines, boarding schools in particular. Many boarding schools, under the control of religious authorities, were isolated from the life of the wider community, with routines of schoolroom, study,

Table 2: **Expansion of secondary education in Ireland, 1924-60**

Year	Number of secondary schools	Number of pupils in attendance
1924-25	278	22,897
1930-31	300	28,994
1940-41	352	38,713
1950-51	424	48,559
1960-61	526	76,843

Source: *Annual Reports of Department of Education*

prayer and recreation plotted with the order of an enclosed community, punctuated by holidays and annual open days. Secondary school authorities allowed very little involvement of teachers, parents or pupils in devising school policy, insofar as policy existed other than teaching for the public examinations. High levels of performance, particularly in academic subjects, were frequently attained with the restricted pupil clientele. The uneven geographic distribution of schools placed children in counties such as Donegal, Monaghan and Cavan at a disadvantage. The period following 1960 was to witness a dramatic change in state policy on secondary education, and of second-level education generally, which led to a large expansion in pupil participation, the re-organisation of the rules and regulations of existing schools as well as the institution of new state-funded post-primary schools.

One of the significant steps taken by the government in 1924 had been the abolition of closely prescribed courses and textbooks so as to give the schools 'the maximum of freedom both as regards the range of their programmes and the choice of books to suit their particular needs'. For teachers so accustomed to the clear directions hitherto available and in the context of uniform public examinations for the whole country, the newly granted freedom was a mixed blessing. In July 1937 Eamon de Valera took the initiative in calling a conference of the Minister of Education, the Secretary of the Department and the secondary school inspectors. In his view the existing programmes were 'too extensive and too vague'. He also urged a narrowing of the subjects of the programme feeling that its range hampered the gaelicisation task. The inspectors were not in agreement with the full changes proposed and no significant curricular changes were made except that prescribed textbooks were reintroduced for the various secondary school subjects between 1939 and 1941. An interesting and surprising feature of this conference was that no concern was expressed about the effect which a solely written examination was having on fluency in oral Irish. An oral Irish examination has been in operation in Northern Ireland since the 1920s.

Another appraisal of the secondary school curriculum was undertaken by the Council of Education in 1954.[41] It was six years before it completed its deliberations in 1960 and for those who patiently awaited guidelines for a reformed system the report proved a big disappointment. It identified the dominant purpose of the schools as the inculcation of religious ideals and values. The report identified the prevailing curriculum as 'the grammar school type, synonymous with general and humanist education'[41] and it endorsed this type of curriculum; science was not made an essential subject for school recognition. The report supported a departmental decision at the time to introduce an oral Irish examination for Leaving Certificate but did not extend this to other modern languages. The Council expressed satisfaction with existing extra-curricular activities and with the informal modes of vocational guidance which it found existing in schools. The report could not see that any greater co-ordination was possible between primary and secondary schooling. A scheme of 'free secondary education for all' was regarded as 'untenable' and 'utopian' but the Council recommended a much greater extension of scholarship provision for secondary education. By the time the Council of Education report was published in 1962 more analytical and dynamic thinking was taking place which would reshape post-primary schooling in the following decades.

Events and reports on secondary (Intermediate) education (1838-1954)

1838	Report of Select Committee on Foundation Schools etc, (Wyse) H.C. 1837-8 (701) VII. 345
1858	Report of Commissioners on the condition of endowed schools (Kildare), H.C. 1857-58 (2336-I) XXII, Part I. I
1878	Intermediate Education Ireland Act, H.C. 1878 (275) III, 543
1881	Report of Commissioners on Endowed Schools (Rosse), H.C. 1881 (C. 2831), XXXV, I
1885-94	Commission to re-structure educational endowments
1890	Local Taxation Act
1892	Introduction of preparatory grade examination
1899	Reports of Commissioners on Intermediate Education (Palles) Final Report, H.C. 1899 (C. 9511) XXII, 629
1900	Intermediate Education Amendment Act
1900	Board raised from seven to twelve members
1901-03	New programmes
1901-03	Temporary inspectors
1905	Report of Dale and Stephens, H.C. 1905 (Cd. 2546) XXVIII, 709
1907	Irish Council (Devolution) Bill
1909	Permanent inspectors

1913   Abolition of preparatory grade
1914   First direct Treasury grant for Intermediate Education
1918   Teachers' Registration Council established
1919   Report of Vice-Regal Committee on teachers in intermediate schools (Molony), H.C. 1919 (Cmd. 66) XXI, 645
1919-20   Education Bill (MacPherson), H.C. 1919 (214) I. 407
1921-22   Dáil Commission on Secondary Education (Report unpublished)
1924   Department of Education set up
1924   Intermediate and Leaving Certificate Courses
1924-25   Incremental state salaries for secondary teachers
1939-41   Set syllabuses re-introduced
1954   Council of Education began examination of the secondary school curriculum — Report (Pr. 5996) published in 1962.

Chapter Three

Technical/Vocational Education

Overview

Ireland lagged behind many other European countries in industrial development in the nineteenth century. But even England which had been the early pacemaker in the industrial revolution neglected for most of the century to build up a structured, co-ordinated system of technical education. However, there were signs at the Great Exhibition of 1851, later confirmed at the Paris Exhibition of 1867, that British manufacturing products were being out-classed by the exhibits of some continental competitors, particularly Germany and France. Their success was popularly attributed to the more purposive approach towards technical education. The Devonshire Commission in 1875 and the Samuelson Commission of 1884 surveyed continental developments and the position in England. They added their weighty endorsement to the view that England needed to adopt much more serious measures to promote a developed system of technical education. Ireland, which did not experience the same spur of industrial competition, waited longer and the establishment of a co-ordinated system of technical education in Ireland is a twentieth-century story.

Various initiatives of a private philanthropic or municipal character did occur in nineteenth-century Ireland but technical education lacked the coherence, sense of purpose and official backing to make an effective contribution to society. Part of this was due to a lack of realisation of its importance and the industrial sluggishness which prevailed. It also suffered from a lack of clarity as to what technical education involved and the methodology and techniques which should be employed. Another important impediment was the low social status enjoyed by manufacturing, manual or trade work generally. It was thought that the skills involved could be learned through formal apprenticeship and informal experience on the factory floor or at the work bench. The old tradition ˜of liberal education undervalued the worth of manual occupations: a humane education might be had from study of languages or history but scarcely from technical or craft studies. The churches also concentrated on the humane disciplines as being the formative experiences in pupil development, a tradition which continued well into the twentieth century. Such a tradition had a big influence on the shaping of public attitudes and the much greater valuation of academic education rather than applied education courses which was prevalent among the public. Although craftsmen might be respected at local level in Ireland, the mode of handing on the craft was direct apprenticeship. Many parents wished their children to go into clerkships and public service occupations, and the passport to these was success in general schooling.

These two features — the late start of a coordinated system of technical education and the relative lack of concern from church interests — facilitated a new administrative structure for technical education. The two landmark dates from the point of view of legislation were the establishment of the Department of Agriculture and Technical Instruction in 1899 and the Vocational Education Act of 1930. In the 1890s politicians from various parts of the Irish political spectrum were united in pressing for the improvement of technical education provision. Technical education was not added to the functions of the existing education boards but rather put under the aegis of a new department. The mode of financing and control coincided with the mode favoured at the time by the Treasury: this was a combination of central funding and finance raised from local rates with the system under the control of departmental and local authorities. In giving local civic authorities such a role in administering education schemes the system, initiated at the turn of the century, was breaking new ground in Irish educational administration. Following independence this pattern was maintained by the Vocational Education Act of 1930 which updated and revamped the earlier legislation but kept its essential features. Having been given ministerial assurances on the limited role of the 'continuation' education being provided under the 1930 Act, the Catholic hierarchy tolerated the system. Individual clergymen did of course play a prominent part in vocational education committees and from 1942 a more religious aura was promoted in the schools, yet they remained non-denominational schools under lay control and financially accountable through official audit. The Department of Agriculture and Technical Instruction was somewhat less constrained for funds than the National Board and, particularly, the Intermediate Board. Indeed, intermediate education was to benefit significantly from the Department's grants for science, drawing, manual instruction and domestic economy in intermediate schools. The Department acted in a supportive role to local technical education committees in approving schemes and allocating grants in support of them. The Department's strategy was one of fostering the initiatives of various agencies rather than the design or imposition of grandiose schemes. A good deal of flexibility was maintained and it was hoped that the schemes devised would meet the real needs and motivations of people at local level. Considerable success was achieved but neither then nor in later decades was there any significant conversion of Irish social attitudes in their valuation of technical and applied education. More so than other European countries there has continued to be up to modern times a much greater participation in academic-type education than in technical education.

Early initiatives on technical education

An organised system of technical instruction did not develop in Ireland until the early years of the twentieth century. However, a number of individual institutions were making contributions in this field from the second half of the previous century. The Metropolitan School of Art, which was set up by the Royal Dublin Society as early as 1749, took on new life when it came under the aegis of the Kensington Science and Art Department in 1854. Several of the Irish institutions benefited from the results payments of the Science and Art Department examinations following their establishment in 1859. A move to have a separate science and art department for Ireland was made following the Dublin Exhibition of 1865 but the report of an investigative commission opposed this in 1868. A school of design was established in the premises of the Royal Cork Institution in 1849. The Athenaeum Society of Limerick built its hall in 1855 and quickly established a school of art there. Mechanics institutes had been established in a number of centres for the education of artisans.[1] The first one was established in Dublin in 1837 and a notable one was set up in Clonmel with the help of the transport entrepreneur Thomas Bianconi in 1845. Most of the mechanics institutes gradually became more literary and social clubs with library facilities and less technical teaching institutes.

The Royal Dublin Society provided lecture courses at its premises in Dublin and also organised 'provincial' lecture series. Courses in technical and industrial education were also provided by the Museum of Irish Industry which was under the direction of Sir Robert Kane, an eminent champion of industrial education.[2] Kane also became Dean of the Royal College of Science which superseded the Museum of Irish Industry in 1867. Its aim was to provide 'a complete course of instruction in science applicable to the industrial arts', in particular to mining, agriculture, engineering and manufacture. However, the number of full-time students at the College of Science courses was small. Following the Artisans' Exhibition of 1885 in Dublin a committee of interested citizens, with the help of an annual grant of £500 from Dublin Corporation, established the City of Dublin Technical School at Kevin Street, while in 1892 Pembroke Technical School at Ringsend, Dublin was set up. In 1884 M.A. Crawford presented Cork with a new science and art institution.

This was the year (1884) which saw the publication of the report of the Samuelson Committee on technical education in Britain. It drew attention to the poor provision being made there for this form of education when compared with some of Britain's industrial competitors. It was followed by a Technical Instruction Act in 1889 which, for the first time, recognised the state's role in giving direct support to technical education and empowered local authorities to aid technical education out of local rates.[3] The Samuelson report had also urged the expansion of technical education with state support in Ireland. Ireland did not have a satisfactory local authority structure at that time, however, and only twelve of the existing 228 urban and rural sanitary authorities, who could have given grants from rates in aid of technical education, chose to do so. The Local Taxation (Customs and Excise) Act of 1890 in Britain allowed the residue grant of the beer and spirits duties to be applied by county and borough councils for the relief of rates and the promotion of technical education. This also applied to Ireland but in the absence of county councils operating technical education schemes, the money accruing to Ireland from this Act — £78,000 per annum — was allotted to primary education and intermediate education benefited from a fluctuating annual grant.

New structures for technical education
The 1890s saw a striking movement for reform in Irish education

and a live public concern about the unsatisfactory plight of technical education in particular. The report of the Commission on Manual and Practical Instruction in Primary Schools (1898) led to radical changes in the primary curriculum in 1900, intended to give a more practical and more child-centred emphasis to primary education. The report of the Commission on Intermediate Education (1899) included much criticism of the academic nature of the school programmes and the rigid, competitive results examinations. New programmes containing a four-course optional structure were introduced in 1902 but, as discussed elsewhere, were not established successfully. The Technical Education Association of Ireland was formed in 1893. A direct call for reform came from the report of the Recess Committee in 1896 which among other things urged that technical education should be put under a new government department set up to administer state aid to agriculture and industry.[4] It urged a new type of post-primary school for agriculture and practical industry. It sought the establishment of evening and continuation classes for those engaged at work during the day and the setting up of higher technical colleges. The Committee felt it imperative for Ireland's economic wellbeing that the cause of 'practical education' be promoted.

The Local Government (Ireland) Act of 1898 prepared the way for an organised local authority structure for Ireland and empowered the new county and borough councils to levy a rate of one penny in the pound for the purposes of technical instruction. The great breakthrough for technical education was the Agricultural and Technical Instruction (Ireland) Act of 1899 which resulted in the establishment of the Department of Agriculture and Technical Instruction.[5] This Department had Horace Plunkett, who had played a major part in the Recess Committee and the co-operative movement, as its vice-president.[6] The Act empowered the transfer to the new Department of the institutions and grants relating to technical education hitherto administered from the Science and Art Department of South Kensington. An endowment of £55,000 per annum was provided for the purposes of technical instruction. The Act defined technical instruction as 'instruction in the principles of science and art applicable to industries and in the application of special branches of science and art to specific industries or employment'. It did not include 'teaching the practice of any trade or industry'.

The administration of technical education took an innovatory form. As well as the Department itself the Act allowed for a board of technical instruction comprised of twenty-three members to advise the Department on all relevant matters submitted to them by the Department. At local level the councils of county boroughs, urban districts and counties set up local statutory committees. These local committees prepared schemes of technical instruction for their areas which, if approved by the Department, were put into operation subject to annual review. The local financial contribution was limited by statute to 2d in the pound. This sum was usually made available in urban areas but in county areas it varied from $^1/_3$d to a little over 1d in the pound. Local funding had to be forthcoming before the Department could assist local schemes from central funds.

Thus a combination of central and local popular control came into being. This of course contrasted with the national and intermediate sectors with their government-nominated boards. Dr Walsh, Archbishop of Dublin, was a supporter of practical education and was instrumental in getting the Catholic hierarchy's acceptance of this secular-controlled and rate-supported branch of education.[7] He also took the initiative in getting a consultative committee established with representatives of national, intermediate and technical education, with a view to getting cohesion and cooperation between the different education sectors. This, however, had no real power and little co-ordination resulted. The key personnel who guided the work of the Department in its early years were Horace Plunkett, vice-president, and T.P. Gill, secretary.

The new Department did not see itself as establishing a separate educational structure in rivalry with existing boards; rather it saw itself as a supportive agency of local effort and resources aimed at improving the industrial potential of the country. It was careful in its early years not to antagonise existing agencies and it saw as an early priority the improvement of scientific and practical subjects in the secondary schools. Science teaching had reached a very low ebb with only 673 pupils presenting in science at the intermediate examinations in 1899; in 1901 there were only six secondary schools in Ireland with laboratories and such science teaching as existed was largely theoretical and verbal. At the end of 1902 with the assistance of the Department 101 permanent and forty-nine provisional laboratories had been established at an overall cost of £30,000.[8] Unlike the Intermediate Board, the Department paid its grant on a capitation basis dependent on favourable inspectors' reports, rather than on the results of written examinations. The Intermediate Board agreed to accept the Department's programmes and mode of operation in the designated subjects of science, drawing, domestic economy and manual instruction. In the year 1901-2 154 day-secondary schools qualified for grants amounting to about £10,000 in respect of 6,614 pupils who took these subjects. By 1919 the number of such schools qualifying for grants was 247, the number of pupils 16,077 and the amount had reached £36,000.[9] The type and amount of support provided a valuable boost to subjects such as science and drawing in the secondary schools. Small grants were also made available to primary schools, mainly Christian Brothers' schools, for drawing and manual crafts. Certificate courses were also provided by the Department for national school teachers in elementary science; the largest number of teachers in any year being 214 in 1907-8. The local authorities also got schemes of technical education under way with the help of the Department. By 1902 there were twenty-seven county schemes, twenty-four urban schemes and plans were well ahead for six schemes for county boroughs. Grants were made available for the conversion of disused buildings into technical education centres. Another important early initiative of the Department was the publication of a good quarterly journal which carried many articles on scientific, technical and agricultural education.

Problems and progress of technical education, 1900-22
A serious difficulty in the path of technical education was the inadequate finance made available for laying the foundations of a whole new system. The Act of 1899 made no provision for the building of technical schools. At first a large number of private or disused buildings such as old distilleries, hospitals and warehouses were converted for use as technical schools. Later, in the large urban areas, organised technical schools were established which offered co-ordinated courses of instruction; in rural districts this was much more impractical and the schemes devised usually involved just itinerant teachers giving six- to eight-week courses in single subjects. In both urban and rural areas most of the work was done at evening courses which imposed serious limitations on what could be achieved.

The general standard of education of many of the entrants to technical courses was found to be unsatisfactorily low. The lack of tight compulsory attendance legislation and the early drop-out patterns from the national schools no doubt contributed significantly to this as did the lack of background in manual subjects. Special introductory classes had to be provided for such students.

A further serious problem for the Department was the shortage of adequately trained teachers. The Department decided to recognise only properly qualified teachers of science, drawing, manual instruction and domestic economy. From 1901 special summer courses were held for teachers of science in Dublin, Belfast and Cork. Practical and written examinations were held at the end of each course and provisional recognition given pending the teachers' success in the examinations of five such courses. Summer courses in drawing were also held to help teachers attain the Teachers' Art Certificate of the Board of Education, London. Teachers of domestic economy were helped through a scholarship scheme to undertake training courses in Dublin or abroad. Open competitive examinations were held for craftsmen who then underwent a twenty-week course followed by written and practical examinations to qualify as manual instructors. Other scholarships for intending teachers were made available for advanced study abroad in aspects of industry and commerce.

Table 3: **List of the subjects taught in technical schools for boys, 1900-01**

Commerce	Science and Art	Industrial
Shorthand	Elementary science	Carpentry
Typewriting	Building construction	Joinery
Commercial	and drawing	Plumbing and cabinet
arithmetic	Machine construction	making
Commercial	and drawing	Coach-building
geography	Drawing and wood-	Paper manufacture
All other subjects	carving	Milling
recognised by the	Drawing and modelling	Book-binding
Department from	Design and workshop	Pottery and porcelain
time to time	Mathematics	Typography
		Breadmaking and con-
		fectionery
		Ship joinery

Source: *Report of the Department of Agriculture and Technical Instruction 1900-01*

The list of subjects for the various courses in technical schools for 1900-01 is set out in Table 3. Grants were paid for instruction in these subjects at rates of 7/6 per pupil per subject per session for commercial subjects, 15/- for science and art subjects and 30/- for industrial subjects. Grants were also paid for instruction to girls in such subjects as lace, crochet, needlework and machine knitting. A session consisted of twenty lessons of 1½ hours duration or thirty 1 hour lessons. In 1906 new programmes were devised which included attendance grants payable for co-ordinated courses of instruction. These allowed urban areas more scope for developing technical schools. Students could take two or three subjects from a range of different groups which were laid out in courses of three and four years' duration. Extra capitation payments were paid for the later stages of the course to encourage students to persevere. This resulted in a dramatic increase in the attendance grants payable, from £4,423 in 1905-6 to £12,057 in 1906-7, but the number of students remained at approximately 42,000.[10] In 1911 the regulations were extended to allow attendance grants to be also paid for single-subject courses and this helped the development of rural schemes of technical education. In 1913 the Department instituted its own schemes of technical school examinations, whereas up to that they used those of English examining bodies which had wide acceptability and recognition.

Day trade preparatory schools were established but these remained few in number, amounting to ten in 1909, and fourteen by 1919.[11] They were seen as a bridge between national school and employment, offering part general and part industrial education. They did not offer religion on the programme, and if these schools had been expanded it is likely they would have caused controversy. However, the outbreak of war and the decrease in the value of money created difficulties in expanding technical education facilities. By 1914 many of the improvised technical school buildings had been replaced by purpose-built schools and at the time of transition to the Irish Free State sixty-five technical schools existed within its area of jurisdiction. In the year 1918-19 the Department paid grants amounting to £69,304 for 37,241 pupils in technical schools and classes. In the same year 4,026 'exercises' were presented for the Technical School Examinations with a success rate of 63.4 per cent.[12]

As was the case with teachers in the other sectors, the level of technical teacher remuneration by no means kept pace with the rising cost of living. In 1918 the British Treasury made funds available to the Department which were distributed in the form of war bonuses but the conditions of employment and tenure remained very unsatisfactory for teachers. The Irish Technical Instruction Association, which had been set up in 1901, made many worthwhile contributions on the theme of technical education and the necessity of improving the conditions for teachers employed in the system, but progress on pay and conditions was slow.

As well as direct problems of a financial or organisational character, technical education faced other difficulties. There was a strong prejudice against technical education among the general public and many parents were anxious that their children should gain white collar employment and they tended to regard practical and manual work, and the preparation for it, as inferior. Some craft-workers opposed the extension of craft teaching fearing that it might have bad effects on employment prospects. Further, nationalist politicians such as John Dillon did not favour the Department of Agriculture and Technical Instruction, seeing it as a weapon in the campaign of 'killing home rule with kindness'. Horace Plunkett, knighted in 1903, became a figure of controversy and he resigned from the Department in 1907. The high hopes entertained at the turn of the century for the impact which technical education would have on industrial and economic development were scarcely realised. Yet, despite these difficulties and problems, technical education made considerable progress and an infrastructure was laid which was capable of great development.

Technical education at the transition to independence

The Government of Ireland Act in 1920 removed the control of technical education in Northern Ireland to the new government established there under the Act. The Board of Technical Education ceased to function and the control of technical education in the Irish Free State came under the Department of Agriculture in 1922. As was the case with national and intermediate education, technical instruction became a branch of the Department of Education on its establishment in 1924 and from June of that year central funds for technical education were to be voted by the Oireachtas. The new Department also took control of the Metropolitan School of Art and the Royal College of Science though the latter was transferred to University College, Dublin in 1926.

The total income of technical instruction committees in the Irish

Free State for the school year 1925-6 was £236,476, of which the state contribution was £161,442 and rates and other contributions amounted to £75,034.[13] Under the Local Government Act of 1925 local authorities became liable for the pensions of whole-time technical teachers and security of tenure was guaranteed to such teachers subject to their giving satisfactory service. Schemes of technical education were devised and conducted by forty-nine committees operating under the aegis of local authorities. The committees appointed executive officers to undertake the secretarial and organising duties associated with the schemes. During the academic year 1924-5 there were sixty-five technical schools operating; twenty-two under county borough and urban committees and forty-three under schemes conducted by county committees. Courses under local authorities can be summarised as follows:

1. whole-time instruction prior to employment
2. evening instruction in technical schools
3. classes in rural areas.

The annual output of pupils from whole-time instruction of an industrial character was about 300, while about 1,200 pupils emerged from full-time commercial courses. The figure of 300 must be regarded as extremely unsatisfactory for the needs of the industrial sector. In 1925 there were about 22,000 students in attendance at evening instruction.[14] The main work of the schools was carried out through voluntary attendance at evening classes of two hours' duration on two or three evenings in the week. The fact that most of the work had to be done in the evenings was a serious impediment to a thorough or systematic approach to technical education. This was further compounded by the irregular attendance, averaging only about 50 per cent. Despite higher grants for continued attendance during the later years of the courses there was a high drop-out rate after the first two years so that, for instance, in 1924-5 only 15 per cent of students were participating in the third or fourth year courses. About 10,000 attended classes in rural areas but these courses were usually of only six or eight weeks' duration conducted by itinerant teachers and often on a single-subject basis. The content and range of the courses was also limited, centring on life on the farm for boys and aspects of domestic life for girls. The range of courses and number of students attending rural classes in 1924, other than established technical schools, may be seen in Table 4.

Table 4: **Number of students attending rural classes at centres other than technical schools, 1924**

Subject	Number of centres	Number of students
Manual instruction	107	2,460 (24%)
Domestic economy	147	4,631 (45%)
Home spinning	30	605 (6%)
Lace and sprigging	16	363 (3%)
Commerce	24	884 (9%)
Other subjects	47	1,352 (13%)
Total	371	10,295 (100%)

Source: *Report of Commission on Technical Instruction* p. 24, par. 53

In the established technical schools, the type of subjects pursued by enrolled students is shown in Table 5. It is important to note that science and handicraft, seen by the Commission on Technical Instruction as the mainstay of technical education, were taken by only 18 and 5 per cent respectively, whereas commerce, languages and domestic economy were the studies predominantly pursued. The introductory courses were intended to help students, who had not completed the top standards of the national school, to catch up on some general and practical subjects. However, the courses evolved to cater for many and various types of students. The variety of standards among the students proved an obstacle to satisfactory work. From 1924 to 1930 the number of students enrolled in classes in technical schools increased from 21,808 to 29,649, an increase of 36 per cent.[15]

The Technical Education Commission of 1926-7 (Ingram)
In the early days of the newly independent state it became clear that the existing schemes of technical instruction, although accomplishing useful work, had many defects. Plans were being made at the time for industrial development and the establishment of state-sponsored bodies and the government thought that technical and industrial education needed an overhaul to come into line with the

Table 5: Number of students and range of courses in established
technical schools, 1924

Subject group	Number of students	Percentage
Introductory	1,757	8%
Commerce and languages	8,811	40%
Science (pure and applied)	3,757	18%
Handicraft	1,009	5%
Domestic economy	5,354	24%
Art	916	4%
Other subjects	204	1%
Total	21,808	100%

Source: *Report of Commission on Technical Instruction*, p. 18,
par. 38

needs of the time. It is also probable that the government felt more free to reform technical education as it was not subject to the denominational controversies which affected the other educational sectors. The Department of Education, at an early stage, carried out an internal survey of the system and came to the conclusion that what was needed was a full-scale commission. This was appointed in 1926 'to enquire into and advise upon the system of technical education in Saorstát Éireann in relation to the requirements of Trade and Industry'.[16] The Commission held its first meeting on 5 October 1926. It received submissions and heard evidence from a wide range of interested parties. Many witnesses from the fields of commerce and industry urged greater development of technical education. The Commission presented its report a year later on 5 October 1927.

The Commission found 'that the work of the schools in the more important districts bears too little relation to the local requirements of trade and industry and that a general change of outlook is required'.[17] Having examined the existing facilities for technical education, the Commission came to the conclusion 'that radical changes are necessary to meet the existing and probable requirements of traditional industry'. It made ninety recommendations. Amongst these were that a school-leaving certificate should be introduced for all sixth standard primary school pupils in an endeavour to improve basic standards of elementary education. It was hoped that the new compulsory attendance legislation would also help in this regard. The Commission urged that drawing be reintroduced as a compulsory subject for national schools and suggested that secondary schools should include science, drawing, manual instruction and domestic economy as compulsory subjects.

A more dramatic proposal of the Commission was that a system of practical continuation schools and classes should be established for young people between the ages of fourteen and sixteen. The absence of such a system was regarded as one of the key weaknesses of the existing situation. The programme of these schools was to be distinct from those of technical schools which, in turn, were seen as catering for the sixteen-plus age group. Attendance at technical schools should be made compulsory in the first two years of apprenticeship to skilled trades, for at least 180 days each year. The report called for an apprenticeship act which would have a wide-ranging impact on apprenticeship. The Commission took note of new state-sponsored industrial enterprises such as the Shannon Electricity Scheme and the Irish Sugar Company and stated that there was a need for a wide development of higher technological work. Other proposals were new schemes for the intensive training of teachers, standard conditions of employment and standard salary scales for whole-time teachers.

Vocational Education Act, 1930

The main recommendations of the Commission on Technical Education formed the basis of the Vocational Education Act of 1930.[18] The term 'vocational' embraced two distinct elements incorporated in the Act — continuation education and technical education.

The administration of continuation and technical education was left in the hands of local statutory committees, as under the Act of 1899. The technical instruction committees, however, were replaced by vocational education committees (VECs) which were intended to be smaller and more effective in their composition. There were thirty-eight such committees, each with fourteen members of whom not less than five or more than eight had to be members of the local rating authority. The remaining members were selected from employers, trade unions or individuals with a special interest or expertise in education. The term of office was to be the same as that of the local authority. Each VEC had a chief executive officer who proposed schemes and implemented policy. Committees were created for each of the following types of categories: borough areas — Dublin, Cork, Limerick, Waterford, Dun Laoghaire; urban districts — Bray, Drogheda, Wexford, Tralee, Sligo, Galway; county areas, excluding the scheduled boroughs and urban districts. Under the new legislation the vocational education committees had the duty to set up schools in each local authority area. Further, a compulsory rate of 1¾d in the pound in county areas and 3d in the pound in borough and urban council districts was to be levied in aid of technical education. This removed the uncertainty which prevailed under the old year-to-year system, and allowed for more satisfactory planning. Amendments to the Act in later years increased the maximum rate levels to cope with expanding needs. The new regulations led to a striking amount of building activity resulting by 1936 in forty-six new schools, extensions to twenty-one others and the initiation of building programmes for forty-eight other schools. The Vocational Education Act of 1930 did not include provision for agricultural education which was left with the Department of Agriculture. Neither did the Act include significant provision for reforming teacher training which was seen as an essential prerequisite for an expanded system by the Commission of 1926-7.

Continuation education

Under the Vocational Education Act, continuation education was seen 'to continue and supplement education provided in elementary schools and to include general and practical training in preparation for employment in trades etc. and also general and practical training for improvement of young persons in the early stages of employment'.[19] It was intended for the age group fourteen to sixteen but was not designated as compulsory though the Act allowed for a raising of the school leaving age later if desired. The schools were under secular control and were non-denominational though committees were encouraged to make provision for religious instruction. In reply to a deputation from the Catholic hierarchy the Minister for Education was at pains to assure them in a written reply that continuation education did not involve 'general education' and was to be severely practical and vocational in its emphasis. It would not be allowed to infringe on the type of education provided in national and secondary schools. He also assured them that he had been most careful not to introduce a new principle of control in education and to secure that the Act did not run counter to established Catholic practice or the Maynooth decrees on such matters. The Minister also tried to allay episcopal apprehensions about co-education and night schools under the Act.[20]

The Department of Education issued guidelines for vocational schools in 1931 but allowed local committees flexibility in the schemes they prepared.[21] The guidelines stressed the practical nature which the courses should reflect. The continuation courses were devised on a two-year basis and they were organised into groups on the following lines:

1. Preparatory course (co-educational for general subjects)
2. Junior technical course (boys)
3. Junior domestic science course (girls)
4. Junior commercial course (girls)
5. Junior commercial course (boys)
6. Junior rural course (boys)
7. Junior rural course (girls).

The main subjects offered for boys were Irish, English, mathematics, general science, rural science, art, mechanical drawing, woodwork and metal work. The subjects for girls generally included Irish, English, arithmetic, commercial subjects and domestic economy. The courses were whole-time and involved between twenty-five and twenty-eight class attendance hours per week.

The new Constitution of 1937 highlighted the state's philosophy on the relative role of the state, the churches and parents in the education system and emphasised the role of religion in society. In the years following, clerical unease at the low profile of religion within the vocational system appeared in several articles. Then in 1942, prompted by the Irish Technical Education Association, the Department issued what was known as Memorandum V. 40 which set out the rationale of continuation education and more precise guidelines than those of 1931 for the guidance of vocational education committees.[22] A key feature of this memorandum was the specific inclusion of religious studies as part of the courses offered and a greater emphasis on the Irish language 'and other distinctive features of national life'. This represented a significant departure from the conception of the 1930 Act as enunciated by the Minister for Education of the previous government in the Dáil at the time of the passing of the Act. Cultural studies became more central to vocational schools and their role in the restoration of Irish as a vernacular became more emphasised.[23] In March 1941 the Department established the first of a series of courses for whole-time teachers of Irish — Timire Gaeilge — who would promote the Irish revival in the vocational sector.

As had been the case with the introduction of the Primary Certificate as a compulsory examination for national schools in 1943, so too a Group Certificate examination was introduced on a nationwide scale for vocational schools in 1947 to be taken at the end of the two-year continuation course. The Group Certificate examination was organised as indicated in Table 6 which also shows the number of pupils who entered and were successful in the first year. To pass in any subject group one had to pass in certain obligatory subjects and one could add a number of optional subjects. The success rate in the first year of examination was poor with a pass rate of 49 per cent and, although an improvement took place in subsequent years, success rates were not impressive. For instance, in 1959-60 out of a total entry of 37,884 pupils, 16,799 passes were secured and 10,148 honour grades, leaving a failure rate of about 30 per cent.[24]

Table 6: **Success rates of students in the Day Group Examinations, 1947**

Subject group	Number of students	
	Entered	Passed
Manual training	561	330
Commerce (general)	413	155
Commerce (secretarial)	102	29
Domestic science	275	168
Rural science	102	29

Source: *Report of the Department of Education for 1946-47*, p. 714

Technical education

The expression 'technical education' was defined in the 1930 Act as 'education pertaining to trades, manufactures, commerce and other industrial pursuits and in subjects bearing thereon or relating thereto and includes education in science and art and also includes physical training'. This was a shift in emphasis from the 1899 legislation which defined it mainly as the study of principles; now there was more scope for the practical application of the principles to trade and industry. Technical education was seen as having two main purposes, to train young people for entry to particular employments and to improve the skills of those already employed. Each vocational education committee was to supply or aid technical education in its area. Technical education was mainly conducted through evening courses though a small number of whole-time schemes were established and a number of schemes in association with apprenticeship arrangements. A great deal of ordinary technical education was craft-based.

Higher technical education was confined to the county boroughs – Dublin, Cork, Limerick and Waterford. In 1935 a special report of the Dublin VEC called for five main colleges of specialisation as follows: College of Technology; High School of Commerce; School of Trades and Crafts; School of Domestic Science; and School of Music. Institutions such as those in Kevin Street, Bolton Street, Cathal Brugha Street, Rathmines, Parnell Square and Ringsend were developing a wide range of technological courses. These institutions served a national as well as a municipal role. Minimum age of entry was sixteen years.

The Department of Education re-organised the Technical School examinations in 1936 with a more practical emphasis to serve not only as evidence of progress at technical schools but also as tests of occupational efficiency. Written and practical examinations were held in the following groups of courses: building and electrical engineering, mechanical engineering, motor car engineering, applied chemistry, commerce, domestic science, art, farriery, telephony and telegraphy. However, there were high failure rates in these first examinations – in 1936 the success rate was 55 per cent rising in the two subsequent years to 61 per cent.[25] Technical schools continued to submit students for the City and Guilds examinations of the London Institute.

The Commission on Vocational Organisation in 1944, as well as regretting what it regarded as the inadequate agricultural and rural emphasis in the vocational schools, considered that technological training which was 'the keystone in the industrial development and economic security of every nation' was not receiving the promotion it deserved.[26]

Apprenticeship

The Commission on Technical Instruction (1926-7) had been very concerned at the lack of proper schemes for apprenticeship training. It made many proposals for improvement including proposing that attendance at a technical school should be made compulsory in the first two years of apprenticeship to skilled trades. It further urged that an Apprenticeship Act should be introduced. An Apprenticeship Act was passed in 1931 enabling the Minister for Industry and Commerce to make an order declaring a trade to be a designated trade in an area, and to constitute such an area as an apprenticeship district for such designated trade. Apprenticeship committees were set up, comprising employer and employee representatives as well as ministerial nominees. The committees were empowered to make rules and regulations relating to the particular apprenticeship. A key element was that committees were enabled rather than obliged to make rules requiring employers to train and instruct apprentices employed by them in a specified manner. In the event most trades did not adopt the provisions and the Act accomplished little.

It was not until 1960, under the provisions of a new Apprenticeship Act of 1959, that a National Apprenticeship Board was established with power to require all employers to send their apprentices to training courses. Possession of the Day Vocational Certificate became the basic qualification for entry to apprenticeship. Various schemes involving block release, day release, part-time release were put into operation whereby apprentices were enabled to attend courses in technical schools. The Board was entitled to lay down the type of instruction to be provided for apprentices in the various trades and to issue certificates to those successful in junior and senior examinations. National apprenticeship committees and local advisory committees were established.

Teacher training

The Commission of Technical Education in 1927 criticised the fact that there was inadequate provision for the training of technical teachers and regarded the existing arrangement as unsystematic and insufficient. If their general recommendations were to be successful the Commission declared it imperative that they 'be preceded by intensive training of teachers'. However, no comprehensive new plan for teacher training was introduced. Various short 'special' courses and summer refresher-type courses were part of a tradition which continued alongside more improved, structured courses. Patterns of training varied considerably for different categories over the years.

Many of the teachers of Irish, English, mathematics, commerce and rural science were university graduates but teacher training was not obligatory for them. Teachers of Irish and general subjects had to obtain the Teastas Muinteóra Gaeilge introduced in 1932 which was awarded after the successful completion of a summer course in Irish and teaching methodology. From January 1944 candidates for posts as full-time teachers of Irish had to hold the Teastas Timthire Gaeilge which was a higher qualification in Irish. A large number of graduates also obtained the Higher Diploma in Education, though such a teacher training qualification was not obligatory. Teachers of woodwork and metalwork were recruited from people who had served approved trade apprenticeships. They had to complete and pass a course which in the early years was of nine months' duration but from 1937 was increased to eighteen months. Coláiste Charman in Gorey, County Wexford became the centre for woodwork and building teachers and the course was further lengthened to two years. Courses for metalwork teachers were held in Ringsend Technical School in Dublin, the courses being of eighteen months' duration. Trainee teachers in these subjects had to acquire the Céard Teastas, a qualification indicating their competence to teach through the medium of Irish. Rural and general science teachers were trained in the Crawford Institute, Cork from 1937. In the 1920s domestic economy teachers were trained at the Department of Education training school, Kilmacud. In 1930 St Catherine's College of Domestic Science, under the control of the Dominican nuns of Sion Hill, Blackrock, got state support as a training centre. In 1941 the school at Kilmacud was closed and St Mary's College, Cathal Brugha Street, Dublin was established. The teacher training section of this college was transferred to St Angela's, Sligo in 1952. The course became a three-year course ending with the award of a diploma. Teachers of art subjects were trained in the Metropolitan School of Art, later the National College of Art.

The vocational education system, c. 1960

Continuation education and technical education were usually conducted within the one building, the vocational school. In 1932 there were ninety-eight schools with 676 full-time teachers and

598 part-time teachers; by 1959 the number of schools had grown to 272 with 1,574 full-time and over 500 part-time teachers. Enrolment in whole-time day continuation courses rose from 7,925 in 1931 to 17,978 in 1950 and 25,608 in 1957. Enrolments in part-time day courses reached 11,992 in 1959. Evening and adult courses had proved very popular and in 1959 there were 86,343 students attending evening classes.[27]

As the 1950s drew to a close, however, there was a great deal of criticism from many quarters including the vocational education sector about the condition of vocational education. Many problems continued to limit the role of vocational education. The full-time continuation course was only of two years' duration and was of a terminal character with little or no transfer value to further formal education. Irish social attitudes still tended to disparage manual and practical-type education and aspiring middle-class parents preferred the more prestigious academic-type education which led to greater opportunities for further education and white-collar employment. Many of the vocational schools were very small and their distribution was often linked to the demand for evening classes rather than the demand for full-time courses for the probable pupil population in the catchment area. The small schools prevented the employment of a range of specialised staff, and some teachers were not attracted by the short duration of the full-time courses and the consequent limitations on professional satisfaction. A further problem was the high pupil drop-out rate from even the short two-year course. Vocational schools were frequently in unequal competition with local secondary schools, each type of school proceeding in splendid isolation from the other. Vocational schools also had to cater for a more than normal distribution of dull or under-motivated pupils who saw the 'tech' as a convenient stop-gap until something better turned up. Some of the pupils may have failed to reach the entrance standards of secondary schools and, in some instances, parents were unable to pay the fees for secondary schools. With a new concern for industrial and economic expansion making itself evident, as symbolised by the publication of the first programme for economic expansion in 1958, it became obvious that the area of vocational and technical education would be brought more to the forefront of Irish education in the following decades.[28]

Events and reports relating to technical education (1837-1960)

1837   First Mechanics Institute in Dublin

1845   Museum of Irish Industry set up

1859   South Kensington Science and Art Examinations

1863   Report of Select Committee on Royal Dublin Society and Scientific Institutions, H.C. 1863 (3180) X VII Pt. 1

1864   Report of Select Committee on Scientific Institutions, H.C. 1864 (495) XIII

1867   Report of the Commission on the College of Science, H.C. 1867 (219) LV. 771

1868   Report of Commission on the Science and Art Department in Ireland, H.C. 1868-69 (4103) XXIV. 1

1884   Royal Commission on Technical Instruction, H.C. 1884 (C. 3981) XXX, XXXI, pt. 1 (Samuelson)

1885   City of Dublin Technical School, Kevin Street

1893   Technical Education Association of Ireland founded

1896   Report of the Recess Committee

1899   Agricultural and Technical Instruction Act, H.C. 1899 (280) 1.73

1907   Report of the Departmental Committee of Inquiry into the provisions of the 1899 Act, H.C. 1907 (Cd. 3572) XVII. 799

1922   Department of Agriculture in charge of technical education

1924   Department of Education in charge of technical education

1926   College of Science transferred to UCD

1927   Report of Commission on Technical Instruction (Ingram)

1930   Vocational Education Act

1931   Apprenticeship Act

1931   Memorandum from Department of Education on Continuation Education (V.1)

1942   Memorandum from the Department of Education on Continuation Education (V. 40)

1947   Day Group Certificate examinations

1959   Apprenticeship Act

1960   National Apprenticeship Board

Chapter Four

University Education

Overview

As was the case with national and secondary education the question of university education in nineteenth-century Ireland was closely intertwined with denominational and political considerations. Up to 1850 Ireland had only one university, the University of Dublin. Various nineteenth-century initiatives failed to set up an overall university structure to the satisfaction of the main interests involved and it was only with the Irish Universities Act of 1908 that an acceptable compromise solution was evolved. Trinity College, the one college in the University of Dublin, was closely linked to Church of Ireland interests and had the advantages of a long tradition and good endowment. Its whole ethos, tradition and structure, however, made it repugnant to Catholic church authorities as an appropriate institution for the higher education of Catholics.

Catholic pressure for a state-endowed and supported denominational university for Catholics gathered momentum from the middle of the nineteenth century and became one of the great political issues of the time.[1] In the prevailing political ethos in England, in which anti-Catholic attitudes were never far below the surface, the state would not agree to give state support to a denominational university. Instead it adopted other strategies including the setting up of a non-denominational university, the Queen's University, in 1850 which acted as the degree-awarding body for three state-built and state-controlled colleges, the Queen's Colleges at Cork, Galway and Belfast. Catholic opinion had hardened against mixed denominational education under Pope Pius IX and these institutions were formally condemned by Rome and the Irish hierarchy as unsuitable for Catholic education. The failure of this initiative was followed by the setting up of the Royal University in 1879 purely as an examining body. This, however, was only a pastiche of university education, and official commissions were set up and other initiatives taken in order to achieve a solution. The main proposals put forward were the opening out of the University of Dublin as a federal university with several affiliated colleges including a new Catholic college, the establishment of a full-scale Catholic university with equal financial endowment as the University of Dublin and the re-organisation of the Royal University as a federal teaching university.

The solution arrived at eventually in 1908 was none of these. Under the 1908 solution the University of Dublin was left intact and two new universities were established. The old Queen's College in Belfast was raised to the status of a full university, non-denominational legally but with a large Presbyterian influence. A federal National University, also non-denominational, was set up which would embrace the colleges at Cork and Galway and an expanded University College in Dublin. It had the right to grant 'recognised' status to other colleges, and this was given to Maynooth College in 1910. Though legally non-denominational the geographic location, the nature of the student body and the religion of the majority of the governing bodies and staff ensured that these institutions would reflect a Catholic ethos and they were accepted by the Catholic hierarchy. While the solution arrived at in 1908 had a slow formulation it proved remarkably durable and survived for three quarters of a century without structural alteration.

The state took several direct initiatives in Irish university education in the nineteenth century. It built and funded the Queen's Colleges in 1845 and retained for itself the right to appoint professors to these colleges. It set up an investigative commission on Trinity College in 1850. Gladstone introduced an Irish University Bill in 1873 attempting to open the University of Dublin as a federal university with affiliated colleges. The defeat of the bill was a major factor in the fall of the Liberal government of the day. The government formally abolished its own creation, the Queen's University, in 1882 and had it replaced by the new Royal University. Under the fellowship scheme of this examining body the state gave indirect support to the Catholic University College and this helped to resuscitate it. With its scheme of prizes and exhibitions the Royal University was an extension to third level of the payment by results type thinking incorporated in the Intermediate Education Act of 1878. Student attendance was not required at any institution in order to enter for the Royal University examinations and this had the unfortunate effect of weakening the public's understanding and valuation of collegiate university education. In the early years of the new century the government set up two commissions on university education — the Robertson and the Fry Commissions. Then, amidst much turbulent academic politics, the chief secretary, Augustine Birrell, steered his Irish Universities Bill of 1908 safely through parliament.

Despite the high profile adopted by the state in university affairs it did not infringe upon academic freedom, the rights of free inquiry, teaching and publication; in fact part of the state's opposition to the Catholic hierarchy's demand for a state-supported university institution largely under their control, was in order to defend against possible encroachment on academic freedom. Under the 1908 Act the state gave an initial capital grant and annual current expenditure grants to the new institutions. But after this, state support for Irish universities was niggardly and hindered their full development. Trinity College could rely on its endowed funds but from 1945 onwards it too became increasingly dependent on state support. The achievement of political independence in 1922 meant little change for Irish universities and the state did not interfere with their internal affairs, though Irish studies were promoted more in the colleges of the National University. Trinity College which had been traditionally Unionist gave its allegiance to the new state but a number of factors including the continued opposition by the Catholic hierarchy to attendance there by Catholic students tended to keep it apart from the main stream of Irish life. By 1960 the need for formal reappraisal of Irish university and higher education was felt by many and the government set up a commission on higher education in that year.

As was the case in other European countries a key element in the debate on Irish university education in the nineteenth century was what type of university education should be provided. Trinity College had been established in 1591 on the Oxbridge model and while Trinity showed greater curricular flexibility than her sister universities, particularly in the eighteeenth century, it largely followed the model of the old universities. It was predominantly the preserve of the Church of Ireland and had a pronounced clerical aura. The administration was hierarchical in structure. It was a small, elite institution whose student numbers even by 1901 numbered less than 1,000. It was fee-paying, residential and linked to strong landed families and those with good positions in the church and state. The curricular emphasis was on the humanities – the classics, philosophy, mathematics and history. Some of its scholars enjoyed international reputations in their fields. From the early nineteenth century, however, trends on the continent and in England were seriously challenging the conception of the traditional university. These trends stressed the importance of scientific and technological studies, of experimental and applied research, and modern languages, and they urged more concern for vocational and professional preparation. There was also a trend to seek for more open access for young people of ordinary means and any denomination, and also for a more democratic administrative framework, as well as graduation by means of written examination.

The pacemaker in England for these new trends was University College, Gower Street, London, established in 1828. What became known as the 'redbrick' universities, linked to the industrial cities, followed the new tradition and, when the government moved to establish university institutions in Ireland through the Queen's Colleges Bill in 1845, it was this new model that was chosen. The Queen's Colleges were to be non-denominational and non-residential with low fees. The curriculum was to place a greater emphasis on science, modern languages and applied studies than had been the case in the traditional pattern. Written examinations were the norm for determining standards and governing committees were set up. Catholic opposition to the colleges was primarily directed against their non-denominational character but it was also influenced by a suspicion that this type of university institution was associated with the forces of secularisation. The utilitarians and radicals had been the main agents behind University College, London and some churchmen felt that what was afoot was a campaign against the established order. For people such as Sir Thomas Wyse and Sir Robert Kane, who were familiar with developments on the continent, the hope was that the new institutions would be closely aligned to the industrial and economic needs of mid-nineteenth-century Ireland.

Ireland shared in the great contemporary debates on liberal versus utilitarian education, secular versus religious-controlled universities, research versus teaching.[2] The Queen's Colleges favoured utilitarian, generalised modern learning conducted in secular institutions with an applied science research orientation. In the 1850s Dublin provided the stage for one of the great statements on liberal education when, as rector of the newly established Catholic University (1854), Newman delivered his famous discourse on university education. The Catholic University had been set up by the Catholic hierarchy in opposition to the government-sponsored Queen's University. Against vocationalism, Newman argued for the development of the moral and intellectual qualities, for the training of man as man rather than training for a particular profession. He spoke of the disinterested pursuit of knowledge rather than its application to social and economic life. For him residence and the 'sense of place' were important educational influences on the formation of young adults. Theological studies had an integral part to play. The cultivation of gentlemanly and courtly virtues evoked memories of the leisured society for whom Castiglione had written in Renaissance Italy. Although Newman gave a masterly exposition of the traditional ideal of liberal education in his writings, it is interesting to note that in his arrangements for the Catholic University there was a much more modern and professional aura to the course of studies than one might have been led to expect. Newman's dreams of a great Catholic university in Dublin catering for the English-speaking world did not materialise. However, when this college merged with the colleges of Galway and Cork to form the federal National University of Ireland in 1908, the tradition which became uppermost was that of the modern university allied to the needs of its society in terms of the skills and professions required.

University education was not a highly valued commodity amongst the majority of the Irish middle class in the nineteenth century. Denominational disputes no doubt affected attitudes but, even allowing for this, the demand for the facilities available remained very low. Even by 1900 there were only 3,200 students at university. University education had the aura of being for the elite in the upper echelons of society; it was, moreover, mainly people who could afford such a long education for their children who also had the money or position to place their children in professions who interested themselves in it. The small number of students also affected the range and quality of what could be provided in the various institutions: the Queen's Colleges and the Catholic University particularly suffered from small numbers. A further difficulty was the lack of satisfactory intermediate education standards for much of the century and the problems this posed for university matriculation. When the Intermediate Board was set up in 1878 it was the learning associated with the traditional university which was fostered and university men set and corrected the examination papers. The shaping influence of the university on the curriculum of secondary schools has been a perennial issue of contention up to recent times.

The range of scholarships to university was very limited. The legislation of 1908 allowed for local authorities to provide scholarships to university and to be represented on the governing bodies of the various colleges. There has continued to be a very pronounced social imbalance in the student composition of Irish universities in that students from families of low socio-economic status hold only a very small proportion of the places in universities. The introduction of a student grant scheme in 1968 has done little to change the pattern.

Ireland, like other countries, also suffered from the prejudices which existed in the nineteenth century against university education for women. It was only towards the end of the century that formal disabilities and restrictions were removed. Even then social attitudes were not in favour of advanced education for women and it was only a small minority who went forward to achieve positions of scholarship and eminence in and through university education. As the twentieth century progressed women assumed their rightful place in all faculties though women still form only a small minority in senior academic or administrative positions within Irish universities.

Until recent years industry and commerce have shown little direct involvement in, or patronage of, university education. During long decades of limited state funding, industry contributed little to establishing chairs or promoting research projects. Lack of funds was an important factor in the universities being largely teaching institutions, with limited research activity. Thus, the universities' links with the economic, industrial and commercial life of Ireland were mainly indirect through training of graduates in appropriate disciplines. The lack of a more direct innovatory involvement was particularly important in that universities had an almost total monopoly of third-level education, apart from some specialist colleges. Recent decades have seen the emergence of a binary third-level system in Ireland wherein, as well as the universities, there are many non-university state-funded research and teaching institutions specialising in applied studies.

The University of Dublin (Trinity College)

Ireland did not benefit from the great flowering of universities which many other European countries experienced in the middle ages. Several initiatives to establish a university failed and Ireland had to wait until 1591 for the establishment of the University of Dublin which received its royal charter in 1592. This was to remain Ireland's only university until the mid-nineteenth century. The university was established as a 'mater universitatis' with one college, that of the 'Holy and Undivided Trinity' and so it has remained despite a number of efforts to extend the University of Dublin to include more colleges. In popular parlance Trinity College has become synonymous with the University of Dublin. The original grant of Queen Elizabeth I made it clear that Trinity College was to be based on the Oxbridge model — 'we license the provost and fellows of the said college that they may establish amongst themselves whatever well-constituted laws they may perceive in either of our universities of Cambridge or Oxford, provided that they shall consider them proper and suitable for themselves.'[3] As well as the promotion of learning Trinity College was seen as an instrument for the 'cultivation of virtue and religion', the religion being that of the Established Church.

In the early years it seems that Trinity College did not exact religious tests from its students and some lay Catholic students attended. In 1637, however, Charles I took back under royal authority the right of making statutes and a series of tests and oaths were introduced which made it impossible on the grounds of conscience for Catholics or dissenters to attend or to graduate from the college. It was only towards the close of the eighteenth century, following the period of penal legislation, that relaxations were made which allowed other than Established Church adherents to benefit from the educational facilities of Ireland's only university. A section of the Catholic Relief Act of 1793 and royal letters of 1794 enabled Catholics and non-conformists legally to enter and obtain degrees, though professorships, fellowships and scholarships of the college continued to be confined to members of the Established Church. Following the Relief Acts a small number of Catholics entered Trinity, some of whom were to attain positions of influence in public affairs in later years.

Despite trends towards intellectual and social radicalism in its early curriculum, by the end of the seventeenth century Trinity had become the intellectual institution of the Anglo-Irish gentleman and- the Church of Ireland minister, and a buttress of the social, political and religious values of the ruling elite.[4] However, in the eighteenth century initiatives were taken which indicate an effort to keep abreast of new branches of learning. Thus, in 1724 a chair of natural and expèrimental philosophy was established, in 1762 chairs of mathematics and oriental languages, in 1776 two royal chairs of modern languages, in 1785 chairs of chemistry and botany, and in 1791 a chair of Irish. The founding of such chairs did not always mean that such subject areas were actively taught and promoted. Yet, more than at her sister colleges Oxford and Cambridge at this time, contemporary studies and modern authors were favoured – as one commentator remarked in 1759: 'The Newtonian philosophy, the excellent Mr Boyle's philosophy, Mr Locke's metaphysics prevail much in the College of Dublin.'[5]

Residence was not necessary for the obtaining of a degree and the BA could be obtained without attendance at lectures at all. Attendance was necessary for medicine, law, divinity and engineering. In the 1830s many changes were introduced which had the effect of tightening up on the examination procedures. Two royal commissions of inquiry were set up for Oxford and Cambridge in 1850 and were critical of much of the academic life and practices of these institutions. The inquiry on Trinity College of 1850, however, which reported in 1852, was much more favourable. It found that 'the general state of the university is satisfactory' and that 'the spirit of improvement has been especially shown in the changes which have been introduced in the course of education to adapt it to the requirements of the age'.[6] In 1873 all religious tests were finally abolished in Trinity College except in the divinity faculty. Sexist barriers were also beginning to be eroded with the provision of special examinations for women in 1870 and their admittance to ordinary university examinations in 1896.

The founding of Maynooth College
The operation of religious tests by the University of Dublin in the seventeenth and eighteenth centuries forced Catholics who sought formal third-level education to go to colleges abroad. Irish colleges had been established in the late sixteenth and early seventeenth centuries in many European centres of learning such as Rome, Paris, Salamanca, Douai and Louvain, and it was in such colleges that Irish Catholic students usually received their education, par-

ticularly clerical students in preparation for the priesthood.[7] Following the spread of revolutionary thought and fervour on the continent in the last quarter of the eighteenth century, political and ecclesiastical authorities became apprehensive of allowing Irish students to be exposed to the 'contagion of sedition and infidelity'. In the year of the French Revolution, 1789, there were 478 Irish students abroad, 348 of them in France. In 1795 the government agreed to give direct funding for the establishment of a Catholic college at Maynooth. Initially it was not confined to clerical students and between 1800 and 1817 a number of secular male students attended, but from 1817 this practice ceased and it became the national seminary for the education and preparation of Catholic priests. In 1845 the government gave it a capital grant of £30,000 and its annual grant was increased from £9,000 per annum to £26,000, despite considerable parliamentary opposition.[8] This sum continued to be paid until 1869 when in conjunction with the disestablishment of the Established Church a compensatory grant of about £370,000 was allocated instead of the annual grant. In 1899 Maynooth got approval to award degrees of the Pontifical University in Rome in philosophy, theology and canon law.

The Queen's Colleges

The problem still remained of providing opportunities for university education for lay Catholics as the atmosphere and control of Trinity remained essentially Protestant. In the wake of the granting of Catholic emancipation the government established the Board of National Education to foster a state-supported mixed education system for elementary education. The period also saw the establishment in England of University College, which opened at Gower Street, London in 1828 as an alternative university model to the Oxbridge tradition. London University, which received its charter in 1836, was designed on more utilitarian lines, was non-residential and its degrees could be obtained by sitting for its examination without attendance at the London College. The curriculum incorporated much modern learning with a concern for its application to the contemporary social and industrial situation.

A Select Committee on Foundation Schools and Education in Ireland was established in 1835 with Thomas Wyse, MP as chairman. It presented a very wide-ranging report in 1838, in the course of which it was urged that four provincial colleges be established to help provide higher education for the middle classes in Ireland.[9] These colleges would be inter-denominational, non-residential, governed by management committees and offer a curriculum on the lines being pioneered by London University. There was no immediate result from these proposals though a committee was formed in Cork to press for a modern university there. Wyse and Thomas Spring-Rice, MP kept the issue alive through meetings and petitions.

In May 1845 the prime minister, Sir Robert Peel, took the initiative and introduced a Colleges Bill which provided for the setting up of three 'Queen's Colleges' in Ireland to be sited in Cork, Galway and Belfast.[10] The government had mixed motives in introducing this measure as is clear from Peel's correspondence when he remarked on his aim 'of weaning from repeal the great body of the wealthy and intellectual Roman Catholics by the steady manifestation of a desire to act with impartiality and to do that which is just. One of the consequences of this may be (and one little to be deplored) refusal on the part of the laity to submit to an intolerant spiritual dictation on political matters'.[11] Peel further felt that there was no possibility in the prevailing political climate of getting parliament to approve financial support for denominational university education for Catholics.

The new Queen's Colleges were to be non-denominational though religious facilities could be provided on a voluntary basis by private endowment. The colleges were to be non-residential though provisions for deans of residence who would have a supervisory role for students' lodgings was included. The government would have the right, at least in the early years, of appointing the college authorities and professors. The curriculum was to be along modern utilitarian lines with three faculties — arts, law and medicine. The fees were to be low. Graduation was to follow tight examination procedures.

Reaction to the Colleges Bill in Ireland was divided. Daniel O'Connell, the prestigious leader of the Repeal Association, denounced the proposed colleges as 'the godless colleges', using the emotive phrase coined by Sir Robert Inglis with regard to University College London, and said that nothing but Catholic colleges would satisfy Catholic demands. Thomas Davis, leader of the Young Ireland Group, praised the measure seeing it as an opportunity for promoting understanding and fellowship among young Irish people of different religious beliefs.[12] The Catholic hierarchy was divided: a minority led by Dr Murray of Dublin and Dr Crolly of Armagh, who had already been sounded on the measure, looked with some favour on the bill; the majority, led by Dr MacHale of Tuam, condemned the bill. A compromise was reached among the bishops in that amendments to the bill were agreed by the hierarchy and forwarded to the government. These were of central significance and included the call for dual professorships, Catholic and Protestant, for a number of subject areas, the demand that a proportion of other professors and office holders be Catholics approved by the bishop, and that all officers should be appointed by a board of trustees which should include the Catholic prelates of the provinces involved. The government refused to make such changes. The three main churches were divided on the measure and the split deepened between the Young Irelanders and the O'Connellites, though the two main protagonists, Davis and O'Connell, died in 1846 and 1847 respectively. The Irish Colleges Bill with slight amendments was passed in the House of Commons on 10 July and received royal assent on 31 July 1845. The autumn of the same year, 1845, saw the start of several years of famine and hunger which had profound social and economic repercussions throughout Ireland. However, the attitude of the church of the majority was the factor which would have the most significant bearing on the success or failure of the colleges. While the eminent scientist Sir Robert Kane acted as chairman of the planning committee drawing up the statutes and planning arrangements for the institution of the colleges, the newly elected Pope, Pius IX, was deliberating on a request from the Irish hierarchy to decide on whether they should accept the colleges. In papal rescripts of October of 1847 and 1848 the colleges were condemned as 'harmful to religion'. Rome at this time was very disturbed at the growing secularisation of European society and had hardened its position on mixed denominational education.

The three Queen's Colleges at Cork, Galway and Belfast were opened in October 1849 for the start of the academic year. In the following year the Queen's University was established to act as the examining and degree awarding body for the colleges. Its headquarters were in Dublin Castle and the examinations were conducted in St Patrick's Hall in the Castle. This year, 1850, also saw a clear affirmation of Catholic opposition to the Queen's

Colleges. In April 1850 a third rescript was issued from Rome which condemned the Colleges as 'detrimental to religion by reason of their grave and intrinsic dangers'.[13] The rescript prohibited the clergy from taking up teaching appointments and urged the bishops to dissuade the laity from attending the colleges. A synod of the Catholic church was held at Thurles in August 1850 and was presided over by the newly-appointed Archbishop of Armagh, Dr Paul Cullen, who had the further authority of apostolic delegate from the Pope. The synod issued a strong statement on the alleged dangers of inter-denominational education and in particular issued a detailed condemnation of the Queen's Colleges as centres of higher education for Catholic students. Despite Dr Cullen's assertion that 'all controversy is now at an end – the Judge has spoken – the question is decided', a large minority of bishops opposed the decrees which forbad priests to hold any office in the Colleges and which urged the laity to repudiate and shun the Colleges.[14] The synod of Thurles was a watershed in the Catholic church's opposition to inter-denominational education. The sustained opposition of the Catholic church proved to be a daunting obstacle to the Colleges realising their potential, particularly in the case of Cork and Galway. Queen's College, Belfast had a predominantly Presbyterian student intake and progressed better than the other two sister colleges.

Another severe problem was the lack of a satisfactory intermediate education system which would serve as preparatory ground for students aspiring to university-type education. The Kildare Commission was set up in 1854 to inquire into existing endowed schools and to see if a public intermediate school system could be built on existing endowments. The Commission in 1858 recommended the establishment of such a state-supported system but on the basis of mixed denominational schools with regulations for separate religious instruction. In the prevailing climate of hostility to mixed education there was little chance of these recommendations being accepted and intermediate education continued on in its haphazard and under-financed state with a consequent shortage of students who were suitably prepared for university. It was also the case that in the social and economic circumstances which existed in post-famine Ireland there was no great demand among the middle classes for higher education.

The model of university education represented by Trinity College had little appeal for the Catholic middle class and the concepts of liberal education set forth by Newman did not fire them with enthusiasm. It is possible, despite the harsh economic conditions which prevailed generally, that more of the middle class would have been attracted by the type of education provided by the Queen's Colleges, with their practical emphasis, if it had been better explained and if they had not been affected by the strong clerical disapprobation. But the lack of a more developed industrial base in the predominantly agricultural economy limited employment opportunities for applied science graduates and this was also a disincentive.[15]

The Queen's Colleges with their impressive new buildings did have some eminent staff members and drew a student body of mixed denominations. By 1864 the three colleges combined had 750 students and their graduates were successful in various fields such as the civil service, army, navy and academic life. Yet the colleges never realised their full potential nor the expectations held for them.

The Royal University
A government initiative of 1866 to allow students not attending the Queen's Colleges to have access to the degrees of the Queen's University was met with strong opposition by Queen's graduates and by some Protestants and it was dropped. However, a somewhat similar scheme was adopted in 1879 with the establishment of the Royal University of Ireland as a purely examining body. [16] Students attending the Queen's Colleges as well as other students could enter for its degrees. The Royal University replaced the Queen's University when the latter was formally dissolved in 1882.

The senate of the Royal University, composed of equal numbers of Catholics and Protestants, was appointed by the crown in April 1880. As an examining board whose examinations were open to all candidates, whether collegiate students or not, and which had the power to award prizes and exhibitions on examination performance, it reflected the type of thinking which had set up the Intermediate Board in 1878. By offering a scheme of thirty-two fellowships valued at £400 per annum, half of which went to the Catholic University, it gave indirect support to denominational university education. The Royal University now made degrees available to those Catholic students who, through conscientious objections, were not in a position to benefit from the degrees of Trinity College or Queen's University. However, the Royal University was open to grave objection because of its concentration on examinations and its tendency to undermine the value of university education by allowing entry to degree examinations without prerequisite college attendance. This last factor dealt a heavy blow to the Queen's Colleges, which not alone lost their Queen's University but saw student attendance decline even further. In the year 1881-2 there had been 567 students in the Belfast College, 402 in Cork and 201 in Galway, but by 1901-2 these numbers had fallen to 349, 190 and 93 in the respective colleges.[17] Indeed at the examinations of 1901 only 500 of the 1,779 successful candidates came from the five principal colleges of a university character — the three Queen's Colleges, University College, Dublin and Magee College. The majority came from miscellaneous schools or through 'private study'.[18] Parliament provided funds for the administrative and examining functions of the Royal University at Earlsfort Terrace, Dublin. A further £20,000 per annum was made available for fellowships, exhibitions and scholarships for secular studies. The establishment of the Royal University was not a satisfactory long-term solution but it did allow students of all denominations and both sexes from different parts of Ireland to sit for the same examinations and compete for the scholarships and prizes made available. The Royal University ceased to exist following the new arrangements established by the Irish Universities Act of 1908.

The Catholic University

In the rescripts from Rome opposing the Queen's Colleges the Pope had urged the Catholic hierarchy to set up a purely Catholic university on the lines of that which had been re-organised in Louvain, Belgium in 1835. A committee for this purpose was set up at the synod of Thurles in 1850. Fund-raising campaigns were launched in Ireland, England and the United States and these yielded about £30,000 in 1851. John Henry Newman, the distinguished scholar of Oriel College, Oxford and a recent convert to catholicism, was appointed rector of the new university in November 1851. Newman had a grand conception of the university becoming a great Catholic university for the English-speaking world. His views on the nature of university education are strikingly set forth in his *Discourses on university education* (some of which were delivered in the form of public lectures in Dublin in 1852), and in what became known as his *University sketches* which appeared in the *University gazette* in the 1850s.

Newman expressed strong opposition to the utilitarian tradition which the London University and the Queen's Colleges embodied.

The Catholic University was formally established in 1854. There were to be five faculties: theology, law, medicine, philosophy and letters. It ought to be noted that science and engineering were associated with the faculty of letters. Certain planning difficulties had arisen over the relative authority of the rector and the Catholic bishops, and delays and uncertainties had ensued. Finally, however, the bishops retained overall authority but entrusted the administration of the university to Newman who was formally installed as rector on 4 June 1854. The university was formally opened on 3 November 1854 at 86 St Stephen's Green, Dublin, when twenty students were admitted. The medical school, which had existed in St Cecilia Street since 1837, was incorporated into the Catholic University and by having its qualifications recognised by professional bodies in Ireland and England it gave a valuable boost to the new institution. Inaugural lectures by new professors attracted public attention. In the first academic year a staff of seventeen, exclusive of the medical school, was appointed. Student numbers increased quickly to forty and reached 152 by 1859, and some students lived in residences associated with the university. As the university had no government charter to award degrees it adopted the titles of 'Licentiate' and 'Fellow'. Interesting features of the new university included the regulation which required all students to undertake a preliminary two-year course of general education, which was a tradition of some older universities, and also the establishment of evening lectures leading to a university qualification. University press and publications were initiated, a library begun and a university church founded in St Stephen's Green. In the hope of improving secondary education a scheme was devised of affiliated schools with a scholarship fund for students.

During these early foundation years Newman had retained his position as Superior of the Oratory in Birmingham. Eventually, in November 1858, he carried out his intention of resigning from the Catholic University of Ireland and returning to his duties and interests in England.[19] This was a blow to the infant university. Newman had put a great deal of time and energy into laying the foundations of the Catholic University but the Irish hierarchy never shared his vision of the great international Catholic university nor was his curriculum to the liking of some bishops. Problems of finance and poor public response caused Newman considerable frustration. Fundamental problems for the university were the continued refusal of the government to grant a charter for the awarding of degrees and the lack of state financial support.[20]

The year 1863 represented the highest point of success: the number of students in the arts and science faculties reached ninety-one, in the medical school 108 and in the evening courses 100. The evening courses were discontinued after 1865.[21] While ambitious hopes continued to be harboured, as instanced by the purchase of a site and grand foundation-stone ceremony for a new university at Drumcondra in 1862, various difficulties persisted and the Catholic University went into decline. Its continued existence became problematic but it was useful to apply as a pressure on the government to support a denominational initiative. Having declined to a low ebb in the late 1870s, the Catholic University was to get an injection of life following the establishment of the Royal University through the degrees and fellowships which were made available to it. In 1882 the bishops remodelled the Catholic University to consist of a group of Catholic institutions. The old Catholic University was one of these and was henceforth to be known as University College. The college came under the control of the Jesuit Order in 1883. Under the arrangements arrived at for distributing the fellowships of the Royal University, University College, Dublin as it was now known, got thirteen fellowships which provided a valuable yearly income of about £6,000. There were 180 students in University College at the turn of the century.

Presbyterian institutions

During the eras of persecution a tradition grew up of Presbyterians seeking higher education in Scottish universities, particularly Glasgow. The Belfast Academical Institution was founded on the initiative of a group of Protestants in 1814. It was a part-school and part-collegiate institution. It had hopes of being a multi-denominational university but this did not happen. A parliamentary subsidy for a divinity school for Presbyterians was granted annually from 1828. It merged with the general assembly's Theological College, Belfast in 1849.

Many Presbyterians accepted the Queen's College, Belfast as a suitable institution for the higher education of Presbyterian youth but others pressed for state support of a 'complete college' for the education of Presbyterian clergymen. State support was not forthcoming but such a college was set up in 1865 in Derry as a result of private benefactions and became known as Magee College. It included two faculties – arts and theology. The College remained small, with sixty students in 1900. From 1879 its students could graduate from the Royal University and it was awarded one fellowship by the University. In 1883 female students were fully incorporated within the college. Magee was disappointed at getting no specific mention in the University Act of 1908. In 1909 Magee College made arrangements whereby its students could take degrees from Trinity College, Dublin.[23]

Museum of Irish Industry – College of Science
As part of the new drive for utilitarian learning the mid-nineteenth century saw the establishment of a number of public museums and non-university societies focusing on inventions and industrial education. Robert Kane had published his monumental *The industrial resources of Ireland* in 1844 and was pressing for the establishment of a teaching museum with an emphasis on practical education. In 1845, the same year as the Queen's Colleges Bill was introduced, the museum of economic geology was instituted with Kane as its director. In 1846 the museum was housed at 51 St Stephen's Green, Dublin. Officially it was seen mainly as a museum but Kane shaped it so that its educational functions were expanded as well as its materials and it became known as the Museum of Irish Industry. For a period it worked in conjunction with the Royal Dublin Society, offering part-time as well as systematic lecture courses. This institution was to evolve into the Royal College of Science, formally established in 1867 with an annual parliamentary grant of £7,000 and with Robert Kane as its dean until his retirement in 1873.

There were two kinds of student admitted to the college. Associated students attended for three years and, on the successful completion of the course, were awarded the diploma of associateship (ARCSI). Non-associated students attended individual courses of their choice and were in many cases teachers. The number of associated students was small, averaging between twenty and thirty in the years up to 1900 though increasing to about 100 in later years. The non-associated students were more numerous, frequently reaching 100 per annum. The dropout rate amongst the associated students was large. A further problem was that in its first forty years of existence, at least 50 per cent of the students were non-Irish.

The College of Science came under the control of the Department of Agriculture and Technical Instruction in 1899 and following this an effort was made to broaden its work on the lines of a continental polytechnic. Considerable expansion took place including new premises in Upper Merrion Street, opened in 1911.[24] A more favourable climate for industrial and scientific education was a factor in the greater success of the college in these years and there was an increase in the industrial enterprises in which some of the graduates might gain employment. In 1926 the College was incorporated into the faculty of science of University College, Dublin.

Initiatives towards resolving the question of university provision for Catholics

By the 1870s it was quite clear that the Queen's Colleges were not going to be a satisfactory solution to the needs of Irish university education. The Catholic University was languishing in the absence of a charter and sufficient endowment. With the disestablishment of the Church of Ireland in 1869 it became increasingly difficult for a government to grant direct state support for a denominational third-level institution. It proved a long and difficult process before a tolerable solution was arrived at. The following account touches on the key stages through which the debate proceeded.

In 1873 Gladstone introduced a bill which proposed one federal university for Ireland — the University of Dublin. The university would comprise Trinity College, Queen's Colleges, Belfast and Cork, the Catholic University and Magee College, with provision for other institutions to affiliate. The university would be open to all but the colleges could be denominational. Attendance at the colleges would not be necessary for entering for the university examinations. This proposal met with opposition from Trinity College which resented the interference with its position; the Catholic authorities opposed it because it gave no endowment to any Catholic institution and the university would be secular in tone; authorities in the Queen's Colleges were also unhappy. The bill was narrowly defeated in parliament, a fact which influenced the fall of the Liberals from power at the time.[25] Shortly after the defeat of the bill all remaining religious tests were abolished in Trinity College. This did nothing to mollify the ire of the Catholic hierarchy who in 1875 imposed a ban on the attendance of Catholic students at Trinity College.

The next significant initiative was the introduction of a private member's bill by˚the O'Conor Don in 1879 which prompted the government to sponsor its own legislation for a Royal University in 1879. As has been noted this was to be a purely examining body open to all male and female students from any college or none. Queen's University ceased to exist from 1882 and the Catholic University got a lease of life from the distribution of fellowships and prizes from the Royal University. Discussions between Dr Walsh, appointed Archbishop of Dublin in 1885, and Chief Secretary Hicks-Beach[26] in 1886 and Balfour in 1889 promised, but did not lead to, progress. From 1897 the bishops indicated that they were no longer insisting on a de jure Catholic university, state-supported and under the hierarchy's control.[27]

Various proposals were in the air and in 1901 the Robertson Commission was set up to report on university education exclusive of Trinity College. Its report was published in 1903.[28] It recommended the re-organisation of the Royal University as a federal teaching university with four constituent colleges – the three Queen's Colleges and a new Catholic college in Dublin. Even this did not prove a satisfactory guideline for policy as the signatories included many notes of reservation indicating divided councils. A further commission, the Fry Commission, was established in 1906 and its terms of reference concentrated on Trinity College. It issued a report in 1907 which was again divided.[29] The majority favoured the opening of the University of Dublin to become a 'national' university with five colleges: Trinity, Cork, Belfast, Galway and a new college in Dublin. The minority favoured the Robertson plan. Two chief secretaries, Wyndham in 1903 and Bryce in 1907, also toyed with the idea of one federal university for Ireland. The final solution emerged under Chief Secretary Birrell and became law as the Irish Universities Act in 1908.[30]

The Irish Universities Act of 1908 allowed the University of Dublin with its single college, Trinity, to continue its existence unaffected. It abolished the Royal University. Queen's University, Belfast and a new National University of Ireland (NUI) were set up. This latter was to be a federal university with the Queen's Colleges of Cork and Galway, now called University College, Cork, and University College, Galway respectively, joined with University College, Dublin. A measure of continuity between the new UCD and the existing University College was maintained by the inclusion of its graduates as members of the new university and most of its professors were transferred. The Queen's University and the National University were to be non-denominational and non-residential, with student attendance at courses necessary to enter for the university examinations. Provision was made for the addition of 'recognised' colleges, which was to have particular relevance to Maynooth College in that it became a recognised college of NUI in 1910. Not everybody was pleased with the overall outcome but in practice Trinity was happy to be left alone, the majority of Catholic bishops felt that no more could be achieved and that because of their geographical situation and student intake the prevailing ethos of the colleges would be Catholic. Presbyterians could attend Queen's University which reflected their traditions, though a fair mixture of students of varying denominations attended there. The university settlement arrived at in 1908 continued for over seventy years without significant structural change.

Statutory bodies known as the Dublin Commissioners and the Belfast Commissioners drew up the statutes for the two new universities. In July 1911 the university senate of the National University and the governing bodies of each constituent college assumed their full powers. In accordance with the federal nature of the National University the university senate approved the statutes for the colleges and appointed the president, professors and statutory lecturers of each college.

The National University had the responsibility of awarding degrees and maintaining course standards. With effect from 1913 Irish became a compulsory matriculation subject in NUI for all native-born Irish candidates. The Act of 1908 provided for annual endowments of £32,000 to University College, Dublin, £20,000 to University College, Cork, £18,000 to Queen's, Belfast, and £12,000 to University College, Galway. Building grants of £110,000 for Dublin, £14,000 for Cork, £60,000 for Belfast, and £6,000 for Galway were also disbursed.[31] Building grants were niggardly for the next fifty years, however, and the limited state subsidisation of university education hindered developments and was a factor in the tendency of the new university colleges to become predominantly teaching rather than research institutions.

Trinity College suffered a decline in student numbers and in revenue during World War I. A royal commission in 1920 urged a direct state grant of £113,000 and an annual subsidy of £49,000 for Trinity.[32] The Government of Ireland Act, 1920 reduced these awards to an annual grant of £30,000. This did not become operative and no mention of a grant was included in the terms of the Anglo-Irish Treaty. The board of Trinity College passed a resolution in 'support of the terms of settlement for the future government of Ireland',[33] but they were disappointed with their financial position. In 1923 the Free State government gave Trinity a non-recurrent grant of £5,000 and an annual grant of £3,000.

Under the provisions of the Universities Education (Agriculture and Dairy Science) Act of 1926 the Royal College of Science was transferred to University College, Dublin and a faculty of dairy science was established in University College, Cork. In 1929 improved financial provision was made for University College, Galway in recognition of the college's special efforts to foster the Irish language in academic life.[34] In 1960 the academic work of the veterinary college, which had been conducted under the Department of Agriculture, was transferred to the two veterinary faculties in Trinity College and University College, Dublin.

Following the great debates and various initiatives which Irish university education had experienced over the sixty years prior to 1908, the subsequent fifty years were years of considerable calm. The focus shifted from structural and administrative debate, and concerns became much quieter as different institutions applied themselves to their various academic affairs. The achievement of political independence caused no significant change. Any hopes which were entertained for greater financial support by an independent Irish government did not materialise. Trinity College had preferred to stay on its own rather than become part of a great federal Irish university. This, coupled with its past political and religious allegiances as well as the continued ban by the Catholic hierarchy on attendance there, which was more strictly enforced under Dr McQuaid as Archbishop of Dublin, tended to isolate Trinity from full-scale acceptance and involvement in Irish society. It retained its eminent position in the world of learning and housed students from England and other countries among its student body. In 1958, for instance, British students formed 39 per cent of the undergraduate student body in Trinity College.[35]

The growth of student numbers in universities was steady rather than dramatic — the total full-time student body in the NUI colleges and Trinity on the eve of World War II was about 5,000 students.[36] Whereas the census of 1871 had listed no woman in the student body of university colleges, and that of 1901 listed only ninety-one female students, later decades were to see considerable redress of this situation. Between 1938 and 1960 the percentage of female students in the total full-time student body ranged from 26 to 30 per cent.[37] The provision of scholarships and awards for university students was meagre; as late as 1964 only 15 per cent of Irish students were benefiting from such awards, amounting to £295,000.[38]

The growth of student numbers within the various colleges can be observed in the statistics for selected years in Table 7. The most striking growth in student numbers occurred in UCD and this put considerable strain on the facilities available on its site in Earlsfort Terrace. Between 1949 and 1958 the College acquired a large site at Belfield on the Stillorgan Rd in the southern suburbs of Dublin. In 1959 the government gave its approval for the transfer of UCD to these spacious surroundings at Belfield and plans for the building of a new university on this site were put in motion. The setting up by the government of a Commission on Higher Education in 1960 was an indication of the felt need for a new appraisal of existing third-level provision and of the need for new guidelines for development.

The founding of some other institutes and cultural societies
There were other developments in higher and general education outside the main university and college ambit of activity in the eighteenth and nineteenth centuries. The Royal College of Physicians was established under charters of 1692 and 1878. It acted as an examining body for various physician qualifications. Another such institution was the Royal College of Surgeons, founded by charter in 1784, whose main function was the development of training in surgery and its related subjects. Societies

Table 7: **Number of full-time students in UCD, UCC, UCG and TCD in certain years 1938-60**

Year	UCD	UCC	UCG	TCD	Total all colleges
1938/9	1,998	853	584	1,543	4,978
1948/9	2,862	936	762	2,236	6,796
1959/60	3,961	1,304	945	2,443	8,653

Source: Table 12 *Report of Commission on Higher Education* Vol. 1, p. 31

charged with professional training duties in the legal profession include the Honourable Society of King's Inns and the Incorporated Law Society of Ireland. Other professional bodies were also established such as the Royal Institute of Architects founded 1839 and the Royal Institute of Chartered Surveyors in 1886.

Other societies were established to foster scholarship and general culture. These included the Royal Dublin Society founded in 1731 and incorporated by royal charter in 1750, the Royal Irish Academy founded in 1785 and incorporated by royal charter in the following year, the Royal Hibernian Academy of Arts which received its charter in 1823 and was re-organised under a new charter in 1861. Great national repositories of books, historical materials and works of art were set up. The National Museum and the National Library were founded in 1877 while the National Gallery of Art was established in 1864.

Events and reports relating to university education (1591-1960)

1591	University of Dublin (Trinity College) founded
1795	Foundation of Maynooth College
1814	Belfast Academical Institution founded
1845	Irish Colleges Act, setting up Queen's Colleges, H.C. 1845 (299) (400) 1.357,365
1850	Queen's University established
1850	Synod of Thurles — Catholic hierarchy condemns Queen's Colleges
1852	Report of Commission of Inquiry on Trinity College, H.C. 1852-53 (1637) XLV. 1
1854	The Catholic University formally opened
1858	Report of Commission on Queen's Colleges, H.C. 1857-58 (2413) XXI. 53
1865	Magee College set up
1873	Defeat of Gladstone's bill on university education
1873	All religious tests abolished in Trinity College
1875	Catholic hierarchy oppose Catholic attendance at Trinity College
1879	The Royal University set up
1882	Abolition of Queen's University
1903	Report of Commissioners on University Education (Robertson), H.C. 1903 (Cd. 1483-4), XXXII. 1
1907	Report of Royal Commission on Trinity College (Fry), H.C. 1907 (Cd. 3311-12), XLI. 1

1908   The Irish Universities Act, H.C. 1908 (358) 11. 1097
1910   Maynooth a recognised college of NUI
1920   Report of Royal Commission on University of Dublin, H.C. 1920 (Cnd. 1678) XIII, 1189
1959   Government approval for new site for UCD at Belfield
1960   Appointment of Commission on Higher Education

Part II: The Irish Education System since 1960

Chapter Five

An Overview of educational change, 1960-80

Compared with previous decades, the period 1960-80 witnessed a dramatic increase in government and public interest in education. A range of investigative bodies, such as the Investment in Education team, the Commission on Higher Education, the Committee on Mental Handicap, the Committee on Adult Education, the Committee on Reformatory and Industrial Schools, examined and reported on many facets of the educational system. Many striking policy initiatives resulted which have altered significantly the shape of the education system. The extent and range of the changes during this transitional epoch were such that they require to be seen against the background of wider social and attitudinal change during the period.

Educational change formed a part of significant changes of attitude which were occurring in Irish society generally. A notable landmark in this was the publication in 1958 of the government White Paper on Economic Expansion which led to the first economic programme and changed attitudes to economic and industrial development. Economists were now emphasising education as an economic investment rather than taking the traditional view of education as a consumer service. The returns on investment in education, both individually and socially, were held to be as high as investment in capital plant.[1] The prosperity of a modern technological society depended on the availability of an educated workforce. Increased economic growth and production in turn allowed for greater financial resources to be applied to education. An expanding economy allows for and needs an expanded education system; new emphasis was placed on slogans such as 'a nation's wealth is its people'. Further, it was felt that a society needs to draw on the full potential of its pool of talent and many commentators remarked that existing educational provision was not facilitating that.

Attitudinal change in Ireland was also influenced by Ireland's expanding links with international organisations such as the United Nations, UNESCO, the Council of Europe and OECD, and hopes of joining the EEC were high in the early 1960s. Irish representatives participated in international conferences and symposia on educational affairs which tended to give a wider perspective and reduce insularity. Irish teachers, with the aid of Irish Teacher Projects, began participating in organised educational visits to Europe and America, while the Irish section of the European Association of Teachers was founded in 1962. In many countries in post-war Europe the slogan 'equality of educational opportunity' gained general currency and this was also to be frequently voiced in the Ireland of the 1960s. The fact that politicians tended to use the slogan in a simplistic manner did not lessen its electoral appeal and high expectations were entertained by many for a better future for their children, education being the social escalator. On the other hand, the expansion of research and teaching in the behavioural sciences, such as psychology and sociology, in the universities helped to focus the attention of educationists and planners on problems involved in removing educational inequality. They also led to an enrichment of educational and pedagogic studies.

Educational groups such as the Teachers' Study Group, Tuairim, the Federation of Irish Secondary Schools and various teacher organisations provided forums where discussion, debate, criticism and proposals on education took place. Several individuals also produced pamphlets which contained trenchant criticisms of the system. Political parties became more conscious of the importance of education as an electoral issue and published policies on educational reform. The introduction of television in 1961, as well as the increasing interest taken by newspapers in educational matters, helped to cultivate and inform public interest in education. Ireland experienced also the breakdown of the old paternalist ethos which tended to confine educational policy to the authority figures, church and state. A greater tolerance and more scope for the expression of group and individual opinion by teachers, parents and students was in evidence. Third-level students, in particular, collectively took a more direct role in educational affairs. A sense of excitement followed the findings of the census of 1966 which recorded an increase in the population of 62,000, the first increase since the famine of the 1840s. This heralded the increase in the youth population-which was to continue in later years.

Many of the educational policy measures introduced were closely linked to perceived socio-economic needs. The state attempted to amalgamate schools at primary and post-primary level, so that larger units would allow for more economical capital and running costs, more satisfactory use of teaching resources and the provision of better equipment and facilities. The proliferation of small national schools in Ireland, as well as the continued decline in population up to 1966, had left many rural schools with small numbers on the roll. It was difficult to equip and staff them in line with modern thinking and requirements. Many of the schools were old and in disrepair and public expectations of the standards of hygiene, heating and facilities had risen in line with general improvements in domestic housing. The drop in enrolments after the school-leaving age had been reached made it difficult for many post-primary schools to offer a wide or balanced curriculum. The development of educational technology in the form of language laboratories, tape recorders, educational radio and television, film projectors, etc. highlighted the need for rationalisation of school provision. The policy of closure or amalgamation of small national schools was adopted and larger post-primary units were also encouraged. The increasing availability of motor cars reduced the physical hardship of travel to school and a bus transport scheme was introduced to facilitate further centralisation of schools.

In October 1959 Seán Lemass, then Taoiseach, announced that an immediate policy of the government was to increase the facilities for post-primary education.[2] Extended scholarship schemes were introduced in 1961 but a more significant development was the more direct role taken by the state in providing post-primary facilities. In 1964, for the first time, the state gave capital grants for secondary school expansion. It also provided fully state-funded comprehensive schools and later it developed community schools. Interestingly, these new forms of school emerged as a result of changes in government policy rather than in response to general demand. This more direct involvement by the state in post-primary schooling gave rise to considerable public controversy and some suspicions within the private secondary school sector. The mode by which some of the government's decisions were announced and communicated indicated a new leadership emphasis. But it was also open to criticism because of lack of clarity and in-adequate thinking through the consequences of the policy measures.

This gave rise to many practical problems of accommodation and staffing and also contributed to difficulties in realising the original conception of the new types of schools.

A key policy was to encourage greater participation in post-primary schooling by pupils with widely-varying abilities and from diverse social backgrounds. This policy got a great boost from what became known as 'the free education scheme' of 1967. Enrolments increased dramatically and this took care of the problems of small post-primary schools, though much controversy surrounded the issue of the most appropriate school size. On many occasions the target date for raising the school leaving age was given as 1970; eventually it was raised to fifteen years in 1972. With the transition to post-primary schools occurring predominantly about the age of twelve years, this also meant larger numbers of pupils in post-primary schools.

Coincident with the policy of increased participation was a changed conception of the appropriate form of post-primary school. Hitherto, the post-primary system had been bi-partite — academic secondary schools on the one hand, and vocational schools, emphasising technical and applied studies, on the other — and there was little liaison between them. The policy now adopted was one of eroding the academic/technical division by raising the status of the vocational schools and encouraging a more comprehensive-type curriculum in both vocational and secondary schools. This was a somewhat mixed blessing for vocational schools, as they were forced to compete with existing secondary schools on unequal terms. The raising of the status of vocational schools so that they could offer full post-primary courses was a cancellation of the Minister for Education's promises to the Catholic hierarchy in 1930 that the vocational schools would not offer the full range of post-primary studies. The new comprehensive schools and later community schools were to point the way for post-primary schooling. These moves were influenced by contemporary trends in Britain and in some continental countries which were promoting comprehensive schooling, and also by the desire to redress an imbalance which existed in Ireland between the number of pupils engaged in academic and those engaged in technical-type education. There was very little change in the actual numbers of secondary and vocational schools from 1960 to 1980 but the number of pupils in each type of school almost trebled over the period. The 'secondary top' as a form of schooling virtually disappeared. The preparatory colleges also changed their function, most of them becoming 'A'-type secondary schools. The number of secondary schools teaching through the medium of Irish decreased significantly during this period.

Many curricular changes were introduced into post-primary schools. A highly influential factor here was the pressure for a closer alignment of school curricula with the needs of a more industrialised economy. Changes occurred in the content of existing subjects and the pedagogic approach to them, with technical and applied subjects getting more official support. These curricular changes preceded and took little account of curricular developments at primary level. However, the later 1960s saw the preparation of a new curriculum for national schools which became official policy in 1971. This curriculum, in its ideology, content and format, was a radical contrast to that which had existed previously. Based on the ideology of child-centred education, it offered a wide subject range and encouraged 'discovery-type' teaching methods with pupil interest and involvement as the prime objectives. However, the lack of co-ordination and the failure to plan an educational programme in sequential stages appropriate to age and intellectual capacities from the early primary level upwards was to cause considerable problems for pupils and teachers. It led to the setting up in 1978 of a special committee on the transition from primary to post-primary schooling.

The extent and range of curricular change in post-primary schools was hampered by the lack of fundamental change in the public examination structure. Critical appraisals of these examinations were published and resulted in some changes in the mode of questioning, but the examinations continued to be operated largely in the same manner except that they now carried an increased strain of high competitiveness. This in turn gave rise to an expansion in private tuition and 'grind' institutions aimed at increasing the examination chances of those who availed of them.

An area which received serious attention from the Department of Education for the first time in the 1960s was educational provision for groups of people suffering from various forms of handicap and disadvantage. A better informed awareness of the educational needs of mentally-handicapped people as well as those afflicted by blindness, deafness or dumbness was in evidence. Although much remains to be done, there have been improvements in the quantity and quality of the education provided for such people and specialised training for educational and medical personnel has been made available. In line with developments in other countries, more attention has been focused on the education of children suffering from social and economic hardship and some experiments and improvements have been made for them. The government appointed a committee to examine the existing provisions and to make recommendations for the development of adult education. The concern for community and adult education gathered a new momentum and plans were proposed for improved, co-ordinated and up-dated forms of such education. Some of these proposals have been implemented.

The state took a much more active role in regard to third-level education than previously. It greatly increased capital and current expenditure on existing institutions and founded many new third-level institutions. Two new planning authorities were set up, though the canons of academic freedom were not infringed.

The most striking feature of third-level education policy has been the establishment of a binary system. This has entailed the building-up of the hitherto neglected non-university sector. New institutions such as regional colleges and national institutions of higher education have been added to the colleges of technology. This sector has its own statutory award-giving body — the National Council for Educational Awards (NCEA) — which validates courses and awards certificates, diplomas and degrees. The promotion of technological and applied studies at third level has been a key part of government policy. The Higher Education Authority (HEA) was established primarily as a co-ordinating, planning and financing body, liaising between the government and the universities. New building programmes were undertaken in all third-level institutions to cater for the greatly expanded student numbers which increased by about 60 per cent from 23,000 in 1968-9 to 37,000 by 1978-9. Interestingly, in the former year the universities accounted for 76 per cent of the total but by 1978-9 this proportion had been reduced to 61 per cent of the larger total. The period since 1960 saw considerable debate on the future structure of the universities, particularly the colleges of the National University. However, a final resolution in legislative form was very slow to emerge. A further significant development which has gathered momentum since the early 1960s has been the foundation and development of many non-university research institutes.

The unification of the teaching profession received a large boost by the establishment of a common salary scale in 1969. Teacher unions, although retaining their independence, have lessened the areas of disagreement among themselves, and they cooperate on many issues. Teacher training courses have undergone significant changes, the most obvious being the move towards an all-graduate profession. The awarding of university degrees to primary teachers and of NCEA degrees to physical education teachers and the planned extension of these to craft teachers, rural science and art teachers are important milestones in the history of teacher training. A tendency which became very pronounced over the years was the growing predominance of females within the profession, particularly at primary level.

Another feature of the education system which became pronounced is the decline in the number of religious in the overall teaching body. This was due to a decline in vocations and the greatly increased numbers of teachers needed at post-primary level to cater for the expanded number of pupils. Teachers in secondary schools were anxious for greater promotional opportunities and the right to principalships. This resulted in certain tensions between the religious proprietors of the schools and the teachers. Such tensions emerged also on the wider issue of the management of schools. Management boards were first set up for national schools in 1975. Secondary teachers rejected proposals made by Catholic school authorities in 1976 for management boards in secondary schools, finding the proposals unsatisfactory. Considerable acrimony and prolonged negotiation between church interests, teachers and the vocational education authorities attended the deed of trust document setting out the governing structure for community schools. During the 1970s vocational education authorities became concerned at what they viewed as the erosion of their traditional role in providing non-denominational vocational schools, in favour of new community schools. They initiated moves whereby some new schools would come under their control, be run on community school lines and be termed community colleges. This too gave rise to some tension with church authorities. The trend towards a diminution in church control of schooling could also be detected in the call by some suburban communities for multi-denominational national schools. Such calls were not favoured by the churches which saw them as part of a growing trend towards secularisation. By 1980 the Dalkey School Project had succeeded in opening a multi-denominational national school, followed by Bray in 1981. There have also been calls to establish all-Irish national schools in some suburban districts. Notable instances have been those set up in Ballymun and Rathcoole in County Dublin. Such developments are important not for the numbers involved but as signs of a more alert and concerned interest in educational needs and rights on the part of local communities.

The greatly increased impetus of educational improvement since 1960 is reflected in the increased levels of state financing of education. In 1960 this amounted to about £16,500,00; by 1965 it was £32,000,000; by 1970 it was £61,000,000; by 1975 it had reached £214,500,000 and the educational estimates for 1980 amounted to £550,000,000. Public expenditure on education as a percentage of GNP more than doubled from 3.05 per cent in 1960-1 to 6.29 per cent in 1973-4. Within the same period education's share of public current expenditure rose from 9.37 per cent to 12.75 per cent, and its share of all public capital expenditure increased from 4.22 per cent to 8.09 per cent.[3] The percentage of GNP devoted to education remained at about 6 per cent up to 1978-9. Even allowing for inflation, particularly rapid in the 1970s, the increase in the state financing of education is striking.

The period from 1960 to 1980 was a remarkable one in the history of Irish education. The wide range of reports on so many aspects of educational provision reflected the amount of investigation and appraisal which was undertaken. The state adopted a much more active role in educational planning and many new institutions were established at second level and third level. Participation rates at these levels soared. Important changes also took place at primary level. The areas of special education and adult education got new and welcome attention. Some less than radical changes were made in the administration of schools. Teacher training benefited from the reforming zeal and the goal of an all-graduate profession was virtually realised. Despite certain tensions created by such a period of change, for much of the time public opinion was buoyantly optimistic about the developments. The educational debate tended to reflect preoccupations with economic and industrial development more than purely educational considerations, but there is no doubt that this period represents a watershed in Irish education. Developments during this era have had a profound influence on the present-day system, and a treatment of these developments is interwoven with the appropriate sections in this part of the book. So as to allow a comprehensive treatment of the developments of the recent past combined with an accurate account of the existing system some overlap of material occurs.

Events and reports for the period 1960-80

1960   Commission on Higher Education set up
            Diploma course for teachers in special education
1961   Local Authorities Scholarships Act
1962   Council of Education Report on Curriculum of Secondary Schools
            Mathematics, science, modern language curricular changes
1963   Minister Hillery's policy speech
            National school library scheme
1965   Report of Commission on Mental Handicap (Pr. 8234)
            Psychological service set up in Department of Education
            Policy of closure of small national schools
1966   Investment in Education Report (Pr. 8311), Appendices (Pr. 8527)
            Maynooth College opened to lay students
            First three comprehensive schools opened
            Common Intermediate Course started
1967   'Free Education' scheme
            School transport scheme
            Abolition of Primary Certificate
            Report of Commission on Higher Education (Vol. I, Pr. 9389) (Vol. II, Pr. 9588; Summary Pr. 9326)
            Report on regional technical colleges (Prl. 371)
            Minister O'Malley's university 'Merger' proposals
1968   Government proposals on university re-organisation
            Third-level student grants introduced
            Higher Education Authority (HEA) set up on ad hoc basis (statutorily in 1971)
1969   Opening of first regional technical colleges
            Common salary scale for teachers
            Rutland Street pre-school project
            Grading introduced for public examination results
1970   Thomond College set up
            NIHEL received first students
            Report by Madaus and McNamara on Leaving Certificate
            Report on reformatory and industrial schools (Prl. 1342)

Department of Education Report on the education of itinerants

Joint Trinity and UCD plan for university education

Catholic hierarchy lifts attendance ban from Trinity

Community schools announced

1971   New curriculum for national schools

New equipment grants for national schools

Opening of first teacher centre

1972   Report on Education of the Deaf

School-leaving age raised to fifteen

NCEA established on ad hoc basis (statutorily in 1979)

1973   First community schools opened

Report on adult education

1974   BEd degrees instituted for national teachers

Three colleges of education become 'recognised' colleges of NUI

Report on An Chomhairle Mhúinteoirachta

New government proposals for third-level education

Report on Irish in education

1975   Boards of management for national schools

Intermediate Certificate Report (ICE)

1976   Central Applications Office (CAO) established

1977   Royal College of Surgeons in Ireland becomes a recognised college of NUI

New government proposals on third-level education

1978   St Angela's College, Sligo, a recognised college of NUI

VEC third-level colleges in Dublin combine to form DIT

Ministerial committee on problems of transition

1980   *White Paper on Educational Development*

Ministerial committee on educational broadcasting

Report of review body on teachers' salaries

Opening of Dublin NIHE

Deeds of trust agreed for community schools

Chapter Six

The Education System today with some trends and problems

As earlier sections of the book have indicated, factors in modern Irish history such as the colonial past, the religious affiliations of the population, the cultural traditions of the people, the economic structure and the goals set for education have all shaped the unusual, interesting and complex structure of the present-day Irish education system. Ireland's educational tradition is deeply-rooted in its past and the regard displayed by the people for education, even at periods of great political and economic difficulty, is a most striking feature of her history. However, as Ireland enters the last decades of the twentieth century, some daunting challenges face her in providing the range and standard of educational facilities appropriate to the needs of contemporary society.

The republic of Ireland, though a small island state of about three and a half million people, has a developed and intricate education system. Almost the entire population belongs to one of the christian denominations, over 90 per cent being Catholic. The churches have been deeply involved in education and this has had a large influence on the nature of the educational patterns which have evolved. The education system is predominantly a state-aided one, with the state providing the vast proportion of finance for capital and current expenditure although most of the institutions are not publicly owned or controlled. The state, through the Department of Education, exercises a preponderant role in determining educational policy.

The great majority of schools are denominational. An earlier tradition of single-sex schools has been changing, so that now about 80 per cent of the state-supported primary schools are mixed male and female pupil clientele and almost half of the post-primary schools are sexually mixed. Attendance at school is compulsory from the age of six to the age of fifteen, unless parents undertake to provide alternative education of an appropriate standard for their children. Participation up to the end of junior cycle post-primary schooling is over 90 per cent, and about 60 per cent of an age group now complete the senior cycle. About 85 per cent of children aged four and five also attend school.

The main institutions in the traditional, three-level structure of Irish education are as follows. At first level the predominant institution is that known as the national school. There are about 3,500 such schools catering for more than half a million children. The national schools are almost all owned by church authorities, with over 90 per cent under Catholic control. The state provides a minimum of two-thirds of the building costs of such schools, most of the current expenditure and all of the teachers' salaries, the teachers being employed by the local management board of the school. Local communities have to provide the school site which places a heavy burden on groups of ordinary citizens who may seek to set up a national school particularly in urban districts. There are a small number of private primary schools catering for less than 4 per cent of first-level pupils. These private schools receive no state aid and are not bound by the regulations of the Department of Education. About 63 per cent of the students enrolled in full-time education are at first-level.

The oldest institution of second-level schooling is the secondary school. These are almost all denominational schools built by religious groups. Up to 1964 they received no direct state grant for building, though now the state provides about 80 per cent of building costs but does not contribute to the site. Provided the secondary schools satisfy the regulations for 'recognised' status, the state pays building grants, capitation grants and most of the teachers' salaries. The school pays a nominal sum towards teachers' salaries to emphasise that the teachers are in their employ rather than direct public employees. Grants in lieu of school fees are paid to schools which offer free education, which amounts to over 90 per cent of the schools. Traditionally the secondary schools have followed the grammar-school pattern, though recent years have seen some alteration of this. They cater for about 70 per cent of all the second-level pupils.

The vocational schools are second-level public schools under the control of local authorities. They are built and maintained jointly by central government and local authority. Since 1966 most of the vocational schools offer the full-cycle of post-primary education. The local authority appoints the teachers under ministerial sanction and the state pays almost all the costs of the vocational schools. These schools are non-denominational but religion is part of the curriculum and churchmen usually play a part in the vocational education authorities who run the schools. About 21 per cent of second-level pupils attend vocational schools. These schools also cater for many forms of adult education.

Comprehensive and community schools are new forms of post-primary schools which provide a comprehensive curriculum blending academic and applied subjects and cater for all pupils in their catchment areas. They are mostly co-educational schools and no selection occurs at entry. The state builds and funds the comprehensive schools completely and it undertakes almost the total costs of community schools also. These types of school are public schools run by management boards with representatives of different interest groups, including church and local authority representatives. They are mostly denominational schools and have responsibilities for adult education and community development in their areas. They cater for about 8 per cent of the second-level pupils but as more community schools are established it is expected that this proportion will increase considerably. The state has shown considerable support for the community school as the preferred form for the future.

At third level the two universities – the University of Dublin (Trinity College) and the National University of Ireland, with its three constituent colleges – were by far the main providers of third-level education up to recent years. Trinity College was traditionally associated with the Church of Ireland interest and the National University though non-denominational had a predominantly Catholic ethos. Recent years have seen a large growth in the universities, and their students and atmosphere now reflect a more pluralistic composition. The universities have come increasingly to depend on the state for their funding, and over 85 per cent of their income now comes from the state. The Higher Education Authority (HEA) exists as a funding and planning authority for the universities and some other third-level institutions. In 1979 the universities catered for about 60 per cent of the full-time students in higher education.

Training colleges for national school teachers have also been in existence for a long period. In recent years they have become associated with the universities for academic purposes. They are private institutions owned by various denominational interests.

Again, they reflect the unusual Irish arrangement whereby the state pays for capital and current expenditure through the Department of Education, but the institutions remain in private ownership. College authorities employ the staff subject to ministerial approval and the state pays their salaries through the colleges.

Recent years have seen highly significant developments in the non-university third-level sector, which reflect the binary nature of the system. Firstly, there are third-level colleges under the vocational education committees (VECs): the six main ones are in Dublin and they have combined to form the Dublin Institute of Technology. Secondly, there are the regional colleges which also operate under the VEC network, and are built and supported by the state. Thirdly, national institutes of higher education have been established by the state in Limerick and in Dublin. The emphasis of all these institutions is on technology, applied sciences and business studies. They receive most of their academic awards from the National Council for Educational Awards, established in 1972.

Overall, the third-level sector caters for only about 4 per cent of the total enrolled fulltime in educational institutions. A higher education grants scheme, linked to academic performance and parental income, exists and about 30 per cent of higher education students benefit from it. There is a very significant social imbalance in the representation of the various social classes in third-level education.

The Irish education system is highly centralised with the Department of Education exercising a great deal of direct and indirect control over most aspects of the system. The bitter conflicts which existed between church and state under the British administration in Ireland largely disappeared following independence; the new state acquiesced in the churches' ownership and control of most of the institutions and their powers in such matters as teacher appointments and school ethos. On the other hand, church authorities were prepared to concede to the state the responsibility for laying down regulations with regard to curricula, examinations and so on, and responsibility for the payment of teachers and various grants. There have been very few occasions of open dispute, the main periods of unease being when the state passed the Vocational Education Act in 1930 and again when the state took initiatives in second-level education in the 1960s. The Department of Education in earlier decades tended to see its role primarily as an administrative body with little concern for educational research or innovation.

Recent years have seen a modification of this and the 1960s, in particular, saw the Department taking significant initiatives in educational policy. However, the pace of this has slackened and the role of the development unit with its concern for forward planning, which was set up following the Investment in Education Report of 1965, has been diminished. In the 1960s the Department ceased to publish its annual reports which could have contributed much to educational debate. It publishes annual statistical reports but policy or discussion documents are seldom issued by the Department. Since 1968 it has published a journal *Oideas* which carries articles on general education. A white paper setting out government long-term thinking on Irish education was sought and promised for a long time and was finally published in December 1980.[1]

Although the Irish Constitution of 1937 pays generous attention to the prior rights of parents in education, neither church nor state had made efforts until recently to involve parents closely in policy making, consultation or administration of schooling. Organised groups of parents are likely to exercise a much greater influence on educational affairs in coming years, however. The vocational education committees are the sole public authority other than central government involved in the education system and their role is confined to specific types of institutions. In the early 1970s discussions took place on the desirability of regional educational authorities but no action on the establishment of such bodies has taken place. Neither do any agencies exist distinct from the Department such as a national advisory council on education, a council for the curriculum or an examination council. A registration council for secondary teachers was inherited from the British regime but the government has refused to establish a teachers' council, as recommended to it in 1974 by a special committee appointed by the Minister for Education. The White Paper of 1980, however, proposed the setting up of a curriculum council for second-level education.

In line with some changes in the mode of financing and the increased size of many schools in recent years, changes have been made in the administrative structure of some schools. Comprehensive and community schools are run by management boards and many vocational schools have set up management boards. Management boards have also been established in national schools. However, the establishment of the boards has been notable more for the jockeying for power by interested parties than for the quality of the debate concerning what constitutes good management. Formal management boards do not exist in the vast majority of secondary schools, as the owners of these schools and their teachers cannot agree on an acceptable format for the division of power and responsibility. The progress which has been made in changing the management of Irish schools to a more broadly-based democratic mode has been a halting one, accompanied by some bitter debate.

Whether the school is managed by a private agency or public board the whole area of educational administration is receiving more attention. The increased size of many schools, the expanded curricula, the large numbers of pupils of varied background and ability, the availability of specialist staff, the more formal account-keeping and so on have highlighted the need for greater attention to training of school authorities in administrative skills. Educational administration has already become available in academic and in-service courses for teachers and it is likely to be an area of increasing popularity in the years ahead.

Perhaps the greatest problem facing Irish education is the provision of facilities to meet the needs, aptitudes and aspirations of an increasing youth population. Unlike most other European countries Ireland is experiencing a rising youth population with a consequent explosion in the number of young people seeking education. They have high expectations of education and its relationship to job opportunities. The political slogan of the 1960s was equality of educational opportunity. This has proved an elusive goal and, although many of the initiatives taken have improved the educational provision for a wider band of the population, the optimism which accompanied them has palled in the light of harsh realities.

About half of the population of Ireland is under twenty-five years of age, which reflects a high dependency age range within the overall population. In 1979 there were over 894,000 young people in full-time education, amounting to more than a quarter of the total population of 3.3 million. When adult education and various forms of training are included it means that almost one out of every three in the Irish population is engaged in formal learning activities. In recent years a number of demographers and economists have been endeavouring to make projections on population trends and future educational demand. Demographic projection is an inexact science but, nevertheless, the projections pose serious challenges for educational planners and politicians. One projection, that of Professor Tussing in 1978, predicted an increase in school enrolment at all levels of 188,700 or 23 per cent by 1986 over the figure for 1974. The highest growth would be in the senior age groups, 50 per cent in the group aged sixteen to nineteen years, and 159 per cent in the group aged nineteen years and over.[2] Participation in third-level education has been strikingly low, with about 11 per cent of the age cohort participating. Studies by Sheehan and others have indicated the need for a great expansion of the number of third-level places available in the years ahead. Calculating on the basis of about 17 per cent of second-level pupils looking for places in third-level education, Sheehan predicted that about 10,000 new places would be required by 1986 over the 1976 level. If Ireland were to reach EEC levels of participation, the increase would be much greater.[3] It is likely that a significant part of the expansion will occur in the non-university sector because of its close alignment with industrial and commercial job opportunities. The White Paper of 1980 projected an increase of 12,000 places over the decade to 1990, of which 9,000 would be in the non-university sector.[4] Many commentators hold that this projection will fall short of demand.

The expansion of educational demand and enrolment is coinciding with a time of high inflation and economic recession. Some of the changes brought about since the mid-1960s, such as free post-primary education, an expanded teaching force, student third-level grants, school transport, higher capitation and maintenance allowances, are now absorbing large amounts of public funds. The cost of the school transport scheme alone rose from £1.7 million in 1968 to about £20 million in 1980, benefiting about 158,000 school pupils.[5] The government toyed with the idea of a school transport levy on parents but in the face of political unpopularity the projected scheme was withdrawn. Other factors operate within the education system to make it more expensive. The standards of school building, furnishing and equipment have improved to meet pedagogic patterns and public expectations. The shift from traditional, largely literary curricula to a wider subject range with a more technical, scientific and applied component has involved increased expenditure on equipment and facilities. The official policy of reducing class sizes, particularly at primary level, to facilitate greater individual and small-group teaching has had significant effects for teacher costs. The Catholic church's contribution, particularly at second level, has declined and the state has had to assume a greater share of the burden of supplying new schools and making higher grants available. The decline in the number of religious teachers, who traditionally devoted some of their salaries to the general educational costs borne by the Orders, has also had consequences for public expenditure. The needs of large schools and the pressures by teacher unions have led to an increase in the number of ancillary staff such as secretaries and caretakers in the schools. The expansion of special education, as well as improved medical and social services linked to schools, has further increased the bill. The expansion in enrolments at second and third levels since the mid-1960s has necessitated a huge increase in the number of new teachers employed. Many of these were recruited at young ages, leading to a large bulge in the number reaching their salary maxima in the immediate years ahead. Education being highly labour-intensive, teacher costs absorb almost 80 per cent of the overall government educational expenditure. Schemes for the qualitative improvement of other aspects of the system tend to be postponed, involving less political inconvenience.

To cope with the increased demand for education at a time of rapidly increasing costs and to maintain, if not improve, the quality of the education provided is a serious problem facing Irish education in the early 1980s. Tussing has calculated that real public expenditures on first- and second-level education are likely to double in the period 1974 to 1986 and that for third-level will more than double. In 1978 Education was second only to Health as the highest-spending government department and as such it is a big drain on public financial resources, supplemented by various forms of private expenditure on education. With increases in teachers' salaries following the salary review body's report and subsequent negotiations in 1980, the Education estimate will rise significantly and present further challenges. Further, the hoped-for political goals of many of the initiatives such as the promotion of equality of educational opportunity have proved elusive. Participation and achievement levels have remained relatively low in certain districts, and among those parts of the population where this was traditionally the case. A study of the socio-economic background of all students in university in 1977/8 revealed that no significant change had taken place from the position in 1965/6. Of Dublin entrants to higher education in 1978/9, 72 per cent came from the four higher socio-economic groups although these groups constituted less than

21 per cent of the population of the county.[6]

The per pupil costs at the different educational levels have caused considerable disquiet among some politicians, economists and primary teachers. In 1980 the average cost per primary pupil in public expenditure was £303, for each second-level pupil it was £542 and for third-level students it amounted to £1,343, exclusive of the third-level grants scheme.[7] Realising that 'the quality of education received by children during the years when they are compelled to attend school is of fundamental importance to their progress in later life', the National Economic and Social Council in a report published in 1975 urged greater provision for the first-level sector.[8] At the same time the potential benefits accruing to third-level students were such that the Council urged that a mixed system of loans and grants with a graduated fee system should be considered so as to shift some of the burden of additional expenditure from the general tax payer to the graduate.[9] Tussing in his report, *Irish educational expenditures – past, present and future* (1978), based his proposals on the principle that 'scarce resources available for education should be reserved, in general, for those aspects of schooling which benefit society at large as opposed to the individual learner, and in particular Irish society, and for the less advantaged'.[10] He urged a much greater private subvention of senior cycle second-level and also of third-level education with state support more specifically targeted to the needs of the more economically disadvantaged students. The government has made no move on the second-level issue but in the white paper, *Programme for national development 1978/81*, published in 1979, it indicated that third-level institutions should collect a greater proportion of their income through fees, recommended an improved grants scheme for poorer students and also recommended that the existing subsidies for student teachers should be reduced.[11] The Minister for Education has also declared that government priorities in education will relate more to first- and second-level education in the years ahead. The white paper on educational development of 1980 stated that a loan scheme allied to student grants was under consideration.[12]

Whatever about the actual decisions which may be taken it is clear that a climate of economic scrutiny and accountability for educational expenditure is prevalent. The in-built momentum for greater expenditure may be realised but new projects or expansionary schemes are likely to be kept on a very tight rein, at least in the years immediately ahead. Table 8 shows the general level of estimated public expenditure on education for 1980 and gives a breakdown of the main elements. The cost of the education system to the state has been estimated by the government at over £500 million for 1980. Supplementary estimates for 1980 brought the figure to £550 million, and the estimate for 1981 is £685 million. Considering the high level of expenditure on the education system it is interesting that only £210,000 was allotted in 1980 under the specific heading 'research activities'.

Table 8: **Main components of estimated state educational expenditure, 1980**

	£
Primary education	190,570,000
Secondary education (including comprehensive and community schools)	134,347,000
Vocational education	82,221,000
Higher education	54,568,000
Transport services	16,000,000
Salaries and wages of Department of Education	7,869,000
Higher education grants	3,340,000
Residential homes and special schools	2,189,000
Clerical assistance for national and secondary schools	1,160,000
Grant for youth and sport organisations	1,392,000

Source: *Estimates for Public Services 1980* Stationery Office (Prl. 8699) pp. 39-50

Although formal educational provision at the three levels — primary, post-primary and third-level — has formed the main concern of planners, the needs of adult education have also received more attention in recent years. The adult education report of 1973 calculated that about 10 per cent of the adult population participated in formal classes and about the same percentage in adult-training, in-service and retraining programmes.[13] It would seem that these proportions have increased in recent years. The number of agencies which provide adult education and the range of courses are very large indeed. There is no overall authority for adult education and no special section of the Department of Education has been formally set up to deal with it though it has been designated as a responsibility of one of the assistant secretaries.

Aontas acts as a general advisory and consultative agency for those involved. The need for adult education has been highlighted from the social justice point of view. It was recorded in the 1971 census that 51 per cent of the population had left full-time education at under fifteen years of age.[14] The idea of a second chance for education, in line with rising educational expectations in society at large, led to calls for greater provisions for adult education.

The increased pace of technological and social change in recent years has emphasised the need for a good basic education to facilitate re-training and further education. This is more necessary because of the changing work patterns and job opportunities. Groups such as the Industrial Training Authority (AnCO) and the National Manpower Service have increased the level of their activity enormously to help cater for re-training and redeployment as well as for apprentice training. The reduction of working hours of those in employment has allowed more scope for leisure and self-development courses. Further, the electronic revolution associated with the micro-chip and the possible consequences for employment and life-style are likely to increase the need and demand for forms of adult education and retraining. It may be that ideals such as life-long, permanent and recurrent education will become realised and the formal school will become less a preparation for adult life and more an on-going, integral part of living. Ireland needs a more co-ordinated framework than that which exists at present to meet the challenges.

The great changes in technology including computers, video recorders, television, recording instruments etc. are likely to affect schooling and the process of education at an accelerating rate. As yet in Ireland they have been employed within the education institutions to improve the teaching/learning and administrative work. But already plans are being mooted for more radical utilisation of such resources such as making institutional programmes available to wider audiences through various forms of distance-learning. Some people hope that the improvement in information and communication systems may help to bring skilled personnel to wide audiences without incurring the full costs of building pro- grammes and transport. However, the potential of such develop- ments for changing traditional forms of education, as well as adult education, lies in the future. The limited contribution at present of Irish television and radio services to education programmes urges caution in one's expectations.

A key feature of curricular policy for Irish schools following political independence was the promotion of the Irish language in the hope that it would be revived as a general vernacular language. This was an important factor in the narrow subject range which prevailed in Irish national schools up to 1971. The cause of the Irish language continues to be officially espoused and the white paper of 1980 emphasised the role of the school in helping to achieve true bilingualism in Ireland.

Since 1971 a wide, balanced curriculum has operated in national schools with greater concern for individual learning and utilising more source materials. At second level the secondary schools favoured the traditional grammar school curriculum with its heavy reliance on literary studies. The vocational schools offered a two-year continuation course with an emphasis on applied studies. Since the late 1960s all types of post-primary school have moved towards the provision of a comprehensive curriculum with a wide range of literary, scientific, practical and aesthetic subjects. The majority of pupils, however, still favour the academic and literary subjects.

Curricular and examination policy at second level has been the cause of a good deal of debate. Many consider that the policy has not been flexible enough. A number of experiments have taken place along the lines of more integrated courses at junior cycle and a greater linking of the world of school to that of social and work life outside the school. A recent report of the Arts Council itemised and criticised the position held by the arts in the education system.[15] Others have pressed for more direct preparation for personal and social development of the pupils, including sex and health education. Other groups have been pressing the claims of new areas such as computer study and electronics in schools, in line with advancing technology. Religion is usually taught at second level by clergy or others trained in catechetics. At national-school-level religion has been traditionally taught by the ordinary classroom teachers but in a society with declining religious affiliations some teachers have objected to having to teach religion.

In line with the general movement towards greater equality for women in society, women are participating more at the higher levels of education. They form a majority of the teaching force at first and second level, a proportion which is not reflected in the number who hold senior positions in the schools or in teacher unions. Women also form only a small proportion of those holding senior positions in third-level institutions. With greater job mobility and acceptance of women in general society, many more women are taking up varied and professional careers than did so in the past. Despite such trends the curricular choices at second level still reflect traditional sex-role expectations for boys and girls, and some school textbooks cause offence on sexist grounds. It is likely that the years ahead will witness considerable change in all these areas.

As educational matters have not been a central concern of the European Economic Community, Ireland's participation within that body has not meant significant adjustments in the education system. The Directorate-General for Research, Science and Education tends to concentrate on aspects such as training, the links between school and work, the educational needs of minority groups. Ireland has benefited considerably from training grants through the Social Fund which has allowed agencies such as AnCO to expand their programmes. A number of education research projects, focused on the interface between school and work, have been partly financed by the EEC. Of the European languages, French is the only one which has made significant strides in the number of pupils studying it. Some subjects such as history have benefited from a greater consciousness of the European heritage.

In indirect ways the frequent contact with EEC countries at ministerial, official and fraternal organisational level has influenced educational outlook and attitudes. The interchange of ideas has widened mental horizons on contemporary educational problems and trends. Comparative tables on expenditure on education and pupil participation rates are frequently referred to in educational debate, usually as a lever towards improving Ireland's position. A number of schemes exist which allow transfer and exchange between education personnel of the different EEC countries. Schemes also exist to encourage co-operation in the mounting of courses or joint research projects between third-level institutions.

Ireland expresses confidence in its educational and schooling system and the debate by the de-schooling movement has had little influence on the Irish system. However, the years ahead are likely to see considerable changes in educational institutions in Ireland. Pointers to the changes are the development of community schools, varied forms of adult and life-long educational patterns, increased concern for blending the world of school with the world of work, the many new dynamic agencies engaged in training and education, highly important changes in educational technology and resources, changes in the administrative structures of schools and their architectural design. Such portents indicate the closer involvement of the school as an institution with the general life of the community and emphasise the need for flexible arrangements so that society's educational resources may be used by the population at large. Although the education system faces daunting challenges, it may also be on the verge of an exciting new era in which the patterns may differ greatly from the structures which were shaped by and served the needs of Irish society in the past.

With the many changes involved in the recent history of Irish education it is noteworthy that legislative measures have been few and that they have tended to be confined to giving a statutory basis to various new institutions. The document setting forth the rights and duties of the citizen and the state in relation to education is the Irish Constitution of 1937. As the main touchstone of rights it is being frequently referred to and appeal to its provisions is increasingly being made in the courts. It has important implications for present and future policy and, accordingly, the articles relating to education are treated as a specific issue in chapter 7 which follows.

The Department of Education is the area of government with pervasive power and influence throughout the education system. Established in 1924 its role in the educational and administrative policy of a highly centralised system has increased, particularly at second and third level. The structure and functions of the Department are also of pivotal importance and are discussed as a unit in Chapter 8, prior to examining recent changes and the present position within the various components of the education system. The overall structure of the education system is set out in diagramatic form at the end of the book, in Appendix One.

Chapter Seven.

Education and the Irish Constitution

The Constitutional position

Whereas the Constitution of the new Irish Free State in 1922 referred to education in Article 10 in simple terms — 'All citizens of the Irish Free State have the right to free elementary education' — the Constitution of 1937 contained much more detail on constitutional rights and duties in education. The articles of the 1937 Constitution are in accord with Catholic social teaching on the rights of parents, churches, the state and the child in the matter of education. The predominant rights of parents are stressed and the supporting and subsidiary role of the state in education is emphasised. A number of important court cases seeking educational rights based on the Constitution have taken place. In line with developments in other countries it seems likely that there will be more frequent resort to the courts to settle matters of educational dispute.

The constitutional position with regard to education in Ireland is set out in Articles 42, 44.2.4° and 44.2.6° of the Constitution of Ireland, 1937.

Article 42

1. The State acknowledges that the primary and natural educator of the child is the Family and guarantees to respect the inalienable right and duty of parents to provide, according to their means, for the religious and moral, intellectual, physical and social education of their children.
2. Parents shall be free to provide this education in their homes or in private schools or in schools recognised or established by the State.
3.1 The State shall not oblige parents in violation of their conscience and lawful preference to send their children to schools established by the State, or to any particular type of school

155

designated by the State.

3.2 The State shall, however, as guardian of the common good, require in view of actual conditions that the children receive a certain minimum education, moral, intellectual and social.

4. The State shall provide for free primary education and shall endeavour to supplement and give reasonable aid to private and corporate educational initiative, and, when the public good requires it, provide other educational facilities or institutions with due regard, however, for the rights of parents, especially in the matter of religious and moral formation.

5. In exceptional cases, where the parents for physical or moral reasons fail in their duty towards their children, the State as guardian of the common good, by appropriate means shall endeavour to supply the place of the parents, but always with due regard for the natural and imprescriptible rights of the child.

Article 44

2.4 Legislation providing State aid for schools shall not discriminate between schools under the management of different religious denominations, nor be such as to affect prejudicially the right of any child to attend a school receiving public money without attending religious instruction at that school.

2.6 The property of any religious denomination or any educational institution shall not be diverted save for necessary works of public utility and on payment of compensation.

Comment

Some comment on these articles is desirable. Article 42 clearly establishes the parents as having the primary rights and responsibilities for the education of their children. The role of the state is to protect and promote these parental rights with a limited right to prescribe that 'a certain minimum education' be attained. However, the potential role of parents within the education system in terms of management, setting up schools and affecting policy has been little exercised. In recent years parents have become more organised and the various parent associations are exerting pressure to have their voices heard by legislators and school authorities.

A number of court judgments have clarified the meaning of sections of the articles on education. A judgment in 1965 in relation to Article 42.1 declared that the term 'education' was not broad enough to include the general process of nurturing and rearing but must be of 'a scholastic nature'.[1] Under the School Attendance Act of 1926 attendance at school was made compulsory from the age of six to fourteen but, as Article 42.2 makes clear, provided parents make educational provision for their children in their homes, school attendance is not obligatory. The role of the state in directing schooling activity is also severely curtailed by Article 42.3.1 which prohibits the state from designating the schools children should attend. An effort by the School Attendance Bill of 1942 to confer on the Minister for Education the express power to prescribe the content and the manner of imparting the education which children might receive other than by attending a national school, a suitable school or a recognised school, was adjudged to be unconstitutional when referred by the President of Ireland to the Supreme Court in 1943. This underlined the limited power of the Minister to define 'a certain minimum education' as set out in Article 43.3.2. Article 42.4, by which the state undertakes to provide for free primary education, has been expanded by the raising of the school leaving age in 1972 to fifteen years of age, and the pattern whereby, nowadays, this involves about three years' post-primary schooling for participating children. Further, since 1967 tuition is free for the full range of post-primary education in the great majority of schools.

Since the 1960s the provision in Article 42.4 for the state to 'provide other educational facilities or institutions' has been much more exercised than formerly and the state has become a much more central agent in the planning and provision of facilities. The state assists children to exercise their constitutional rights by the provision of a free transport service to children living certain distances from school. As the result of an industrial dispute involving the withdrawal by INTO members from schools in the area of Drimoleague, County Cork, in 1976 a case was brought against the state alleging that it was in breach of its obligation to ensure that education was provided for the children. The courts ruled that the state was not obliged to provide free primary education in the children's own parish once the education was made reasonably accessible, for instance through a transport scheme to schools in neighbouring parishes. Article 42.5 provides the constitutional framework for the limited action of the state for 'care and protection' where parents fail in their duty to their children. This also covers state provision of institutional care for young offenders.

Articles 42.2.4. and 44.2.6. relate to the state's acceptance and protection of denominational interests in education and makes explicit the state's role in providing state aid for denominational schooling. This was further emphasised in the *Rules for national schools* which, following a setting forth of the constitutional provisions, added the following note: 'In pursuance of these Articles the State provides for free primary education for children in national schools, and gives explicit recognition to the denominational character of these schools'.[2] The Constitution does not rule out recognition of non-denominational or multi-denominational schools. Recognition for a multi-denominational national school was given to the pilot school at Dalkey, County Dublin.[3]

There has been some evidence that parents in a number of suburban districts favour setting up multi-denominational schools though the churches have opposed the initiatives and the state has been slow in its support for them. A problem facing groups of private individuals as distinct from church organisations is the departmental regulation that the site and about 15 per cent of the building costs must be provided by the local group which, in the context of land prices in suburban districts, is a daunting obstacle.

The place of religious instruction within school life is clearly enunciated in the official *Rules for national schools*, as follows:

> Of all parts of a school curriculum Religious Instruction is by far the most important, as its subject-matter, God's honour and service, includes the proper use of all man's faculties, and affords the most powerful inducements to their proper use. Religious instruction is, therefore, a fundamental part of the school course, and a religious spirit should inform and vivify the whole work of the school.[4]

The periods of formal religious instruction have to be indicated on the timetable but conscience clauses exist so that children whose parents disapprove of the religious instruction given may withdraw. Under Article 44.4 children have the right not to attend the religious instruction provided in the school. In the *Rules for national schools* teachers are urged to practise the moral virtues. National teachers traditionally have taught the religion classes and prepared children for various religious ceremonies. However, in recent years teachers have called for the right to refuse to give religious instruction without this affecting their employment or promotion prospects. At the moment, in the case of non-believing teachers, local arrangements are arrived at, but legal opinion is being sought by the various interests on the position.

Departmental rules require vocational, community and comprehensive schools to provide religious instruction. Secondary schools also do so and in second-level schools there is frequently a catechetical teacher or clergyman to give the instruction. The conscience clause of withdrawal by pupils also applies in second-level schools.

Although the Constitution has set forth some fundamental principles on the rights and responsibilities of the state and citizens relating to education, a notable feature of the Irish education system is the paucity of educational legislation. The system relies heavily for its mode of operation on rules, memoranda and circulars issued on the authority of the Minister for Education. Apart from brief mentions in national economic programmes the state has been reluctant to issue white or green papers on education which would set forth planning in a co-ordinated manner. The long-awaited white paper on educational development published in 1980 has been heavily criticised as a planning document. This trend has inhibited informed educational debate and, when coupled with the lack of departmental annual and other reports, the lack of information gives rise to misunderstanding and frustration. There is also a tardiness in updating rules which allows anomalies to occur.

Chapter Eight

The role of the Department of Education

The authority of the state in education is vested in the Minister for Education who is a member of the government and responsible to Dáil Éireann (Parliament). There is also a Minister of State for Education with special responsibility for youth and sport. The Minister for Education's administrative agency is the Department of Education. The Department was established in June 1924 under the Ministers and Secretaries Act, 1924. At the head of the department is the secretariat led by the secretary and assistant secretaries. The administrative sections of the department include the primary education branch; post-primary education branch; accounts branch; publications; school transport section; youth; physical education and recreation section; examinations section and reproduction unit. The Department has its central offices in Marlborough Street, Dublin.

The Department of Education exercises varying degrees of power and influence over the different educational institutions but its overall influence on educational policy and administrative procedures is very great. At first level it has large powers. It draws up the rules and regulations for national schools. Management boards become responsible for the conduct of the schools following a written undertaking by them to the Minister that they will comply with the rules. The management boards appoint teachers subject to the Minister's approval. The Department pays the salaries of the teachers; devises the curriculum and sanctions the textbooks which may be employed; and ensures that the curriculum is being satisfactorily implemented and monitors teacher efficiency, through the agency of the national school inspector. The Department usually pays about 85 per cent of the building costs of national schools and most of the operating expenses, subject to local contributions of about 25 per cent of the state's funding for maintenance. In a similar way the Department exercises control over special national schools and liaises with health and social services where appropriate.

At post-primary level the Department of Education is responsible for setting the syllabuses for the public examinations – Group, Intermediate and Leaving Certificates – and for the operation and correction of these examinations. The Department has the right to refuse to sanction the appointment of most types of teacher and can withdraw official recognition from any teacher. The Department of Education pays the salaries of all post-primary teachers, though secondary school authorities pay the small 'basic' salary of £400 per annum to their teachers usually from funds provided by the Department. The secondary schools are private institutions but if they wish to benefit from departmental grants they have to comply with the regulations of the Department for recognised status. Inspectors of secondary schools visit the schools less regularly than inspectors at national school level and traditionally they have adopted a low profile in these private schools. The Department has representation on the registration council for secondary teachers and the regulations of this council are subject to ministerial approval. The state provides complete funding for comprehensive schools and the vast proportion of that for vocational and community schools. The Department has a representative on the management boards of comprehensive schools but not on the boards of vocational and community schools. Teacher appointees in these three types of school are all subject to ministerial approval. These schools also have to furnish formal annual financial reports and are subject to inspection. The Department retains the right of prior examination and approval of all plans for new schools which are to receive state aid. The Department also has joint administrative functions with the vocational education committees on their other educational programmes: these include the regional technical colleges and other third-level colleges operated by VECs.

The colleges of education, except for Thomond College, are linked with the universities for their academic work, but they are funded by the Department of Education which also has a major say in regulating entry. The colleges are private institutions but the staff are paid by the Department of Education through the colleges, and the Department recognises the colleges as the appropriate centres for training teachers. Departmental inspectors monitor the final teaching practice of students on behalf of the Minister to ensure that appropriate standards are maintained. Thomond College and the two national institutes of higher education in Limerick and Dublin have their own governing bodies with ministerial appointees and are linked to the National Council for Educational Awards (NCEA) for the purpose of approval of their courses and conferring of awards. The National College of Art and Design comes under the control of the Department of Education for some financial and academic affairs, though its main academic work is now validated by the NCEA.

The full-time chairman and all members of the Higher Education Authority are appointed by the government. The government also appoints the chairman of the National Council for Educational Awards and the Minister for Education has nine appointees on the council. The Department maintains close liaison with these bodies in the conduct of their affairs. The universities are academically independent but are subject to certain financial and planning constraints exercised by the HEA. The government appoints the Provost of Trinity College following selection procedures within the university.

Other national educational and cultural institutions, such as the National Library, the National Museum, the Irish Manuscripts Commission, the Linguistics Institute and the Institute for Advanced Studies, come under the direct control of the Department of Education. In 1981 the government announced its intention of removing some of the national cultural institutions from the jurisdiction of the Department of Education to that of a new national heritage council. The provision of textbooks is largely in the hands of private enterprise publishers with whom the Department maintains liaison. The Department has a publishing section which concentrates mainly on providing textbooks in Irish as well as some scholarly works linked to the Irish language.

The influence of the Department of Education pervades the whole education system by direct and indirect means. Its influence is strongest at first and second levels where it largely controls the regulations, curricula and examinations: this results in a strong, centralised system of first- and second-level education. The vocational system is the only one where local authorities and elected public representatives have a role to play. The lack of regional education authorities, and of curricular, examination or teacher councils gives great power to the Department. New legislation for third-level institutions such as the national institutes for higher education and Thomond College also binds such institutions closely under ministerial and departmental influence. Although an abundance of educational authorities for a population of under 4 million might prove cumbersome, it is also true that the centralised system has led to a uniformity in schooling practice and it has not fostered direct involvement in educational affairs by the public at large. Outside bodies have representation on certain departmental committees such as the second-level syllabus committees, and occasionally special committees are set up by the Minister in which non-departmental personnel participate. However, even in such instances, the Department of Education's influence is usually pronounced. From another perspective, however, considering its extensive role as paymaster of staff and provider of capital and current expenditure for privately-owned educational institutions such as secondary schools and colleges of education, it is surprising that the Department or public representatives have no say in the governing of these institutions.

As well as the Department of Education there are other departments which have a role in educational provision. The provision of care and educational facilities for young offenders is the responsibility of the Department of Justice. The Department of Agriculture is involved in facets of agricultural education and provides funds for some university education. The Department of Health and the regional health boards are involved in the school health services and special education. The Department of the Environment, through the local authorities, provides meals to necessitous children as well as helping in school library schemes. Local authorities also provide grants for third-level education. The Department of Labour is involved in funding education/training courses for apprentices and for people in their places of work. The Department of the Taoiseach funds the Arts Council and through this is linked with aspects of education in the arts. To facilitate planning between the different agencies, inter-departmental committees are established where appropriate but problems of split responsibility arise.

The personnel in the Department of Education are loosely grouped into the administrative and the professional staff. The former comprise the greater body of staff and, in line with general civil service procedure, they deal with policy formulation, general administration and information. The professional personnel are usually recruited on the basis of qualifications and experience directly related to the education system. The two main groups on the professional side are the inspectorate and the psychological service. The inspectorate is headed by the chief inspector and three deputy chief inspectors and is divided into the national and post-primary school inspectorates. The inspectors are the main liaison personnel between the schools and the Department of Education. Their duties are many and varied and include inspection and evaluation of teachers; counselling and demonstrating; planning of curricula and administration of examinations; participation in in-service courses for teachers; liaising with teacher training colleges and the National College of Art and Design; interviewing teachers for some posts and generally acting as information officers on behalf of the Department of Education. At senior level they assist in policy formulation and may advise the Minister. The psychological service, which was established in 1965, has expanded significantly and it too liaises between the Department and schools. The service is organised regionally and is focused mainly on pupils in post-primary schools. As well as providing psychological advice in schools the unit has also developed standardised attainment tests for use in schools. The unit participates in training and in-service courses for guidance and remedial teachers. The psychological service also engages in research on various aspects of education.

Chapter Nine .

The Investment in Education Report

The *Investment in Education Report*, published in 1966,[1] is one of the foundation documents of modern Irish education and merits close attention. It was a major analysis of the education system, initiated in 1962 by the Department of Education in co-operation with the OECD. The terms of reference of the survey included an assessment of existing educational provision and projections of future lines of development, bearing in mind the overall needs for skilled manpower in the Irish economy. The report was intended to be fact-finding and analytical in character. It was to analyse the existing system and to lay the basis for informed decision-making in education. It was a large-scale, detailed report but its main findings can be summarised under four headings — manpower, participation, curricula and use of resources.

From a comparison of the probable manpower requirements and the probable supply of suitably-educated personnel for the labour force projected for 1971, it was estimated that there would be serious deficiencies in the number of persons holding educational certificates at different levels of achievement. The survey team pointed out that there would probably be shortages of technically-qualified personnel, unless remedial action was undertaken. It was estimated that during the decade 1961-71 there would be a short-fall of 76,000 in the number of workers with junior post-primary certificates newly entering the labour force.

When pupil participation rates in schooling were studied, some very disturbing findings emerged. Analysing a cohort of 55,000 pupils, it was estimated that 17,500 of them left full-time education at primary level and 11,000 of these without having obtained the Primary School Certificate. Of the 37,500 who went on to second level, 13,500, or 36 per cent, left without sitting for a junior post-primary certificate. The drop-out rate was most striking in the vocational sector where, from an entrance group of 16,000 to the two-year course, 7,000,or 44 per cent, left without having sat for the Group Certificate. Of those who sat the Intermediate in 1963, it was estimated that only about 2,000 pupils left full-time education. Of those who continued into senior cycle, a further 2,000 dropped out without sitting for the Leaving Certificate. Of the approximate 10,000 who sat for the Leaving Certificate examination, only 2,000 entered university. The huge drop-out rates occurred at the transition from primary to post-primary and before sitting for the post-primary junior cycle examinations.

Very disturbing statistics also emerged when the social class pattern of pupil participation was examined. A matrix of occupational categories was devised which indicated a very marked association between social and economic status and participation in full-time education. For instance, students aged fifteen to nineteen years of age and belonging to categories A, B, and C (farmers, professional, senior employees, clerks, etc.) were shown to have a four to five times greater chance of participating in post-primary education than those belonging to categories D, E and F (skilled, semi-skilled and unskilled workers). It was disclosed, moreover, that students from categories A, B and C made up 85 per cent of university students. Further significant participation differences were noted with regard to geographical location. For instance, the participation rate of thirteen to seventeen-year-olds in second-level education in County Cork was 49 per cent but in County Donegal only 30 per cent. Pupils in counties Donegal, Cavan, Monaghan, Laois, Meath and Kildare fared worst in terms of participation. Of course Ireland was by no means unique in this situation of inequality of educational opportunity but the stark statistics emphasised the urgency for remedial action.

Concerning curricula, it was calculated that the teaching week in national schools amounted to about 22½ hours. Ten hours were devoted to the Irish and English languages; about 5 hours to mathematics with another 5 hours for other subjects and 2½ hours for religion. The use of Irish as a teaching medium was felt to be very limited outside infant classes. Pupils in smaller schools, in particular, were regarded as having a restricted curriculum available to them. The curricula of a great many secondary schools were seen to be limited and to be in the traditional secondary grammar tradition, with nearly half of the pupils' time in school devoted to languages. Modern continental languages, however, were not emphasised; for instance, less than 200 boys obtained honours in a continental language at the Leaving Certificate in 1963. It should be borne in mind, however, that Irish and English were taken by almost all pupils. Latin was emphasised with 95 per cent of boys presenting it for Intermediate Certificate and 88 per cent for Leaving Certificate. The strong position of Latin was no doubt linked to its requirement as a university matriculation subject and its place in the pre-Vatican II Catholic Church. Concern was expressed at the relative lack of success at honours level in mathematics and science. It was noted that only 44 per cent of the instruction in mathematics was given by teachers who had mathematics in their degree and 64 per cent of science teaching was conducted by non-science graduates. Science teaching also suffered from a lack of laboratories and the mode of conduct of public examinations. The attention paid to aesthetic subjects and practical subjects was seen as inadequate. The size of vocational schools had a large bearing on the range of curriculum that could be provided and in most schools students could exercise little or no choice of subjects. From probings made by the survey team, they concluded that mathematics and science teaching in vocational schools was generally conducted by non-specialists in those subjects.

The survey team examined the use made of existing resources in national schools and found that about two-thirds of national schools were one- and two-teacher schools situated mainly in rural areas. Factors such as density and mobility of population and separation by religion and sex had led to large numbers of small schools. Such small schools absorbed a disproportionate amount of the teaching force leading to imbalance in the teacher/pupil ratio. The ratio oscillated from 18:1 in one-teacher schools to 45:1 in schools of seven teachers or more. The costs of providing national school education varied significantly depending on school size; the costs for the erection and operation of small schools were considerably greater. This extra expense did not appear to be compensated for by greater educational benefits. About 2,000 small schools were deficient in facilities, lacking good sanitary arrangements and drinking water. Small schools mostly depended on open fires for heating; many did not have electricity and were poorly supplied with school equipment, library facilities etc. The survey team raised the question of whether the existing distribution of schools was the most suitable, satisfactory or economical method of providing primary education.

A pattern of small schools was also revealed in the post-primary sector with 388 or 64 per cent out of 608 secondary schools having less than 150 pupils, and 179 or 73 per cent out of 245 day vocational schools having less than 150 pupils on the roll. It was also noted that, in terms of teaching resources used, smaller schools cost from one-third to one-half more than larger schools per pupil and small schools experienced difficulties in providing a varied course.

Many implications for educational planning arose from *Investment in Education*'s findings, some of which were drawn together in chapter twelve of the report. Schemes for improving participation levels, co-ordination of post-primary schooling within a matrix of catchment areas, rationalisation of national school provision, including the merging of many of the small one- and two-teacher schools, were urged. To ensure continuous review and forward planning of the education system, the report called for the establishment of a special development unit within the Department of Education which would shift the emphasis of the Department from ordinary administration to active initiation and development of educational policy. The publication of *Investment in Education* caused a considerable stir in Irish education circles. The Minister for Education, Donogh O'Malley, remarked of it in 1966: 'It has certainly been a guideline and basic document for us to work on for the future'.[2] Seán O'Connor, then head of the development unit which had been set up within the Department of Education, remarked in 1968 that the report 'has sign-posted the direction of educational reform and, by highlighting our deficiencies, has offered a challenge that cannot be ignored'.[3] Succeeding chapters indicate how this challenge was faced.

Chapter Ten

First-level education

Developments in national school education, 1960-80

One of the main administrative policies in the national school system in this period was the closure of small national schools. This was in line with 'investment' thinking but, as could have been expected, the move was resisted at local level by many communities who had looked on the school as one of the focal points of the community and saw its demise as symbolic of a decline in the community. However, the availability of school transport and the increasing availability of private cars tended to reduce the hardship which long walks to school in harsh weather might otherwise have entailed. The Department of Education hoped that the centralised school would make better use of teacher resources, reduce the spread of classes which any one teacher would have to teach and enable new equipment to be provided which would assist in the implementation of the new child-centred curriculum introduced nationwide in 1971. During the period 1962-79 the number of one- and two-teacher ordinary national schools was reduced from 3,194 to 1,168.[1] Many of the small schools in the worst condition have now been abolished and the pace of closure has largely slackened off.

A useful innovation was the introduction in 1963 of a basic reference library scheme for national schools. The vast majority of national schools now benefit from liaison schemes with local authorities whereby the authority provides books for school libraries on an organised basis. These school libraries have been a boon to schools and they were in line with new curricular thinking which encouraged pupil investigation, project work and the undermining of the dominance of the class textbook. Special rooms for remedial teaching and guidance functions as well as better staff facilities have made many new national schools much more satisfactory educational centres. Special equipment grants were introduced in 1971 which helped to provide teaching equipment in line with changing curricular requirements.

Expansion and development of post-primary education was the priority of government policy in the 1960s and curricular changes in that sector tended to precede those at primary level. However, important curricular changes were introduced in 1967 with the abolition of the Primary Certificate examination and its replacement by a personal record card system in the senior classes. With the introduction of free post-primary education, the scholarship examinations for primary pupils were also dropped. These developments allowed much more freedom at senior level in the national schools to pay attention to aspects other than Irish, English and arithmetic. Following considerable personal experiment by teachers and pilot schemes by the Department of Education, a new programme, *The primary school curriculum*, was launched in 1971.[2] This involved a radical shift of ideological position and methodological approach to primary education. It formally adopted a child-centred ideology and urged that school work should be closely aligned to the cognitive and affective stages of young children's development and be closely related to children's needs and interests. More stress was laid on individual and small group learning with a more active and heuristic approach to pedagogy. The curriculum, and investigations carried out on the success of its implementation, are discussed later.

The problem of large classes which existed in many urban schools was highlighted by the new concern for individual pupil attention. This became a continuing bone of contention among teachers and much rhetoric was expended on the issue. Table 9 shows changes

Table 9: **Number of national school pupils, teachers and student teachers in 1964 and 1978/9**

	1964	1978/79	Percentage increase
Pupils	472,124	545,197	15.5
Teachers	13,875	18,387	31.8
Student teachers	1,108	2,751	147.3

Source: *Investment in Education Report*, Table 1.1, p. 4 and *Statistical Report of the Department of Education* 1978/79 (Pr. 8704) Table 25, p. 32

in the number of pupils enrolled and the number of full-time teachers employed over the period 1964 to 1978/9.

The increase in teacher stock resulted in an improvement in the national average teacher-pupil ratio over the whole period from 34:1 in 1962 to 30:1 in 1980. The closure of small schools was an important factor in the reduction of multi-grade classes (more than two classes grouped under one teacher). Such statistics became available from 1974 and between then and 1978 the number of multi-grade classes reduced from 3,748 with 93,639 pupils to 3,134 with 80, 024 pupils.[3]

During the period under review a special effort was made to reduce the number of very large classes (45+) and the number of relatively small classes of (30—) so that, as Table 10 shows, the number of classes catering for between 30 and 44 pupils has increased. As a further indication of the reduction of large classes in recent years it should be noted that the number of classes having more than 40 pupils per class declined from 3,620 in 1977/78 to 980 in 1979/80, with 41,679 pupils,[4] so about half of national school pupils are now in classes of 30 — 39 pupils. The *White paper on educational development* (1980) projected an increased enrolment in national schools over the decade 1980-90 of 38,100, rising from 550,500 to 588,600.[5] In the context of this increase in pupils and in a climate of economic recession, it seems likely that gradual rather than dramatic reductions will be the pattern in improving the teacher-pupil ratio in the years immediately ahead.

Table 10: **Percentage distribution of national school pupils by class size at triennial periods, 1967-80**

Year	Class size			
	0 — 14	15 — 29	30 — 44	45+
1967-68	1.8	25.1	41.2	31.9
1970-71	1.3	23.4	46.5	28.8
1973-74	1.1	22.3	62.9	13.7
1976-77	.7	20.1	70.6	8.6
1979-80	.6	21.6	76.6	1.2

Source: Based on statistical reports of Department of Education and information supplied by the Department

A noticeable trend in the national schools over the period was the policy of promoting children more quickly through the national schools and the earlier transfer of pupils, at about the age of twelve years, to post-primary level. In 1964 there were 37,176 pupils aged thirteen and over in ordinary national schools but by 1978/9 this number had dropped to 6,866.[6] A number of factors such as the earlier transfer age, the wider range of ability going forward and the more open curriculum at primary level as well as the large classes in primary school contributed to the problem of a proportion of pupils arriving in post-primary diagnosed as having remedial problems in literacy and numeracy. The lack of alignment between the curriculum at senior primary and junior post-primary levels also contributed to transition problems.

There was an important change in the administrative structure of national schools in 1975. It was the first significant change in the management of national schools since the establishment of the system in 1831. Management boards for national schools were instituted in that year. For the first time, parents and teachers were involved directly in a minority position with the patron's nominees in the management of schools. The structure of management boards is discussed later.

Parents, who traditionally played little direct role in the Irish schooling system, have assumed a much more active role since the mid-sixties. Many parent associations have been formed and the organised voice of parents is likely to exercise much more influence in the decades ahead.

National school education in Ireland today
Types of school
More than 95 per cent of primary education in Ireland is state-aided and is conducted in national schools. Some of these schools are vested schools — their title deeds are either vested in the Minister for Education or in trustees under deeds to which the Minister is a party — for the purpose of being maintained as national schools. Vested schools must be used exclusively for the education of the pupils attending them, unless with the special approval of the Minister. There are other non-vested schools over which no control is exercised by the Minister after school hours, except in their use for political meetings. All national schools have to comply with the rules and regulations set out by the Department of Education. The schools are at all times open to inspection by the Minister or

his appointees. Further, any member of the public may, with the management board's approval, visit a national school to observe the ordinary working of the school.

About one sixth of all national schools are convent or monastery schools and, being situated in large population centres, they cater for about one-third of the national school pupils. A small number of model national schools, numbering thirteen in 1979, survive from the state's nineteenth-century initiative of fully-state-financed schools, and they are under the direct patronage of the Minister for Education. Where there are children whose home language is Irish or who otherwise have acquired a good knowledge of oral Irish, the Minister may grant recognition to a national school in which the instruction of the pupils in subjects, other than English, will be through the medium of the Irish language, even though another national school may already be in operation in the same neighbourhood. Recognition may also be given to 'fosterage' schools which are residential in character and situated in intensely Irish-speaking districts. In 1979 there were 166 national schools in which all subjects except English were taught through the medium of Irish, and these schools were attended by about 14,000 pupils. Only twenty-three of these schools with about 3,400 pupils were outside Gaeltacht areas.

School attendance and the school year

About 96 per cent of Irish children of primary school age attend the national schools. Universal compulsory schooling was brought into force for children aged six to fourteen from 1 January 1927, under the provisions of the School Attendance Act of 1926. The compulsory schooling age was raised to fifteen years on 1 July 1972. However, unlike the general European pattern, there is a strong tradition of school attendance among the pre-compulsory age group, whereby about 85 per cent of those aged four and five are in regular attendance in both urban and rural areas. The average daily attendance at national schools as a percentage of average enrolment is a little over 90 per cent. A child who has reached the age of twelve on 1 January of the school year may be recognised as a post-primary pupil, and the practice has developed in recent years of transferring the great majority of children to post-primary schools about the age of twelve, after they have completed sixth standard in national schools.

The school year begins on 1 September and the school must be in operation for not less than 184 days during the school year. The period of secular instruction to be provided for in the time-table of each school day must be at least four hours and ten minutes, though the infant-school day may be reduced by one hour. At least one half-hour in each school day must be devoted to religious instruction. Management boards have some discretion in planning the hours of opening and closing of the school day to suit local circumstances and teachers have freedom to arrange the time-table to suit their professional work.

Management of national schools

Traditionally the management of national schools was the prerogative of the patron, usually the bishop of the diocese, who appointed a local manager, usually a clergyman, to carry out the functions of the school manager. In 1975, with the offer of increased state support for schools with boards of management, such boards became established. The composition of the boards varies with the size of school. The structures are as follows:

1. For schools having a recognised staff of not more than six teachers:
   — four members appointed by and representative of the patron;
   — two members, parents of children enrolled in the school (one being a mother), elected by the general body of parents of children attending the school;
   — the principal teacher of the school.

2. For schools having a recognised staff of seven teachers or more:
   — six members appointed by the representative of the patron;
   — two members, parents of children enrolled in the school (one being a mother), elected by the general body of parents of children attending the school;
   — the principal teacher of the school;
   — one other teacher on the staff of the school elected by the teaching staff.

In the case of a school conducted by a religious order where lay teachers form 50 per cent or more of the recognised staff, a board of ten members as at (2) above would be recognised.

The patron of the school nominates the chairman of the management board, usually the local clergyman, and he is responsible for convening meetings, arranging the agenda and the general functions of chairmanship. The term of office is three years from the date of the board's establishment and out-going members are eligible for re-nomination or re-election.

The Irish National Teachers' Organisation was dissatisfied with the preponderant number of patron nominees on the boards and in 1978 withdrew from participation pending a more satisfactory restructuring. In 1980 the churches agreed to reduce the patron's nominees from six to four in the large schools and from four to three in the small schools, leaving the churches with 50 per cent of the representation on the boards and parents and teachers with 25 per cent each. As part of this agreement the place usually held by a parent's representative on the selection board of assistant teachers was given over to a professional assessor nominated by the patron. Parent groups have objected to this development and many parents consider that their role on the boards is already too restricted. Nevertheless, it is expected that the restructured management boards will come into operation in the school year 1981/2.

The management boards function according to a detailed schedule of regulations and procedures issued by the Department of Education. Each member of the board signs an undertaking that the rules for national schools shall be complied with. The duties of the board are administrative in character and do not impinge directly on curricular or formal educational policy. The board is responsible for the appointment of all teachers subject to the prior approval of the patron and the Minister for Education. The board is responsible for raising the local contribution for operating and maintenance costs and for disbursing state grants for such purposes. The school accounts have to be available for official audit. The chairman is responsible for correspondence with the Department. Appointment to posts of vice-principal and other posts of responsibility are functions of the board of management. The school salary returns must be checked and signed by the chairman of the board. Matters discussed at board meetings have to be treated as confidential unless the board determines otherwise.

Although the boards of management have been a step towards more democratic participation by involved parties in primary education, a number of matters such as the composition of the boards, the restricted area of responsibility, and some of the modes of procedure have tended to limit the impact of the boards. Each of the three groups represented on the management boards have associations, membership of which is not obligatory for any individual on the boards. The organisation for national teachers is the Irish National Teachers' Organisation (INTO), and clerical and religious interests have various denominational bodies such as the Catholic Primary School Managers' Association (CPSMA). Parents have formed a Council for Parents' Elected Representatives on National School Boards of Management and the council has been spearheading a campaign to widen the scope of parental involvement on the boards. With the build-up of experience and trust it may be that the boards will assume greater powers in national schooling.

Financial arrangements and ancillary services
The estimated cost to the state of primary education for the year 1980 was £191 million though later supplementary estimates raised this figure. The main components of that cost are indicated in Table 11. It can be seen from the figures that teacher salaries and superannuation account for 83 per cent of the overall expenditure. Various elements of financial responsibilities and school services are set out in the following pages.

Table 11: **Main components of estimated state cost for primary education, 1980**

	£000
Teacher salaries	137,410
Superannuation of teachers	21,894
Building and furnishing of national schools	17,000
Capitation grants	6,500
Caretakers in national schools	890
Loans and grants to training college students	830

Source: *Estimates for Public Services 1980* pp. 42, 43

Financing the schools   The local community, through the patron and trustees, is responsible for providing the site for national schools (except in the case of all-Irish schools outside Gaeltacht areas). It must also pay a contribution which averages about 15 per cent of the capital costs for the construction and furnishing of the school. The state pays about 85 per cent of the capital costs and about 80 per cent of the recurrent costs of running the schools. The Department of Education pays capitation grants per pupil for such things as heating, cleaning, maintenance, provision of teaching materials and caretaking. A contribution equivalent to at least 25 per cent of the state capitation grant must be provided from local sources. In ordinary national schools the capitation grant per pupil for 1980 was £11. In February 1981 the Minister for Education announced in the Dáil that this would be raised in 1981/82 to £13 subject to a local contribution of £4 per pupil. The grant for special schools for pupils with impaired hearing, impaired sight and emotionally disturbed children is £40 per pupil; special schools for the physically handicapped are allotted capitation grants of £28; and in other special schools £23 is paid per pupil. The local contributions emphasise that the system is a state-aided one and the contributions are the price the local community pays for local management of the system. It is not specified how the local contributions are to be raised but it is forbidden to impose a compulsory levy on parents. The Department of Education pays the full salary of national teachers on the basis of a monthly return form from each school. Such return forms contain all the appropriate information on the teachers employed during the month in question. A small number of teachers in one convent school continue to be paid on an older system of capitation grant payments rather than personal salaries. The Department contributes to the contributory pension scheme that operates for teachers.

School transport   A school transport system is provided by the state. Apart from a number of exceptional situations its terms of eligibility apply to children between four and ten years of age who live not less than two miles from the nearest suitable national school and to children over ten years who live not less than three miles from the nearest suitable national school. Where spare seats are available on special school services after all children entitled to free transport have been accommodated, fare-paying facilities may be granted to other children. Special provisions exist for the conveyance of Protestant children to national schools under Protestant management. Special transport provision may also be authorised in the case of amalgamations between schools in a particular locality. With the increase in petrol and transport costs experienced in the 1970s, the costs of school transport have greatly increased; in 1977/78 the transport scheme for national school pupils cost about £6½ million.

School health services   Under the auspices of the health boards a medical examination service is supplied to the national schools through regular visits by doctors and nurses. Parental consent is necessary before a medical examination takes place. Pupils are tested for vision, hearing and dental defects. Referral and free treatment services are available to pupils. Various forms of immunisation against disease form part of the service. As well as examination and treatment, civics and health education packs focus on preventative medicine, discouraging children from developing habits injurious to health. The Health Education Bureau has made much more curricular material on health available to schools. School meals are made available to children in national schools who, through insufficient food, might be unable to take full advantage of the education provided. The Minister for Social Welfare sanctions applications for school meals and they are provided by local authorities. The boards of management decide on the number of children in need of the food which usually takes the form of milk and sandwiches. Slightly less than 20 per cent of national school pupils benefit from this scheme and more than half are in the Dublin Corporation area.

School books scheme   There is no universal scheme of free books for national school pupils. The books and associated materials have to be paid for by parents. Small grants (£4 in 1981/2) are made available to provide books for what are termed 'necessitous' pupils, that is pupils whose parents have very limited financial resources. Formal application has to be made to the principal of the school for such grants and he or she is responsible for distributing the grants in strict confidence. Some principal teachers have expressed unease at the embarrassment which the administration of this discriminatory scheme sometimes causes them. In 1978/9 the scheme cost £238,000 and this assisted about 22 per cent of the pupils attending national schools.

Grants for school libraries and school equipment   National school library books are provided through the joint efforts of the Department of Education and the local authorities. The Department contributes a sum per pupil (25 pence in 1979) and the local authority contributes a minimum of 10 pence per pupil, though many authorities exceed this figure. The county librarian is the chief executive of the scheme which he or she operates in conjunction with a committee. The existence of school libraries has allowed for a much greater variety in children's reading at all stages in the schools and has facilitated the implementation of the curricular policy introduced in 1971. State grants are also payable to schools for the purchase of audio-visual equipment and materials on a basis of not more than 75 per cent of the approved, vouched-for expenditure, and subject to a maximum figure related to the size of the school. Further, state grants are payable for the first stock of a new school, for school furniture, for basic physical education equipment, and for special and remedial classes in ordinary national schools.

The Department of Education initiated support grants for the provision of clerical assistants to national schools with seven or more teachers in 1978. From 1 April 1979 a scheme of grants for the employment of caretakers in full-time posts in national schools with a staff of sixteen or more was introduced. Despite considerable pressure for the establishment of a psychological service for ordinary national schools, such a service has not been introduced.

The curriculum of national schools

The present national school curriculum was introduced in 1971. The curriculum allows a wide measure of freedom to the teacher and to the pupil. It is based on a child-centred ideology and is designed 'to enable the child to live a full life as a child and to equip him to avail of further education so that he may go on to live a full and useful life as an adult in society'.[7] The wide range of obligatory subjects includes religion, Irish, English, mathematics, arts and crafts, social and environmental studies, history, civics, geography, music and physical education. Guidelines and approaches are suggested but teachers are encouraged to adapt the programme to suit the needs and educational environment of the district in which the school is situated.

Small-group and individual teaching is urged to complement class teaching. Teachers are advised to adopt activity and heuristic pedagogical approaches as far as possible. Integration of various subject areas is also encouraged. Many of the new large national schools are designed to include shared-teaching areas which facilitate team-work on the part of staff as well as allowing more space for activity and movement by the pupils. Schools are encouraged to make excursions to localities outside the school so as to pursue local environmental studies as well as to avail of cultural amenities in the area.

Many of the new national schools are very impressive buildings, with exciting design features and providing a pleasant environment for the education of young pupils. In many classrooms the rigid rows of desks of a former era have been replaced by small tables and children's chairs. Most of the furniture and apparatus is light and easily moved. The decor involves light colours and pastel shades, and floor carpeting reduces the sounds of movement. The nature tables, art corners and library reference corners reflect the new curricular emphases. General purpose halls in the large schools allow for indoor physical education, dance, drama, concerts etc which have become more regular features in schools. Many teachers have used the freedom allowed them to explore the local environment for its historical, geographical, botanical and general cultural richness. Project learning and individual research have become more common teaching/learning techniques in the senior classes. More individual attention is given to pupils having learning difficulties through various forms of remedial teaching. Most observers note that the general atmosphere in schools has become more enlivening for pupils and the resort to forms of punishment such as corporal punishment has declined considerably. Although corporal punishment is still legal for misconduct, humane and pastoral modes of discipline are more frequent. This has probably been aided by the closer links which have been established between the school and the home through more frequent contact between individual parents and teachers, through parent-teacher meetings and through fund raising and social activities centred on the schools.

Yet the picture is not universally satisfactory. Many sub-standard schools still exist. In 1980 the INTO launched a strong campaign urging management authorities to remedy sub-standard and dilapidated schools. The Minister for Education gave the INTO Congress at Easter 1981, an undertaking that the Department would provide significant financial support for such a scheme. The level of implementation of the new curriculum varies between different schools. The large number of pupils in many classes, in the early years after 1971 at least, was a great obstacle to teachers trying to implement child-centred approaches. Many teachers availed of in-service courses to up-date their skills, but others were not in favour of the new curriculum and were reluctant to change their pedagogic style. The guidelines of the new curriculum have not been fully implemented but a significant change in the subjects taught and a modification of the formal approaches of the older system has taken place; the pendulum is shifting gradually. No formal examination exists at the end of the national school period; instead, report cards are filled in on senior pupils setting out their scholastic and social education profiles and these cards are available to the authorities of the post-primary school to which the pupil transfers. However, these report cards are less used than was originally intended and liaison between national and post-primary schools is frequently inadequate.

During the 1970s a number of appraisals were made by agencies such as the Department of Education, the Educational Research Centre, the Conference of Convent National School Teachers and the Irish National Teachers' Organisation on the success achieved in implementing the new curriculum. A significant level of progress was reported but the large classes, unsuitable furniture and inadequate materials as well as the unfamiliarity of some teachers with the new subjects and approaches inhibited full implementation of the curriculum. 92 per cent of teachers who responded to the INTO questionnaire held that the new curriculum was being implemented from a 'moderate' to 'a very great degree'. National teachers considered that all aspects of English and mathematics, with the exception of memorisation of number facts, had improved since the introduction of the new curriculum. It was considered that there was disimprovement in Irish except for reading. The subjects teachers had most difficulty with were arts and crafts, music and physical education.[8] Studies of trends in English reading standards by the Teachers' Study Group over the period indicated significant improvements in the reading standards of Dublin pupils.[9] The Reading Association of Ireland was founded in 1975 and, although it deals with all aspects of reading, most of the association's workshops and published research have concentrated on the primary sector and have improved awareness and fostered skills in that area. During the 1970s many in-service courses were arranged, particularly during vacation time, to assist national teachers and to familiarise them with new subjects and techniques.

Following the publication of the 'new' curriculum in 1971, educational publishers arranged for new schemes of textbooks which reflected the change in emphasis. A wider range of textbooks and alternative readers became available which, in general, were more colourful and better presented than the older schemes.

The Department of Education reserves the right to sanction the textbooks in use in the national schools and officers of the Department liaise with the educational publishers for planning and approval purposes. The Department's publication section publishes and helps finance textbooks in Irish.

Size of national schools and classes
Owing to the policy of small-school closure and amalgamation, discussed earlier, the number of one- and two-teacher schools in 1978/9 was 1,187, or 34 per cent of the total, 3,432.[10] There were 528 schools with ten or more teachers on the staff, and only 229 schools had more than 500 pupils on the roll. The older pattern of single-sex national schools, mainly in urban areas, has declined so that in 1978/9 there were only 654 wholly male or female schools and they catered for about 37 per cent of all pupils.

As has been noted progress was made in reducing the number of large classes in national schools. Considerable disparities still exist in the class sizes in various schools, particularly between urban and rural schools. The national average teacher-pupil ratio stood at 30:1 in 1980 but, as a national average, it masks the very large classes which some teachers encounter and which hamper efforts to give real expression to curricular ideals. The number of children in classes of 45 and over declined to 6,401 in 1979/80 and, overall, there were only 41,679 pupils in classes of more than 40 pupils. Almost half the pupil population, 250,000, were in classes of between 30 and 40 pupils. Apart from indicating a concern about reducing the incidence of classes with more than 40 pupils the white paper (1980) indicated no target plan for radical reduction in class sizes. Neither did its projections for teacher supply reflect planning for this nor, indeed, for a replacement pool for teachers who might be released for in-service training.

Private primary schools
As well as national schools there also exist private primary schools which provide elementary education. These schools are fee-paying, receive no state support and are not normally subject to departmental inspection or regulation. In 1978/9 there were 110 private primary schools with an enrolment of 19,105 pupils. Most of the schools are situated in the urban districts of Dublin and Cork. Such schools are frequently run by religious orders and are linked to state-supported secondary schools run by these communities.

Priority of access to these secondary schools is given to pupils from the private primary schools and this is often a factor in the parents' decision to send their children there, as well as a certain social exclusiveness which many of these schools reflect.

Traditionally these schools did not give the same emphasis to the Irish language as national schools did and they tended to offer a wider curriculum with more out of class activities. However, since the introduction of the new curriculum into national schools, the differences are less. A number of the private primary schools employ particular pedagogical styles such as the Montessori or the Froebel systems and the teacher training experience of staff may vary considerably.

Early childhood and pre-school education
The tradition of beginning formal school attendance at the age of four has been a strong one in Ireland. This early enrolment in the formal school system may have resulted, in the past, in a lack of public concern about pre-school education. However, in recent decades psychologists and others have focused attention on the educational potential of the early childhood years. Many of the research studies, including that at Rutland Street in inner-city Dublin, have concentrated on the needs of young children and their parents who suffer from harsh socio-economic circumstances. Many parents from more favoured backgrounds have come to value pre-formal schooling believing that their children can benefit socially, emotionally and, perhaps, intellectually from being with their peers in play and small-group learning situations. Apart from such concerns society is undergoing employment changes with implications for child-rearing in the home. Whether through voluntary choice or economic necessity many mothers are going out to work, resulting in the closedown of the home for part, or all, of the working day. It seems likely that forms of pre-formal schooling services will become more general, with demands on the state for support.

In common with other countries there has been a considerable growth in pre-school playgroups. There are now several hundred playgroups operated by private individuals, voluntary and community groups, local councils and health boards. The participation of parents, when it occurs, in the activities of the playgroups is regarded as an enriching element. An umbrella body, the Irish Pre-School Playgroups Association (IPPA), aims to promote the extension of playgroups and acts as an advice and registering centre for new playgroups. Nursery schools tend to provide a more formal and planned learning environment than playschools. They are mostly operated by teachers trained in the Montessori method. Most of the nursery schools cater for children up to five but some take children up to the ages of seven or nine. They are mainly private and fee-paying though some health boards assist in the provision of non-Montessori nursery schools. There are also some playgroups and nursery schools conducted through the medium of Irish. An Comhchoiste Réamhscholaíochta associated with Bord na Gaeilge co-ordinates about 80 'naonraí' throughout the country and they are sometimes linked to all-Irish national schools. The state exercises no control over the various types of pre-formal schooling which exist, and teachers or organisers receive no official recognition. The approach and curriculum of the Rutland Street Pre-School Centre have been applied to a number of other disadvantaged areas, but there has been no further state initiative in pre-school education.

Chapter Eleven

Special education

Background

Since the early 1960s Ireland has seen an increased official interest in and support for education provision adapted to the needs of children who, because of mental, physical, sensory or emotional handicaps, are unable, or find it difficult, to participate in ordinary schooling. It is important to chart the growth of these recent developments before dealing with present provision. Some schools for deaf mutes were established by religious communities in the early nineteenth century and similar institutions for the blind were set up after 1870. However, even when such institutions eventually became part of the national school system in this century, no special staffing ratios were operated. It was not until 1962, when the schools for the blind were given a special teacher-pupil ratio of 15:1 and a grant for special equipment, that these schools became what might be regarded as special schools. Special staffing arrangements for the schools of the deaf followed a few years later. A diploma course for teachers of the deaf was set up in University College, Dublin in 1957.

The provision of facilities for the mentally-handicapped in Ireland has been limited up to recent decades. Most of the educational provision that did exist was left to voluntary societies and the range of their activities, although worthy, was limited. In Ireland the state did not involve itself in the education of the mentally-handicapped until the mid-twentieth century, although maintenance and basic medical services had been provided by the state since the early nineteenth century. In 1950 there was only one special school for the mentally handicapped, St Vincent's, Dublin, which was recognised by the Department of Education; by 1960 there were thirty-three such schools. In 1959 an inspector was assigned to special education by the Department of Education. The first Irish training course for teachers of the mentally handicapped was set up in St˙Patrick's Training College, Drumcondra in September 1960. It offered a one-year full-time in-service diploma course for teachers teaching in special schools. About 400 teachers had been awarded this diploma up to 1980.

The government produced a white paper, *The problem of the mentally handicapped*, in April 1960. It was mainly an assessment of the existing situation and it indicated that a commission of inquiry was to be set up. The commission of inquiry on mental handicap was established in February 1961 to recommend a scheme 'for the treatment, care, training and education of mentally-handicapped persons . . .'. In 1963 the first official recognition was given to a school for maladjusted children and, in the following year, the Department of Education also recognised schools for the moderately mentally handicapped as special national schools. Special state-aided transport was extended to children in special schools and from 1965 more emphasis was placed on day schools for the handicapped and on reorganising residential schools with an emphasis on a five-day residence schedule.

The *Report of the commission of inquiry on mental handicap* was presented to the government in March 1965.[1] Many of its ninety-six recommendations had a bearing on educational provision for the mentally handicapped. It proposed that school-linked teams should be established to serve as diagnostic, assessment and advisory services; it made specific proposals about the curriculum, duration of programmes, sizes of schools and classes, equipment relating to schools for the mildly handicapped, and sheltered training workshops; it stressed the importance of preventative measures and the need for more theoretical and practical studies of mental handicap in the training courses of medical and educational personnel whose work dealt with mental handicap. The publication of the report reflected a new awareness of the problems of educating the mentally handicapped and a greater social concern generally that the problems should be grappled with.

Following the publication of this report the number of special schools increased to seventy by 1970 and 108 by 1980.[2] From about 1970 the policy of establishing special classes in ordinary national schools was promoted; a circular from the Department of Education issued in 1977 tightened the criteria for admission to these special classes. By 1980 there were 157 special classes catering for 2,135 pupils. In 1978 the Department, for the first time, issued specific curricular guidelines for the education of the moderately handicapped. In line with international thinking on the subject, policy in the late 1970s has increasingly favoured integrating mild mentally handicapped and physically handicapped children as far as possible into the ordinary schools. However, to achieve this in a satisfactory manner in prevailing circumstances will require a major initiative in planning, training and the provision of resources.

In 1972 there was a report on 'The education of children who are handicapped by impaired hearing'.[3] One result of this was that a new scheme was initiated in 1974 which provided for a visiting teaching service to help children with impaired hearing who attended ordinary national schools and to provide guidance for parents, especially at pre-school stage. In 1978 a similar scheme was introduced for blind or partially-sighted children.

Existing provision

Although only about 2 per cent of school children are involved in special education, this aspect of educational provision has come to assume an important place in the educational system. As has been outlined, Ireland in recent decades – in line with developments in other countries – has devoted more specialised and scientific attention to the educational needs of children suffering from various forms of handicap. Within the general framework of the system, special provision is now made for handicapped and deprived children in special schools which are recognised on the same basis as national schools, in special classes which are attached to ordinary schools and in certain voluntary centres where educational services appropriate to the needs of the children are provided. Categories of handicapped children catered for include the visually handicapped, those with impaired hearing, the physically handicapped, the mentally handicapped, the emotionally disturbed, itinerants and other disadvantaged children. Provision is also being made on an increasing scale for children with dual or multiple handicaps. In each case a programme suited to the needs of the particular kind of handicap is provided and new school buildings have been provided to cater for the special educational requirements of the handicapped child. The number of children in each class is very much smaller than in ordinary classes in a primary school and, because of the wide catchment areas for these schools, an extensive system of school transport has been developed.

Many handicapped children who have spent some years in a special school or class are integrated into normal schools for part of their school career, with special additional facilities, if necessary, such as nursing services, special equipment etc. Others, who cannot progress within ordinary school structures, obtain all their primary and second-level education at special schools or in special classes. In addition to the services provided on a full-time basis many children are catered for by part-time teaching facilities in hospitals, child guidance clinics, rehabilitation workshops, special 'Saturday-morning' centres and home-teaching schemes.

Existing schooling provision, as of 1979, for children who suffer from various forms of physical or mental handicap, include the following.

1. There are two special national schools for blind and partially-sighted children. These are based in Dublin and operate on a residential and day-attendance basis. Arrangements exist in a number of post-primary schools for some older blind and partially-sighted children. A visiting teacher scheme exists with a particular interest in parent guidance and pre-school children whose sight is deficient.

2. There are three residential schools in Dublin for deaf and severely hard-of-hearing children and a further school is sited in Cork. Parent groups have established some further schools for the deaf on a private basis. A visiting teacher scheme for the deaf also exists.

3. There are thirty special schools for the mildly mentally handicapped and others are catered for in about 150 special classes in ordinary schools. There are thirty special schools for moderately mentally-handicapped young people.

4. Physically-handicapped children unable to attend ordinary schools are served by six special schools and by ten schools attached to hospitals. Pilot schemes to provide a comprehensive post-primary curriculum for the physically handicapped have been established in a number of comprehensive and community schools. There is a growing sensitivity apparent in the design of schools to cater for the needs of physically handicapped children.

5. There are fourteen special schools for children who are emotionally disturbed to the extent that they require special schooling either on a temporary basis or for the duration of their school career. These schools range from those for children whose degree of disturbance is mild and can be expected to clear up in a year or two to schools for autistic children. The number of children

being catered for is about 450. Such schools operate in association with child guidance clinics operated by health authorities and voluntary bodies.

Significant reductions exist in the quota of pupils necessary for the appointment of teachers in all kinds of special schools. Overall, in 1979, there were 817 teachers for 8,083 pupils in the various special national schools. The white paper of 1980 indicated a desire to plan provision of special classes for the mildly handicapped in ordinary second-level schools. In March 1980 the Minister for Education set up a special working party to report on education for severely mentally handicapped children. Teachers, through their unions, have urged that the International Year of the Disabled, 1981, should be marked by a special effort to improve educational facilities for the handicapped and, while favouring an integration policy for such pupils, have urged that adequate back-up services be provided.

Table 12: **Number of special national schools for the handicapped and number of pupils in each type of special school, 1979**

	Number of schools	Number of pupils
Mentally handicapped	60	5,535
Children with impaired hearing	4	819
Blind and partially sighted	2	139
Physically handicapped	17	689
Emotionally disturbed	14	451
Other special schools	11	450
Total	108	8,083

Source: *Statistical Report of Department of Education, 1978/9* Table 16, p. 26

Educational provision for slow learners and the socially disadvantaged
There has been a considerable expansion of personnel and facilities for the remedial education of children in ordinary schools who are backward owing to various causes such as poor attendance, adverse

home conditions or special learning difficulties particularly with regard to literacy and numeracy. In schools with a high incidence of such problems, teachers assigned to remedial work may be appointed in addition to the normal quota. In 1980 there were more than 300 such teachers serving about 16,000 pupils. Special facilities can be provided for such pupils in association with some child guidance clinics or in some schools specialising in learning difficulties, but a more general psychological service for diagnosing early difficulties is being sought by educationists. In-service courses for remedial teachers in national schools are provided in St Patrick's College, Dublin, Mary Immaculate College, Limerick, as well as by some other groups and agencies. The psychological service of the Department of Education provides courses for remedial teachers in post-primary schools.

Recent years have also seen a greater awareness of the educational problems and needs of children who suffer educational disadvantage because they are socially and economically deprived. A notable research project in this area was the pre-school centre in Rutland Street in inner-city Dublin, jointly sponsored by the Department of Education and the Van Leer Foundation. The experiment was initiated in 1969 for a five-year period. However, the scheme has continued and some of its techniques have been extended to other areas. Although the results of attainment tests did not show impressive improvements in the scholastic performance of the children involved, it is generally felt that the gains have been considerable in the affective domain, in curriculum techniques and in home-school understanding.[4] As well as positive intervention at the pre-school and early education stages in schools in disadvantaged localities, there is greater public and professional awareness of the need to understand and cope with the educational needs of children of specific disadvantaged groups, in particular the children of itinerant families. Following the report of the commission on itinerancy, the Department of Education set up an internal committee to plan policy for the education of itinerants. Its report published in 1970[5] indicated that the main aim of policy should be to place itinerant children in the ordinary national schools at their appropriate age-level. Such children could, if necessary, benefit from any remedial facilities for backward children existing in the schools. Where large concentrations of itinerant children were involved and where their placing in ordinary schools would present particular educational problems, one of two approaches could be adopted: the special school or the special class in an ordinary school. In recent years the predominant approach has been one of integration within ordinary schools. A number of training centres have been established for itinerant youth, partially financed by the VECs.

Reformatory and industrial schools

Up to the middle of the nineteenth century, the only provision for orphaned and neglected children was in the workhouses. Subsequently, voluntary institutions conducted by religious organisations and charitable persons provided, in some measure, for the care of juvenile offenders. This was at a period when children above the age of seven were subject to the same rigours of the law as adult offenders. The institutions received no public moneys and were not subject to inspection by any state authority. In 1858 Ireland came under the provisions of the Reformatory Schools Act. This act allowed for the certification of a number of existing voluntary institutions as reformatory schools suitable for the reception of youthful offenders committed by the courts. It also provided for the inspection of these institutions and for grants from public funds for the maintenance of children in them. By 1865 ten reformatory schools were certified. The Children Act of 1908 marked a more humane concern for children's welfare; gradually reformatory schools fell into decline and by 1970 only three existed, catering for 100 children.

Industrial schools were introduced into Ireland in 1869 shortly after the reformatory schools and, within a year, twenty-two had been recognised. By 1875 there were fifty with 7,638 pupils. Industrial schools catered for neglected, orphaned or abandoned children. They provided a refuge for such children, made them literate and numerate, and aimed at teaching them a trade. Local authorities were reluctant to take on the job of providing these industrial schools and the onus fell on various religious orders. By 1899 seventy-one such schools existed and catered for 8,422 children.[6] As time went on such schools reduced in number so that by 1970 there were twenty-nine industrial schools catering for 1,513 children.[7] Since 1924 both reformatory and industrial schools have been under the authority of the Minister for Education.

This area of educational endeavour was also affected by the reforming movement of the 1960s. In 1967 the government set up a committee 'to survey the Reformatory and Industrial Schools system and to make a report and recommendations to the Minister of Education'. In its report (Kennedy Report) published in 1970[8] the committee made many recommendations on the need for changed attitudes regarding children in need of care and on improved methods of referral, reception and treatment. The report proposed changes in the training of personnel in charge of such children and in the legal framework and after-care provision. The existing educational provisions were seen as highly inadequate and, because of the deprivation experienced by such children, it was urged that they should be over-compensated. A team approach was recommended involving pre-school work, early diagnosis, psychological and other advisory services as well as the skill of educational personnel attuned to the children's needs. It was urged that children in residential houses should receive their education with other children in schools located outside the houses.

In the aftermath of the Kennedy Report, some improvements have taken place in dealing with children in care. For example, the names 'industrial' and 'reformatory' have been changed to residential homes and special schools and many reforms have been introduced in the operation of these institutions. However, many other suggested reforms were not implemented. In 1979 there were five special schools and twenty-five residential homes catering for a total of 1,208 children in care for various reasons. A report of the task force on child care services published in 1980 urged that residential homes and special schools, with the exception of St Joseph's, Clonmel, should be placed under the authority of the Minister for Health rather than the Minister for Education.[9]

Chapter Twelve.

Second-level education

Developments in second-level education, 1960-80

Even before the publication of *Investment in Education*, the government had made it clear that it was planning significant new initiatives in second-level education. A notable speech in this regard was that made by the Minister for Education, Dr Hillery, in May 1963.[1] This was a major policy speech which contained seminal ideas that were to come to fruition in the following years. The most important announcement was that the government was to undertake the building of post-primary schools of a new type termed 'comprehensive schools'. They were to be co-educational schools open to all classes and levels of ability, offering a wide curriculum to match the aptitudes of their pupils. The comprehensive schools would benefit from a psychological guidance service and would have a transport system laid on in their catchment areas. They were to cater for a minimum of 150 pupils and to offer junior cycle studies only. They were to be run by a management committee of three — a departmental inspector, a representative of the local bishop and of the local vocational educational committee. The management arrangements for the small number of Protestant comprehensive schools, which came to be established, differed in the greater number of denominational representatives appointed. The comprehensive schools were not planned on a nationwide scale but rather were to be situated in regions where there was a lack of post-primary schools. To help put vocational schools on an academic and social par with secondary schools, Dr Hillery announced that the two-year course in vocational schools would be extended to three years and that a wide Intermediate Certificate course would be offered by both secondary and vocatioal schools. As a further indication of concern for raising the status of technical education, it was announced that a Technical Leaving Certificate would be introduced. Another new educational institution was announced in the form of regional technical colleges which would help boost technical education and help align educational provision with manpower needs.

Capital expenditure by the state on secondary schools started in 1964-5, with the introduction of two schemes. The first scheme allowed departmental grants of 70 per cent and allowed borrowing facilities for the remaining 30 per cent of the capital for building projects. The second scheme enabled schools to borrow capital from commercial finance houses for a ten-year period. The Department undertook to pay 70 per cent of the annual capital and interest repayments, and the schools were responsible for repaying the remaining 30 per cent. The latter scheme was terminated in 1973 and under the ten-year terms the last repayments fall due in 1982.

The first three state-run, comprehensive schools opened in 1966, a year which also saw the Minister for Education, George Colley, appealing for co-operation and co-ordination between small post-primary schools in towns where a number of such schools existed. Colley remarked: 'I do not anticipate that the number of public comprehensive schools will be very great. My aim is that secondary and vocational schools, by the exchange of facilities and by other forms of collaboration, should make available the basis of a comprehensive system in each locality.'[2]

It was hoped that such pooling of resources at local level would help to provide a wide curriculum similar to that provided in the comprehensive schools, and also minimise the distinctions between vocational and secondary schools. The common Intermediate Certificate programme was initiated in 1966. However, appeals for local co-operation did not result in significant developments. In the past, co-operation had been minimal and the interested parties felt threatened by the new developments. Meanwhile, planning was being undertaken within the Department which approached the provision of schooling from the point of view of the needs of districts or catchment areas rather than from the needs of individual schools viewed in isolation. Meetings between departmental and local school personnel took place to discuss county surveys during 1966 and 1967.

An obstacle in the path of children of poor parents wishing to participate in second- and third-level education was the cost involved, particularly in the case of large families. The Local Authorities (Education Scholarships, Amendment) Act of 1961 was an effort to improve the meagre and geographically-imbalanced system of scholarships which had prevailed. For the first time, the state now contributed to the scholarship scheme. Two-thirds of the new scholarship fund went to second-level pupils and the remainder to university students. The number of scholarships increased from 2,609 in 1960 to 9,614 in 1966.[3] That year — 1966 — was also to hear of a more elaborate scheme for increasing participation.

In September 1966 the Minister for Education, Donogh O'Malley, made a dramatic announcement. He declared 'free post-primary education' would be made available nationwide from the academic year 1967/8 onwards.[4] This announcement received maximum publicity, though many involved parties felt aggrieved at the lack of prior notice and discussion. Despite misgivings and organisational problems, the scheme got underway as planned, coupled with a new transport scheme which provided free bus transport for pupils living more than three miles from the nearest school.

Traditionally, school fees at many Irish day secondary schools had been small and some school managers felt aggrieved that the Minister, in deciding on a system of state-reimbursement in lieu of school fees, was taking advantage of the low figures obtaining. Enrolments in post-primary schooling had been increasing annually but they now grew more rapidly. The enrolment rose from 148,000 in 1966/7 to 185,000 in 1968/9; succeeding years saw continued increases in participation so that by 1974, for instance, it had reached 239,000 pupils at second level.[5] This huge bulge led to a lot of temporary school building in the form of prefabricated classrooms. Teachers faced new problems with pupils of a wider range of ability and social background in more crowded classrooms.

A further dramatic development was the announcement on community schools in October 1970.[6] The concept of the community school was a development of the comprehensive school. The community school was to provide free schooling of a comprehensive type to all in the catchment area without pupil selection procedures. The schools were described as a further step towards equality of educational opportunity, the reduction of overlapping of resources, and the elimination of the bipartite pattern of vocational and secondary schools. A significant new element, however, was the special emphasis on establishing reciprocal relationships between the school and its surrounding community. No longer was the school seen as an institution concerned solely with the job of educating the young; it was to foster many forms of youth and adult education and to make its facilities available to the wider community. The comprehensive school idea was largely superseded by the wider community school concept and since 1974 no further comprehensive schools have been built.

The mode of administration of community schools was to cause considerable difficulty. The first community schools were run by ad hoc management committees comprising two representatives of the VEC, two of religious orders and two parents. New arrangements are discussed later. The VECs and religious orders are responsible for a local contribution of about 10 per cent of the capital costs of the community schools, and the state pays the rest and also the current expenditure.

A Vocational Education (Amendment) Act was passed in 1970 to facilitate VECs co-operating with other agencies in the provision of schools. A variant on the community school is the community college which differs mainly in that it is solely under the control of the VEC and the Department of Education. The community colleges emerged because the VECs wished to retain their role in providing schools, even if the vocational schools were being displaced by new types of school in areas with expanding school-going populations.

The raising of the school-leaving age to fifteen years in 1972, which had long been promised, meant that most pupils would experience two or three years of post-primary education, as the age of transition from primary school became generally established at about the age of twelve. The raising of the leaving age was, of course, also a factor in the expansion of numbers in post-primary schooling in the early 1970s.

Although the structural changes stole the limelight, there were several important initiatives to change the syllabuses of post-primary subjects as regards both content and method, starting in the early 1960s. Efforts were made to give science teaching a more experimental base and grants for science laboratories as well as special gratuities for science graduates to enter teaching were made available. An annual competition known as 'Young Scientist Exhibition' was sponsored by Aer Lingus and has done a great deal to foster science experiments in schools, as well as promote general public interest in science. Much work was put into changing the mathematics courses and this resulted in the introduction of what were popularly known as 'new maths'. An effort was made to break the dominance of the grammar translation method of teaching modern languages. Language laboratories, film strips and tape recorders were introduced as features of language teaching in schools. The Irish language, which had suffered from the heavy reliance on the written and literary approach, began to benefit from the oral/aural method. An oral examination in Irish was introduced as part of the Leaving Certificate in 1960, accounting for one-sixth of the allocated marks and later one quarter. Various difficulties with regard to payment and mode of examining contrived to prevent full-scale oral examinations in other modern languages, though experiments in the early 1980s are likely to lead to oral examinations, at least in French. More frequent school visits abroad helped in the acquisition of foreign languages.

The introduction of the common Intermediate Certificate course in 1966 contributed to a wider subject range and a greater role for practical subjects. The vocational and new comprehensive schools offered practical subjects and many secondary schools made provision in the late 1960s for a more comprehensive curriculum. A significant indicator of shift in curriculum balance was the steady decline of classical studies with Latin plummeting from its position of prominence. Civics was introduced as a compulsory but non-examinable school subject in the mid-1960s. Courses in history and geography became more varied, were given a greater social and economic input and scope was allowed for individual project work by students. Literature courses were changed to incorporate the works of modern and contemporary authors and pupils were encouraged to be creative and draw from personal experience in writing essays. The Department of Education encouraged a group scheme of subject choice for Leaving Certificate in 1969 but this was not generally successful. From a range of five groups — languages, commerce, science, technical studies and social studies — students were to choose at least three subjects from one of the groups: this would have introduced an element of specialisation at senior cycle but the established tradition of a general education was preferred. The intention to make the group scheme compulsory in 1972 was not proceeded with, nor was the projected Technical Leaving Certificate ever introduced. The proposal of a post-Leaving Advanced Certificate year was only taken by a small number of schools as an optional matter. A significant change of policy occurred in 1973 with the government decision to drop Irish as a compulsory subject for the award of certificates at

Intermediate and Leaving levels. Irish remained an essential subject if schools were to be 'recognised' and an honours award in Irish at Leaving Certificate counted as a double subject for the purposes of student grants at third level. New subjects such as metalwork, engineering workshop theory and practice, accounting and business organisation were introduced. Alternative courses were introduced for subjects such as science, history, geography, music and home economics.

The increased pupil numbers, changes in the ability spectrum and the wider range of social backgrounds of the pupils have lent a sense of urgency to the need for a more thorough approach to curricular policy than had been the pattern. Prompted by such considerations, the 1970s witnessed some interesting experiments in curriculum development and pilot work on assessment procedures and these are described later.

Linked to the curriculum is the mode of pedagogy. At the post-primary level it was subject-centred with a heavy reliance on the expository lecture method and note-giving. The teaching style was didactic or directive. The structured and packaged mode of handling subject content tended to foster pupil dependency, even at senior level. One outcome of this was the lack of preparedness or skill in personal study which many pupils exhibited when removed from the highly-structured teaching with which they were familiar. Some commentators have also remarked that the didactic tradition has inhibited more innovative, creative, problem-solving attitudes among school-leavers. Pedagogic patterns have been influenced by curricular change over recent decades. Another challenge to pedagogy was the changed clientele of schools, following the expansion in participation rates. This posed challenges to the traditional image of the teacher as the authority, some of the new pupils being less amenable to conventional methods of maintaining order and discipline. The expansion also demanded a range of skills to motivate and help pupils of relatively weak ability to master the curriculum. Teachers with specialist skills in remedial education were provided to help pupils of poor standard and weak ability.

This period also saw the introduction of guidance teachers in Irish post-primary schools to help pupils through counselling and vocational guidance. By 1979 about half the post-primary schools benefited from the service of guidance counsellors who, as well as providing guidance and help to students themselves, also liaise with the Department's psychological service and guidance clinics. The Department of Education's psychological service, established in 1965, helped in conducting various educational tests and in the handling of the psychological problems experienced by some pupils. The psychological service has been mainly concerned with pupils in the junior cycle of post-primary schools.

Despite quite considerable curricular change the examination structure tended to remain traditional with its three national certificate examinations – the Group, Intermediate and the Leaving. A study of the Leaving Certificate by Madaus and McNamara in 1968 pointed out that it was not reliable, that it sought too much factual data, and that it placed a heavy burden on pupils because it was used as the test which qualified candidates for entry to many occupations.[7] In 1969 the 'honours-pass' nomenclature was dropped and a grading system with six categories from A to F introduced. The centralised public examinations have continued to exercise a huge influence on the work of the schools. A further pressure was added to the Leaving Certificate examination and the universities' matriculation examination in 1968, when universities began to operate a points system to select candidates for entry into some faculties where student numbers were restricted. The increased number of second-level students competing for limited occupational opportunities and university places has led to greatly increased competitiveness in the examinations. Ironically, the third-level student grant scheme introduced in 1968 tended to lessen the competitiveness which had existed for university scholarships, but the introduction of the points system in the same year reintroduced competitiveness. Many teachers and parents feel that the examinations and the entry requirements to third level have come to exercise a distorting influence on the whole process of second-level education.[8]

The hopes held out in the 1960s for an observation cycle within the junior cycle allowing time for pupils' aptitudes to emerge and be related to appropriate subject choices, has tended to be undermined as parental expectations and society's awards place a premium on examination performance. This has resulted in moulding the new types of school such as community and comprehensive into more traditional roles than the theory had envisaged. All types of post-primary school felt the need to direct their sights at successful examination performance if they were to retain public confidence and esteem.

A special *Report on the intermediate certificate examination* was published in 1975[9] and called for radical changes in the Intermediate Certificate examination. It recommended more school-based assessment procedures and more varied assessment techniques than just the written examination. The final report of the Public Examinations Evaluation Project was presented to the Minister for Education in 1981 and it urged more varied modes of examination with greater teacher involvement in syllabus design and assessment.[10] The public examinations have, therefore, been the subject of considerable debate and investigation and, although some changes have taken place in the type of question set in the examination papers, no fundamental reforms have been made.

Post-primary (second-level) education today

School and pupil numbers

Traditionally post-primary education was conducted on a bipartite system with the secondary schools offering a grammar school education on christian humanist lines and the vocational schools offering a two-year continuation course with a practical orientation, as well as technical education for more senior students. Since the 1960s this has changed dramatically with the policy of establishing post-primary schooling on comprehensive lines, through the secondary and vocational schools and also through two new types of institutions — comprehensive and community schools. With the compulsory school leaving age set at fifteen years of age, most pupils of necessity undergo two or three years of post-primary schooling, but even in the age range fifteen to nineteen the percentage participation rate is high at about 55 per cent.

Table 13: **Main categories of post-primary schools with their pupil numbers, 1978/9**

Type	Number	Pupils
Secondary schools	531	196,606
Vocational schools	246	68,120
Community schools	26	14,204
Comprehensive schools	15	8,152

Source: *Statistical Report of the Department of Education 1978/9*, Table 11, p. 55

Overall there were 882 second-level institutions in 1978-79 catering for a pupil enrolment of 292,674. The main categories of schools with their full-time pupil numbers are set out in Table 13. The secondary schools are still the predominant form of second-level school but it is expected that the number of community schools will increase and, being situated in centres of large population, will cater for larger numbers. No further comprehensive schools are being built. Traditionally post-primary education was available in some national schools known as 'secondary tops' which taught post-primary curricula to advanced pupils. These schools have declined to five in number, catering for 616 pupils. Vocational education committees have begun setting up what they term 'community colleges', on the lines of community schools but under the control of the VECs. A small proportion of students receive second-level education in regional, technological, commercial and some miscellaneous schools and colleges. In order to be accepted as a recognised post-primary pupil the individual must be at least twelve years of age on 1 January of the school year in which he or she wishes to enroll, and must have normally completed a full course of primary education.

The vast majority of second-level schools in Ireland are relatively small by international standards. Despite increased participation, about 25 per cent of post-primary schools had under 200 pupils in attendance during the school year 1978-9. The average school size is between 200 and 500 pupils, and only 20 per cent of schools have over 500 enrolled.

As was the case with national schools there has been a move towards more co-educational schools but these still form less than half the total. The great majority of the vocational, community and comprehensive schools are co-educational but only about 25 per cent of secondary schools are mixed. Most second-level schools are day schools but about 30 per cent of secondary schools take boarders; the number of boarders was 17,767 in 1978-9. Because of the scattered nature of the Protestant population in rural areas, the children tend to be sent to Protestant schools with boarding facilities. Schools operating a five-day week must be open for a minimum of 180 days and schools offering a six-day week must be open for 200 days. Days allotted for public examinations are allowed in calculating these totals.

Education in over 90 per cent of second-level schools is free; a minority of secondary schools continue to charge fees. There are no selection tests for entry to vocational, community or comprehensive schools, but some secondary schools set their own entrance examinations. In the past vocational schools tended to get more than their fair share of the less academically able pupils and, although this has eased considerably, some school principals still feel that the secondary schools are more favourably placed with regard to pupil selection and hence with regard to public examination success. Schools vary in their policies on mixed ability teaching, streaming and setting pupils in relation to individual subjects. Corporal punishment is forbidden in vocational, comprehensive and community schools and is now rarely exercised in secondary schools.

The transition to second-level schools sometimes causes considerable difficulty for pupils. As well as the normal problems of coping with a wider range of subjects, choosing subjects, dealing with different teachers for various subjects and new approaches to study and examinations, there is often a significant change in the curricular and educational policies. This lack of alignment in curricular approach should be modified. Further, many of the pupils now in post-primary schools are the first members of their family receiving such an education and there exists, at times, inadequate information and understanding among families of the demands and expectations of second-level education. With the wider range of social classes and ability among the pupils proceeding to second-level nowadays, there are more pupils with learning difficulties. It is expected that the guidelines of a ministerial committee on the problems of transition, due to report in 1981, will help to resolve the various difficulties being encountered.

Post-primary pupils benefit from a free transport scheme if they live three miles or more from their nearest school, with special arrangements for pupils wishing to attend an all-Irish school. The cost of the transport scheme in 1978-9 was £6½ million but with transport costs rising dramatically this figure is steadily increasing. Special maintenance grants are available for second-level pupils living on islands or remote areas, and in 1978-9 this scheme cost £63,457 and benefited 235 pupils. Grants are also available for free books for 'necessitous' pupils and are distributed at the discretion of principal teachers who disbursed £895,064 in 1978-9 to 105,874 pupils. Health services are available free for pupils aged twelve to sixteen years if their parents are holders of medical cards and students aged sixteen or over are themselves eligible for medical cards and hence free medical services.

The post-primary curriculum
The Department of Education requires that the curriculum of state-supported second-level schools must contain a syllabus approved by the Minister for Education in the following subjects: (1) Irish, (2) English, (3) history and geography (in the case of vocational, comprehensive and community schools, mechanical drawing, art, home economics or commerce may be substituted), (4) mathematics, (5) science, or a language other than Irish or English, or commerce, or a subject from the business studies group, and (6) civics. The curriculum must also include provision for physical education, singing and, in schools for girls, home economics. It is interesting that science is not listed as an essential subject for school recognition. The course approved for junior cycle pupils must include Irish, English, mathematics, civics, history and geography and not less than two other subjects from the approved list of examination subjects. History and geography are taken as one subject in junior cycle examinations and in vocational schools the history and geography requirement is replaced by mechanical drawing or art for boys and home economics or commerce for girls. As well as the subjects listed above there are seventeen other approved subjects for recognised junior cycle. The approved course for recognised senior pupils is less prescriptive, designating Irish as the only essential subject, while at least four other subjects must be taken from a list of thirty-two approved subjects. This list of subjects has been split into 5 groups: Language, Science, Business Studies, Applied Science, Social Studies. Each pupil is recommended to take at least three subjects from the group of subjects for which he is best fitted and at least two subjects from outside that group. However, in practice, the grouping system has had little influence. The tradition of a general rather than a specialist education is pursued up to the end of senior cycle with almost all students studying six subjects and many students pursuing more than that. Although free to do so very few schools submit individual syllabuses for ministerial approval. Schools adopt the subject syllabuses for the three public examinations and so the programmes for the examinations exercise a dominating influence on second-level education.

During the 1970s a number of curricular experiments and innovations took place at second level. Alternative curricula for junior cycle were developed in the humanities, the sciences and environmental studies, with an emphasis on subject integration. These were devised by the Curriculum Development Unit of Dublin VEC, based in Trinity College. Another alternative course termed the Social and Environmental Studies Project (SESP) was developed by a curricular team based in Shannon comprehensive school where another, more recent initiative, the Shannon Project on Interventions for Relevant Adolescent Learning (Spiral), deals with links between the worlds of school and work. Authorities such as the VEC of Tipperary North have promoted curriculum development in social education and mathematics. Pilot programmes in media studies have been introduced in some schools. A small number of schools still operate a 'transition year' programme, sponsored by the Minister for Education in 1974. This course follows the completion of the junior cycle and is a one-year interdisciplinary course. It is directed towards the intellectual, social and emotional maturation of the pupils through educational pursuits outside the examination syllabus. A Department of Education initiative to start an Irish studies integrated course has not been widely adopted or followed through. A new classical studies course has been introduced with the stress on classical civilisation rather than language learning. Pilot courses with an emphasis on aural/oral and communicative French are in operation and it is expected that these developments will have generally influenced modern language teaching by 1985. With the help of the Linguistics Institute new courses in oral Irish are also being experimented with. Computer studies, as a course module in mathematics, were introduced in 1980 and it is intended to expand these. A new syllabus in religious studies is to be introduced for the Leaving Certificate examination.

A number of projects which cover the transition from school to work are benefiting from the support of the European Economic Community. Since 1977 'pre-employment courses' have been introduced in over 120 post-primary schools, particularly in the vocational schools. It is intended to extend these to secondary schools in the years ahead. They are post-junior cycle courses aimed at pupils who do not go on for the Leaving Certificate but who do not wish to, or cannot, go straight into employment. The programmes combine social, general and technical education with work experience in industry or commerce. Many post-primary schools offer one-year secretarial courses which may involve a work experience component. Some of the curricular projects have been of a 'pilot' nature for a good number of years and decisions about their future status are needed. Curriculum development has become a more prominent feature in teacher training courses and a curriculum unit was set up within the Department of Education in 1976. A Curriculum Development Association exists as a discussion and promotion group for curricular reform.

These curricular initiatives reflect the widespread concern about second-level curricula. There has been a lack of a synthesising, co-ordinating statement on overall curricular policy for second level, including the formal programmes offered, the pedagogy employed and the life-style of the schools. Some pressure groups feel that although the content of individual subjects may be adequately covered in school, the presumed values of such study in terms of personal development are not being realised.[11] Spokesmen for parent groups feel that more specific provision should be made for social, health and sex education in the schools as a preparation for adult life.[12] It is felt that the arts are being seriously neglected in the education system.[13] Industrialists and politicians comment that the school programmes are not sufficiently aligned to the technological changes in areas such as electronics and bio-engineering. Scientists feel that the implications of developments in the micro-chip call for curricular change at second level. The post-primary curriculum tends to be subject-centred and subject-compartmentalised, and some teachers and researchers in curriculum development feel that there ought to be more integrated courses, particularly at junior cycle and they seek alternative examination programmes. It may be that society is expecting too much from the schools or poses too many conflicting goals but, nevertheless, it seems that the momentum is gathering for significant appraisals of post-primary curriculum. The white paper in 1980 announced that a curriculum council was to be established to advise the Minister for Education and this may prove to be an important agent of change.[14]

The post-primary curriculum offers a wide range of subjects with twenty-six subjects at junior cycle and thirty-three at senior cycle. This in itself may pose significant problems for pupils in deciding which subjects or combination of subjects they should pursue, bearing in mind their ability and aptitudes as well as the subjects required by certain careers or by third-level institutions. These early decisions have long-term consequences on the options which are open to students at a later stage. There is now a great deal of information and data on regulations for examinations and institutions which need to be communicated intelligibly to students.

Increasingly the importance of pupil and career guidance has been recognised by schools and many schools now have personnel with some professional expertise and experience in this area. There is a high degree of competitiveness, which imposes considerable strain on pupils in their adolescent or early adult years, at Leaving Certificate level. There has been a growth of 'grind' schools which provide extra tuition in the hope of improving examination performance. Some people are concerned that the examinations have become the raison d'être of post-primary schooling to the detriment of the more humane concerns of education. However, as is the case in many other countries, it is not easy to see the public examinations dismantled and the level of competitiveness being reduced, particularly with the increased participation rate in education and without corresponding expansion of job opportunities and third-level places.

The post-primary examinations and some third-level entry requirements
The public examinations exercise a profound influence on the curricula, aspirations and career prospects of second-level pupils. Much of the concern of pupils, parents and teachers at second level is geared towards successful performance in the various examinations. The Department of Education is responsible for holding the three public examinations each year — the Day Vocational Group Certificate (Group Certificate), the Intermediate Certificate and the Leaving Certificate — and for the award of examination certificates to successful pupils. In 1979 about 19,000 candidates sat for the Group Certificate, 50,000 for the Intermediate and 36,000 for the Leaving Certificate. The average age of pupils taking the examinations is about fourteen, fifteen and seventeen years respectively. The National University also sets a matriculation examination which is taken by about 8,000 candidates, but most students matriculate by means of the Leaving Certificate. A small number of schools enter pupils for the English General Certificate examinations at ordinary and advanced levels.

The Group Certificate is offered by most vocational, community and comprehensive schools and, increasingly, by secondary schools. Pupils take it after a two- or three-year post-primary course. They study Irish, English and mathematics and some practical subjects from a range such as mechanical drawing, woodwork, metalwork, shorthand, typewriting, are also essential. It is a flexible examination framework encouraging practical aptitudes. Three D grade results in the Group Certificate represent the minimum qualification for entry to apprenticeships under the AnCO training schemes.

The Intermediate Certificate examination is taken by pupils in all types of post-primary school who have pursued a minimum of a three-year course, though some schools pursue the course over a four-year period. In its *Rules and programmes for secondary schools*, the Department of Education defines the purpose of the Intermediate course as being to provide a well-balanced, general education suitable for pupils who leave full-time education at about sixteen years of age or, alternatively, who wish to enter on more advanced courses of study. With the school leaving age now set at fifteen years of age the Intermediate Certificate acts as the main certificate of general education. Pupils have to present a minimum of six subjects, four of which are specified — Irish, English, mathematics, history and geography or an alternative to history and geography in vocational schools. Most pupils present more than the required six, particularly those pupils who wish to keep their options open for subject choice at senior level. Pupils who wish to proceed to the Leaving Certificate course must have taken the Intermediate course (not necessarily the examination) or its equivalent.

There are higher and lower level courses and examination papers for Irish, English and mathematics and also alternative syllabuses and examination papers for history and geography, science and French. Practicals as well as written examinations exist for art, woodwork, metalwork, home economics and music and musicianship. Some credit can be given to projects and continuous assessment in science and history and geography. In both Intermediate and Leaving Certificate examinations candidates have the option, except in a small number of specified instances, of answering through the medium of Irish or English. Those who answer through the medium of Irish may benefit from bonuses varying from 5 to 10 per cent, subject to certain adjustments on performances of over 75 per cent in the subjects.

To be eligible to sit for the Leaving Certificate a pupil must be at least sixteen years of age by the previous January and have pursued the course for at least two years. The Department defines the aim and purpose of the Leaving Certificate course as being the preparation of pupils for immediate entry into open society or for proceeding to further education. The examination is seen mainly as a test of achievement and those wishing to use it for job selection purposes are advised to use their own supplementary aptitude tests. A minimum of five subjects must be presented for the Leaving examination. Pupils are advised by the Department not to present more than seven subjects because of the high standards expected. The range of subjects have been arranged in five groups — Language, Science, Business Studies, Applied Science and Social Studies. Pupils are advised by the Department to select at least three from the group for which they have the greatest aptitude and at least two from outside that group, but in practice pupils exercise open options on the range of courses. Higher and ordinary level papers exist in all subjects except three technical subjects and music for which only common level papers exist. In this regard the Minister for Education announced in 1981 that engineering workshop theory and practice, building construction and technical drawing were to become Honours subjects. There is a compulsory oral examination for Irish, and orals are being experimented with for modern languages. There are practical as well as written tests for engineering, building construction, mechanics, art, music and musicianship. Credit may be given for continuous assessment projects in mechanics, building construction, agricultural science and agricultural economics.

The syllabuses for the various examination subjects are devised by syllabus committees. The syllabus committees are chaired by a departmental inspector and are composed as follows: one representative of each of the two teacher unions (ASTI and TUI), two representatives of the managers of schools, one representative of the chief executive officers of vocational education committees, and one representative of the appropriate subject association. At Leaving Certificate level one representative from each university (NUI and TCD) sits on the committees because the Leaving Certificate is accepted by the universities for matriculation purposes. The syllabus committees review each programme at intervals of a few years, and their recommendations must be approved by the Minister and by university authorities for matriculation purposes. There is no co-ordinating curriculum council to act in a policy-overseeing capacity, though the proposed curriculum council may remedy this situation. Each subject also has its standardisation committee with somewhat similar representation. These committees usually meet at two-yearly intervals and scrutinise the examinations in the various subjects and comment on them.

The examination papers are prepared under the authority of a senior inspector in the subject area, and he also acts as chief examiner. He is assisted by advising examiners who are other inspectors or invited personnel of proven ability and experience in the subject. Various drafts of question papers are studied and tested until the final draft is agreed. The Intermediate and Leaving Certificate examinations usually begin on the second Wednesday of June each year, in authorised centres throughout the country. They are conducted under the supervision of individuals, usually teachers, appointed by the Department of Education. Meanwhile marking schemes are prepared by the chief examiners with the assistance of panels of advising examiners. Sample scripts are tested by them against the schemes. Meetings are convened between the advising examiners and the general body of examiners, usually teachers in the relevant subject areas, who have been approved as examiners by the Department. Marking of scripts under the monitoring of the advising examiners is done during July and August. The examination scripts bear candidates' numbers only. The results of the Leaving Certificate are usually available by mid-August and those of the Intermediate by the first week of September. An appeal procedure exists whereby, with the authorisation of the school principal and on the payment of a small fee, a candidate may have a re-check carried out on his examination scripts. The examinations branch of the Department of Education is located in Athlone.

The results of the public examinations are issued in the forms of grades, with a grade C or higher corresponding roughly to the older category 'honours'. Candidates are awarded certificates setting forth the grades obtained in the subjects presented for examination. The grading structure is set out in Table 14.

In 1979 almost 50,000 pupils sat for the Intermediate Certificate, 35,500 for the Leaving and 19,000 for the Group Certificate. A detailed breakdown of statistics relating to candidates and success rates in individual subjects of the public examinations is issued in the statistical reports of the Department of Education for each school year. Taking as an example the 1979 examination results, many interesting features are revealed.

Of the 32,146 students who took Irish at Leaving Certificate

Table 14: Grading structure for Group, Intermediate and Leaving
Certificate examinations

Grade	Percentage range
A	85 or over
B	70 but less than 85
C	55 ” ” ” 70
D	40 ” ” ” 55
E	25 ” ” ” 40
F	10 ” ” ” 25
No grade	Less than 10

only 8,992 took the higher level papers, with 65 per cent gaining
grade C or higher. Of the 34,143 who took English at Leaving
Certificate, 15,663 took higher level papers and 47 per cent gained
a grade C or higher. Ordinary level English papers were taken by
18,480 students, and only 36 per cent got a grade C or higher.
Latin had declined very much in popularity with only 1,769
presenting the subject. Of the modern continental languages,
French was the preponderant choice, with 21,542 candidates
sitting it, 61 per cent of them being girls; only 3,273 candidates
took German, Italian or Spanish. Of the 32,981 who sat mathematics only 3,507 of them took the higher level paper, 32 per cent
of these gaining a Grade C or higher. This trend was most striking
in the case of girls where only 924 took the higher paper and
17,121 sat the ordinary level mathematics paper. Of the total of
29,474 students who sat ordinary level mathematics only 36 per
cent got a grade C or higher. Provisional results of the 1980
examinations indicate a significant improvement in mathematics
results. The number of girls presenting physics was also extremely
low at 639. Home economics was virtually completely the preserve
of girls with 11,520 taking papers in the subject, but only 525 boys.
Girls also outnumbered boys by 2 : 1 in the relatively small proportion of the total Leaving Certificate candidates who took art. Of
the 35,510 who sat the Leaving Certificate, 6,045 took art. Girls
also accounted for 527 out of the total 609 candidates who took
music as an examination subject.

At Intermediate Certificate level there were some interesting
parallels to the trends at Leaving Certificate level and some variations. Of the 47,163 pupils who took Irish, only 13,725 sat the

higher course paper with 57 per cent gaining grade C or higher. Of those who took lower course Irish, only 34 per cent got a grade C or higher. A total of 24,879 pupils sat the higher level English paper and 48 per cent got a grade C or higher; only 38 per cent reached such a standard in the lower course English paper. About one in every ten students, mostly boys, took Latin. As was the case with the Leaving Certificate, French dominated among the modern languages with a total of 34,938 candidates, compared with a combined total of 5,916 candidates for German, Italian and Spanish. Less than one third of the boys and less than one-quarter of the girls who sat mathematics took the higher paper. More boys than girls took science as a subject but the girls outnumbered the boys in home economics and commerce. On the other hand only 64 girls took any of the following subjects: woodwork, metalwork, mechanical drawing. Of the pupils who took art as a subject, well over half of them were awarded a grade D or lower. Overall girls performed better than boys at these public examinations.

In the Group Certificate Examination 48.7 per cent of those who sat Irish got a grade E or lower, and 53.6 per cent got a grade D or lower in English. Apart from the two main languages, the most favoured subjects were mathematics, history, geography, woodwork, science, commerce, bookkeeping and metalwork. A striking feature of the results in art was that 97.4 per cent of those who sat the examination got a grade D or lower.

Despite the range of courses the majority of students offer a fairly standard subject core. The policy statements of recent years urging the study of more technical and applied studies, the introduction of several new subjects in this area and the higher level of pupil participation have not led to a significant shift in the proportion of students presenting such subjects for examination, particularly at Leaving Certificate level. The three languages — Irish, English and French — as well as mathematics, history and geography, and a science subject are the predominant subjects presented for examination. This choice is influenced by certain regulations, for instance four subjects are prescribed for the junior cycle course — Irish, English, mathematics, history and geography or a specified alternative to the latter for vocational school pupils. The Department prescribes only one subject, Irish, for study at senior cycle but the entry requirements of the universities and teacher training colleges act as a powerful influence on students' choice in senior cycle. The matriculation requirements of the colleges of the National University of Ireland (NUI) specify Irish, English and another language for all faculties, and mathematics and a science subject are also specified for some faculties. These colleges do not accept all ·the common level subjects, i.e. where higher and lower level courses are not offered and which are of an applied nature, for matriculation purposes. Moreover, they award lower points for common level subjects they do accept than for subjects with higher level papers. Trinity College specifies English, another language and mathematics as essential matriculation subjects but individual faculties have special regulations. The teacher training colleges specify Irish, English, a third matriculation language, and mathematics as essential subjects for entry. As students are recommended to take no more than seven subjects for Leaving Certificate and as the university points system relates only to six subjects, for many students the range of choice is not wide. One of the results of this is that the number of students taking applied science, physical science and technical subjects remains very small. As was noted earlier the number taking higher level mathematics is extremely small. Subjects such as art and music are presented for examination by only a small proportion of the students. In an effort to encourage students to present the subjects at Leaving Certificate examinations, the white paper of 1980 announced that the third-level grants scheme is to be amended so that a grade C on a higher or common level paper in two of the following subjects will fulfil the academic requirements: mathematics, applied mathematics, chemistry, physics and chemistry, agricultural science, agricultural economics and technical drawing.[15]

The success rate of pupils in the Leaving Certificate has a large bearing on future career and occupational prospects. Success in the Leaving Certificate is the main criterion for entry into colleges of education, university and other third-level colleges, and the public service and private employers rely heavily on the Leaving Certificate results when recruiting staff. Student grants from public funds for third-level education require four grade Cs on higher or common papers in subjects accepted for matriculation purposes in the Leaving Certificate. Where one of the subjects is mathematics or Irish, three grade Cs are sufficient and, as has been noted, it is proposed to extend extra weighting to other subjects of a scientific or agricultural character. The matriculation requirements for entry to the colleges of the National University of

Ireland stipulate- a minimum of two grade Cs on higher papers and four grade Ds on ordinary papers. Trinity College requires a minimum of three grade Cs on higher or common level papers and two grade Ds on ordinary level papers. As entry to the colleges of education is highly competitive high grades are important. The minimum entry requirement is three grade Cs on higher course papers including Irish, as well as specified minimum grades in mathematics, English and another language. Other third-level colleges also have minimum entry requirements, based on examination grades, which vary for different types of course.

Apart from basic entry requirements, the universities operate a system known as the points system for entry to various faculties. Because there are more applicants for places than there are places, the points system is used as a mechanism for allocating places. Different university colleges have variations on the scheme but the basic principle is that a number of points are allotted to different levels of performance in Leaving Certificate or matriculation examination subjects, up to a maximum of six subjects, and these are then added together. Students are then placed in order of merit, those with the highest scores securing the available places. The minimum points score for entry to various faculties can vary slightly from year to year depending on the examination achievements of those seeking entry in any particular year. Medicine, dentistry, veterinary, architecture and law require the highest number of points. Table 15 is an outline of the points allocation for various levels of performance in the Leaving Certificate as operated by UCD and UCC. It will be noted that the points for higher level mathematics are greater than for other subjects.

Table 15: **Points system for Leaving Certificate examination as operated by UCD and UCC**

Higher paper	Ordinary paper	Common paper	Mathematics	Other subjects
A			7	5
B			5	4
C		A	4	3
D	A	B	2	2
–	B	C	1	1

The points system in UCG does not make a distinction between higher and common level papers. UCG allows extra weightings to some subjects which are viewed as particularly valuable for study in certain faculties, for instance, engineering and medicine allow extra points for examination grades in mathematics and science. The increased award for higher level mathematics does not apply in all faculties in UCG. Trinity College operates a different model for its points scheme with special weightings for subjects related to the studies in various faculties which the candidate chooses to enter. Most faculties seek high grades in the subjects which they judge particularly relevant to their courses and personal interviews may form part of the selection process. Details on entry requirements and points scheme are published annually by the various universities.

Table 16: **Points system for Leaving Certificate examination as operated by UCG**

Grade	Higher paper	Ordinary paper
A	12	6
B	10	5
C	8	4
D	6	3

Following publication of the report by Madaus and McNamara on the Leaving Certificate in 1970, some changes were introduced into the conduct of that examination. The recommendations of the report on the Intermediate Certificate published in 1975, however, have not been implemented. This report recommended the greater involvement of teachers in local, school-based modes of assessment. A moderation and educational assessment service was called for to help devise school-based tests, organise national monitoring of examination results and train teachers in the skills required. The final report of the public examination evaluation project, which was presented to the Minister for Education in February 1981, also urged action along these lines.

Obstacles in implementing such recommendations are the presumed cost involved and the amount of in-service training required so that the examinations would continue to be reliable and valid tests and would continue to retain public confidence. At both Intermediate and Leaving Certificate level many people would wish to see greater use of oral examinations in languages and of practical tests and continuous assessments in some other areas such as the sciences, technical subjects and the arts. However, as well as the scarcity of sufficiently trained personnel, problems would exist with regard to the remuneration of examiners for the extensive amount of work that would be involved. Thus, the deep-rooted tradition of terminal written examination papers continues to predominate. The current challenge to the Irish education system is to ensure that its public examination system is educationally well founded, is flexible and responsive to the needs of schools and pupils, and that too great a burden is not placed by third-level institutions and society at large on an examination structure which may be too narrow.

Types of post-primary schools
As well as the individual types of post-primary schools which are dealt with hereunder there are a number of specialist schools, services and resources which have a particular relevance to second-level schooling and these are included in Appendix Two.

Secondary schools   Secondary schools form the largest category of post-primary school and they cater for about two-thirds of second-level students. Secondary schools are private institutions and almost all are denominational. In order to be eligible for state support they must be recognised by the Department of Education as offering an approved curriculum and as complying with certain other rules of the Department set forth in the *Rules and programme of secondary schools*, which is published annually. Recognised secondary schools are subject to inspection by officers of the Department. The appointment of teachers rests with the school authorities but the Department's regulations require that schools in receipt of state grants employ a minimum number of registered secondary teachers. The majority of secondary schools are owned by religious groups and are run under the auspices of religious authorities. The management of secondary schools has been exercised, in the main, by religious orders or by denominational boards, each controlling its own network of schools. There is no formal structure whereby teachers and parents can become involved in the management of individual schools. In 1979 there were 531 secondary schools with an enrolment of about 196,600. Of these schools the great majority, 443, were owned by Catholic religious orders and a further thirty-one were Catholic diocesan colleges. There was a small number, thirty-three, owned and controlled by lay Catholics. There were twenty-three Protestant schools and a few schools to cater for other denominations.

Over 90 per cent of secondary schools do not charge fees, the Department of Education giving grants in lieu of fees. Some of these secondary schools hold that the various state grants are not sufficient to cover costs and various fund-raising schemes, including voluntary donations from parents, are put into practice. About 25 per cent of secondary schools are co-educational and about 30 per cent take boarding pupils. The number of boarding pupils has been reduced to about 18,000 and many schools now operate a five-day boarding system, with pupils returning home at weekends. The proportion of junior cycle pupils to senior cycle is roughly two to one, with about 131,500 pupils at junior level and 65,000 at senior cycle.

Table 17: **Number of schools promoting use of Irish as teaching medium and number of pupils in each category, 1978/9**

Category of school	Number of schools	Number of pupils
A*	15	2,952
B^{1}**	5	2,141
B^{2}***	2	808

A*   schools which use Irish as the normal medium of instruction for all subjects except English and foreign languages, and which employ Irish as the normal language of school life.

B^{1}**   schools which use Irish as the teaching medium for at least one class group in the school.

B^{2}***   schools which teach at least one subject other than Irish through the medium of Irish.

There are some secondary schools promoting the use of Irish as a teaching medium and they benefit from bonus grants. There are also nine vocational schools and four comprehensive community schools which provide education through Irish, mainly in Gaeltacht areas.

The estimated public expenditure on secondary, comprehensive and community schools for 1980 was £134 million. The main elements in this total are set out in Table 18.

Since 1924 the state has paid capitation grants to managers of secondary schools for each recognised pupil in attendance. These

Table 18: The main components of the estimated state cost of
secondary, comprehensive and community schools, 1980

	£000
Incremental salary grant	82,586
Running costs of comprehensive and community schools	15,490
Building costs of secondary, comprehensive and community schools	13,380
Grants to secondary schools in lieu of fees	13,700
Capitation grants to secondary schools	6,300
Examinations	2,581

Source: *Estimates for Public Services, 1980* pp. 44, 45

grants are not for particular purposes but are expected to help in
school maintenance and administrative costs and in providing the
'basic' salary of teachers. The basic salary (£400 per annum) is paid
by school management. Teachers receive their incremental salary
direct from the Department of Education. The capitation rate for
1980 ranged from £19 to £36 per pupil. When the great majority of
secondary schools entered the 'free education' scheme in 1967-8,
they agreed to discontinue charging fees and were recompensed
by 'supplemental grants' issued by the Department of Education.
These grants have been increased at intervals since then and in
1980 the supplemental grant amounted to £70 per pupil to be
increased to £77 in 1981-2.[16] In the case of non-Catholic secondary
schools an inter-church committee called the Secondary Education
Committee distributes funds from a block-grant related to pupils'
means. Such pupils may also benefit from extra boarding grants
owing to their special needs as a dispersed minority of the population. Other grants exist for science equipment, for Irish and bilingual schools, for school orchestras and for the annual repayment
of building loans. Since 1975 the Secretariat of Catholic Secondary
Schools has operated a formal account system for its schools from
which financial data on secondary schooling has been accumulated.
Secondary schools do not have to submit their accounts for government audit. The Department of Education gives the school authority
a grant of 80 per cent of the cost of building, furniture and
architects' fees and requires the school to find the remaining 20
per cent from its own resources as well as to supply the site for

the school. Boarding facilities are not eligible for capital grant aid.

Comprehensive schools   The first three comprehensive schools were opened in 1966 in Carraroe, Shannon and Cootehill. These were districts where it was adjudged that existing post-primary facilities were inadequate. Comprehensive schools were established and fully funded by the state. They endeavour to combine academic and practical subjects in one broad curriculum which offers each pupil the opportunity to select the type of education best suited to his or her aptitudes and abilities. Early selection and rigid streaming is avoided and systematised career guidance is available from the Department's psychological service. The first year is a period of observation of the pupil's progress, achievements and aptitudes. As well as the general course of studies each pupil must take at least one practical subject. Pupils may enter for the Day Group Certificate, the Intermediate and Leaving Certificate examinations. The first comprehensive schools were intended to serve as models of comprehensive second-level education.

Most of the comprehensive schools are managed by committees, the members of which represent the diocesan religious authority, the vocational education committee of the area and the Minister for Education. The schools are denominational but may not exclude pupils because of their religious beliefs. Most are co-educational and non-selective in their pupil intake. In 1978-9 there were fifteen comprehensive schools with a total pupil enrolment of 8,152 and a full-time teaching staff of 502. The Department of Education decided that from 1974 onwards no more comprehensive schools would be built.

Table 19: **Pupil enrolments in various courses in comprehensive schools, 1978-9**

General	7,679
Secretarial	212
Pre-employment	102
Technical and other	159
Total	8,152

Community schools   Community schools can be seen as a development of the comprehensive school concept. The first three community schools were opened in 1972 and their numbers grew to twenty-six by 1978-9. As with the comprehensive schools they are part of the Department's policy of creating a unified rather than a bi-partite post-primary system. Some of the community schools have evolved from an amalgamation of existing secondary and vocational schools and others have been established in rapidly expanding urban areas, instead of providing separate secondary and vocational schools in such areas.

The purpose of community schools, in the first instance, is to provide comprehensive second-level educational facilities in one school for all the children in the second-level age range of an area. However, the community schools are intended to have much closer links with their surrounding communities than is usual with schools. They are expected to provide youth and adult education services and to be seen as structures through which recurrent education can be provided. The schools are also to be centres for community activities when their educational, recreational and leisure facilities can be made available to the wider community and its organisations. The schools aim to foster the development of community consciousness and their curricula are intended to reflect the needs and traditions of their surrounding areas. The existing schools have succeeded to varying degrees in giving concrete expression to these aspirations.

The finance for establishing community schools is largely provided by the state, though the local VEC and religious authorities pay about 10 per cent of the capital costs. However, the VEC contribution is provided indirectly by the state. The running costs of the schools are completely paid for by the state. Since their establishment the community schools have been functioning on an ad hoc legal basis. In the majority of schools the management boards comprise two representatives of the VEC, two of religious authorities and two elected parents. Protracted negotiations on proposed deeds of trust for the community schools have been completed and in 1981 the first Deeds of Trust were signed and thus regularised in law. According to the new instrument of management for community schools a management board of eleven members shall be elected or nominated as follows: three nominees of the religious orders involved; three nominees of the VEC; two elected parents of children attending the school; two elected members from the permanent teaching staff; the principal of the school who shall be a non-voting member of the board.

The management board is responsible, on the advice of the selection board, for the appointment of staff. Where existing schools are amalgamated, the existing teachers have prior claim on positions. Further, certain posts are reserved for nominees of the religious orders involved, provided their basic qualifications are satisfactory. The board likewise has responsibility for the general conduct and curriculum of the school. The board is responsible for the maintenance, upkeep and repair of the school premises out of monies provided for the purpose by the Minister. The board determines the community uses to which school buildings or grounds may be put according to regulations which are approved by the Minister.

Table 20: **Enrolments in various courses in community schools (second level) 1978-9**

General	13,556
Secretarial	413
Pre-employment	235
Total	14,204

The full-time teaching staff of community schools in 1978-9 was 896 with an estimated full-time equivalent of part-time teachers of thirty-one.

Vocational schools Since 1966 most vocational schools have offered the full second-level programme of instruction for pupils in the age range twelve to nineteen and some vocational school students sit the Intermediate and Leaving Certificate examinations as well as the Group Certificate. The vocational schools also provide more specialised technical and apprentice education for particular trades or professions and provide evening courses for adults in a very wide range of subjects. Nine of the vocational schools teach through the medium of Irish and have about 840 pupils enrolled. Following a request by the Minister in 1974 most VECs have appointed management boards to manage the majority of individual schools or groups of schools, subject to the authority of the VEC. Most management boards comprise twelve members and the boards are planned to give representation to the VEC teachers, parents and community interests. Since 1978 some VECs have established schools which they have termed community colleges rather than vocational schools. These are second level and similar in conception to community schools but with a different management structure under the aegis of the VECs.

Table 21: **Enrolments in full-time day courses at second-level under the VECs, 1978-9**

	Number of pupils
Vocational schools	
General	59,277
Secretarial	6,228
Pre-employment	2,165
Technical and other	450
Regional technical colleges	
General	126
Secretarial	388
Technical	202
Other technical colleges	
Technical and other	631
Total	69,467

Source: *Statistical Report of Department of Education, 1978/9* Table 1, p. 76

Table 22: **Male and female enrolments in part-time courses under the VECs, 1978-9**

	Male	Female	Total
Apprentices			
Designated courses	11,638	160	11,798
Non-designated courses	1,027	351	1,378
Other part-time	39,278	60,054	99,332
Total	51,943	60,565	112,508

Source: *Statistical Report of Department of Education, 1978/9,* p. 77

As well as vocational schools and community colleges of which there are about 250, the VECs also offer some second-level education in the nine regional technical colleges and the nine other technological type colleges under their control. The latter are old established institutions but the regional technical colleges date from 1969. At second level both types of institution provide advanced courses mainly in technical subjects. There are also courses for technicians, part-time and adult courses and courses for the education of apprentices in the various trades. As these colleges are mainly geared towards third-level education they are dealt with in more detail later in the section on third-level education. Tables 21 and 22 show the numbers of pupils enrolled in second-level courses under the VECs.

The amount of public finance required for vocational education for 1980 was estimated at £82 million. The main cost items are set out in Table 23.

Table 23: **Main components of estimated state cost for vocational education, 1980***

	£000
Annual grants to vocational education committees	66,215
Running costs of regional technical colleges	12,845
Building grant to regional and other colleges	2,000
Superannuation payments	1,800
Training of teachers	806
Total	82,000

Source: *Estimates for Public Services, 1980* pp. 46, 47
*School budgets for vocational, comprehensive and community schools are prepared annually and are submitted to the Department of Education which then allocates finance as it judges appropriate. The accounts of these schools are made available for public audit.

Chapter Thirteen

The position of the
Irish language in the schools

Concern for the Irish language has dominated education debates in
Ireland since independence but, although significant progress has
been made in disseminating a knowledge of the language, the
extent of its restoration as a spoken language of the people has
proved disappointing. This failure has been partly attributed to
the stress laid on the written language rather than on oral fluency.
The period since 1960 has witnessed a shift of emphasis to a promotion of the oral language. Symptomatic of this was the introduction of an oral Irish test as part of the Leaving Certificate
examination in 1960. One of the effects of this was an increase in
the number of pupils who spent holidays in the Gaeltacht or in
Irish summer colleges, as well as the promotion of debating competitions in Irish in post-primary schools. The final report of the
commission on the restoration of the Irish language was published
in January 1964 and the government published its response to it in
January 1965, accepting most of the recommendations.[1] Work on
the standardisation of Irish was continued and the Roman script
was generally adopted. New English-Irish and Irish-English dic-
tionaries were prepared which up-dated vocabulary and translation.
The setting up of the Institiúd Teangeólaíochta was a further step
in promoting the scientific study of the Irish language.

In national schools the abolition of the written primary certificate examination in 1967 allowed more scope for oral work.
But, following the wider curriculum of 1971, the time allotted to
Irish decreased, and many teachers feel that standards in Irish have
declined. In line with developments in language study in other
countries, scientific study was undertaken on the frequency of use
of language forms and vocabulary, and schemes were prepared
based on such research. Grants for language laboratories for
schools and training colleges were made available and these used
the voice recordings of native speakers or highly-skilled Irish

speakers. Tape recorders and slide projectors were used where available to bring a more aural/visual element to the teaching. The Department of Education prepared a scheme for national schools based on a graded system of language development and accompanied by graded schemes of readers.

A significant change in curricular policy at post-primary level occurred in 1973 with the government decision to drop Irish as a compulsory subject for the award of the public examination certificates. An honours standard in Leaving Certificate Irish was at the same time raised to the status of two honours for third-level grant purposes. A new Irish Studies course was promoted which focused on the wider cultural facets of the language as well as on pure language and literary studies. This course remained mainly a pilot study and was not generally adopted. A problem for teaching through the medium of Irish was the lack of Irish language textbooks to cater for the many curricular changes at primary and post-primary levels. The translation and publication section of the Department of Education has made valiant efforts in recent years to cope with this acute pedagogical problem. Further, they have made available translations in Irish of some splendidly illustrated children's general reading books.

The number of national schools teaching all subjects through the medium of Irish has continued to decline over recent decades. In 1958-9 there were eighty infant schools and 391 full national schools teaching all subjects, except English, through the medium of Irish.[2] By 1978-9 the total number of schools had declined to 166 teaching 14,496 pupils and only twenty-three of these schools were outside the Gaeltacht.[3] In 1958-9 there were 2,374 schools in which for two or more classes Irish was the sole medium of instruction; by 1978-9 there were 1,246 schools which taught at least one subject other than Irish through the medium of Irish. Some urban communities in recent years, for instance in Ballymun, Inchicore, Rathcoole and Bray, have been taking the initiative in setting up all-Irish national schools. Further, with support from Bord na Gaeilge, about eighty infant Irish schools — naonraí — have been set up in recent years. The number of A and B type secondary schools has declined sharply over recent decades. In 1958-9 there were 231 A and B type secondary schools with 34,942 pupils.[4] This was out of a grand total of 494 schools and 69,568 pupils. However, twenty years later the A and B schools have dropped to twenty-two schools with 5,901 pupils, out of a total of

531 schools and the greatly increased total of 196,606 pupils.[5] Financial inducements to schools to promote teaching through Irish had been introduced in the 1920s but the value of these declined in real terms and the incentive was diminished.

Some concern has been expressed about the standard of Irish of training college entrants and of some of the graduates from the colleges. It is considered that the decision to discontinue the five main preparatory colleges as all-Irish second-level institutions for intending teachers in 1961 was a factor in the alleged decline of Irish among trainee teachers. Course changes and developments in the study of education have lessened the role traditionally held by the Irish language in training colleges. On the other hand, oral language methods and visits to Gaeltachtaí have helped to improve the standard of oral Irish among the students. The seriousness of the problem of the standard of Irish among training college entrants can be gleaned from the fact that in 1979, for example, out of 35,500 pupils who sat the Leaving Certificate only about 5,800 got a grade C or higher in Irish. Grade C or higher in Irish in the Leaving Certificate examination is a minimum requirement for entry to a teacher training college,[6] and some of those students who went forward did not succeed at the oral Irish entrance interviews.

Comhairle na Gaeilge was appointed by the government in 1969 and it produced a report on Irish in education in 1974. The report re-emphasised a proposal it had made in 1972 that a bord na gaeilge should be set up as the main advisory body to the Department of Education on methods of encouraging the learning and use of Irish. Bord na Gaeilge was established in 1974 and it has endeavoured to give effect to many of the proposals of the *Irish in education report*, as well as develop some schemes of its own. Bord na Gaeilge has endeavoured to re-awaken a general interest among the public in the Irish language in tune with the tastes and life-styles of contemporary living. Other longer established bodies such as Conradh na Gaeilge, Comhdháil Náisiúnta na Gaeilge and Gael-Linn have continued their promotional work for the language. Gael-Linn in particular through school competitions such as Slógadh, debating contests, the provision of records and language courses using new techniques has tried to enlist the interest and support of young people. Various campaigns have been mounted to urge Radio Telefís Éireann to be more actively involved in providing Irish language programmes. Nationwide attitudinal surveys in the 1970s indicated the existence of favourable attitudes towards the Irish language among the general public, but the will to take significant personal action to promote it has been lacking. The interest and active involvement in Irish music and song over recent decades have been more impressive than involvement in speaking Irish.

Most of the evidence suggests that, despite interesting pedagogical and curricular initiatives, the position of the Irish language in the schools has weakened rather than strengthened since 1960. There are some signs that the downward trend may be halted. There is also a greater realisation that Irish within the school needs to be supported by its use in adult society outside the school. The White Paper on Educational Development published in 1980 listed twenty proposals for improvement. It re-emphasised priority for spoken Irish in primary and post-primary schools. In this latter context the marks for oral Irish in the Leaving Certificate are to be raised from one quarter to one third of the total. Extra assistance is to be made available for pre-service and in-service courses so that teachers may improve their proficiency in the language. Irish courses in schools are to be revised and a special effort is to be made to ensure that an adequate supply of suitable textbooks and teaching aids will be made available.[8] It remains to be seen whether these and other such measures will be successful in improving the position of Irish in the school system.

Chapter Fourteen

Teachers and teacher education

Teachers form a central resource of the whole education system and on the quality of the personnel and the standard of their professionalism depend the life and spirit of the educational programmes which are devised. The number of full-time teachers in the main categories of first- and second-level schools increased by about 70 per cent, from 20,872 in 1964 to 35,668 by 1979.[1] It was also an interesting and eventful period for teacher education with changes in institutional provision and in approaches to educational studies at the various levels.

Throughout the 1960s teacher education continued to operate within the traditional structures. Some significant alterations, however, did take place in the content of courses and student conditions. In 1962 the national teacher training colleges assumed a greater degree of academic autonomy by assuming the right to set and correct their own examinations and by being more directly involved in course restructuring, in association with the Department of Education. A shift occurred from the predominant place which practical methodology held in training courses towards a more theoretical grounding in educational studies, notably educational psychology. The large spread of general courses was reduced. Student teachers now did part of their practical teaching in their local areas. The colleges became less closed as institutions and allowed students more freedom in the use of their personal time. A large renovation project with impressive new student accommodation was undertaken in St Patrick's College, Drumcondra, Dublin, and building extensions took place in all the colleges. In 1961 the preparatory colleges, which since 1926 had acted as a mode of entry to training for students highly qualified in Irish, were discontinued, except for Coláiste Móbhí for Protestant students. Open entry through competitive examinations became the norm for the training colleges. Interviews were introduced in 1959 as an aid in the selection of suitable candidates. University graduates could undertake a one-year course in the training college to qualify for national teaching. The student body was further diversified by the acceptance from 1972 of what were known as 'mature students', that is people from a wider age band who evinced an interest in teaching and satisfied entry requirements. With increased numbers and changed attitudes towards the preparation of student teachers, the boarding tradition very much decreased and most students now lodged in outside accommodation, assisted by Department of Education maintenance and travel grants.

The most significant change of all occurred in 1974 with the inauguration of a BEd university degree for teachers. Under new arrangements the three largest colleges, St Patrick's, Drumcondra, Our Lady of Mercy, Carysfort, and Mary Immaculate, Limerick, became recognised colleges of the National University of Ireland. Smaller colleges, such as St Mary's, Marino, St Catherine's, Sion Hill, and Froebel College became associated with Trinity College, with which the Church of Ireland College had long been associated. St Angela's College of Domestic Science in Sligo became a recognised college of NUI in 1978. The BEd offered by NUI is a three-year honours degree; Trinity College requires a fourth year for an honours award, in line with its undergraduate tradition.

The establishment of a university degree had long been sought by national teachers. Recent reports such as that of the Commission on Higher Education in 1967 and a report on teacher training published by the Higher Education Authority in 1970 had both urged a degree for national teachers but not under the direct auspices of the universities. The extended courses and new requirements of the BEd degree led to considerable changes in the course structures of the colleges but a smooth transition took place, the first BEd students graduating in 1977.

Another important development was the building of Thomond College in Limerick which offered a four-year BA degree to physical education students. Initially there were policy differences concerning the validating agency but after the first graduation under NUI it had been settled that the degree would in future be awarded by the National Council for Educational Awards. Trainee craft and rural science teachers have attended Thomond College since 1979 and it is intended that they pursue degree courses validated by the NCEA. The legislative framework for Thomond College was approved by the Oireachtas in 1981. Most teachers of art are trained in the National College of Art and Design.

With the large expansion in the number of pupils in post-primary schools from the mid-1960s, great pressure was placed on the Higher Diploma in Education courses offered for post-primary trainee teachers by the universities. Very large numbers had to be accommodated at a time of change and development of education studies by education departments which had suffered from insufficient staff, resources and funding. The commission on higher education in 1967 and the HEA report on teacher training in 1970 had urged that university education departments should be expanded as a matter of urgency and that facilities for a more active research role should be made available. Gradually progress has been made along these lines. All university departments have recruited more staff, have built up their facilities, have expanded and brought their courses more into line with the development of educational studies overseas. The Higher Diploma in Education has been made a full-time one-year course in Trinity and University College, Dublin, and University College, Cork, and interesting experiments involving such things as block releases are being conducted by various colleges. The Higher Diploma course is a post-graduate one; education is not an undergraduate subject in any of the universities except UCG. Thomond College, Limerick, plans to introduce a graduate diploma course for trainee teachers of Business Studies in 1981/2.

During the 1970s all university education departments established Master of Education degree courses which, as well as the more traditional higher degrees in education such as MA, MLitt and PhD, helped to develop educational studies and to provide opportunities for the acquisition of greater expertise and skill in educational affairs. The establishment of the Educational Studies Association of Ireland in 1976 has fostered co-operation and promoted educational research among educationalists throughout Ireland. It publishes current educational research. Those involved in education have also benefited from diploma courses which cultivate specialist skills, such as the Diploma in Special Education in St Patrick's College, Drumcondra, the Diploma in Psychology, the Diploma in Career Guidance, the Diploma for Teachers of the Deaf, all in UCD, as well as various courses in remedial education. A diploma course in career guidance was established in UCC in 1981. The Mater Dei Institute, Drumcondra, provides courses in teacher training with a special emphasis on catechetics.

The Educational Research Centre was set up on the campus of St Patrick's College, Drumcondra in 1966 and has conducted many valuable empirical research studies into Irish education. It publishes *The journal of Irish education* as well as some other occasional educational research reports. In 1974 a planning committee reported to the Minister for Education on the setting up of a teachers' council with wide-ranging functions. It was to advise the Minister on all matters relating to teacher education and supply, and also to act as a professional body with charge of the professional affairs of teachers, including their registration and probation.[2] Such a council has not been established and the various responsibilities continue to be exercised by diverse agencies. In 1971 the first teacher centres were established. These were set up on a regional basis to serve as focal points for teachers in the various regions to meet together, participate in seminars, lectures, workshops etc., and also to provide resource material and teaching aids for teachers.

Present-day Irish teachers are heirs to a distinguished tradition of professional dedication and service and are generally held in high regard by their local communities. Teaching in Ireland today has come close to being an all-graduate profession. A common basic salary scale exists at first- and second-level supplemented by a scheme of allowances for extra qualifications and the exercise of certain responsibility and administrative roles. The allowances for principals and vice-principals are based on a points rating related to the age and number of pupils in the school. Teachers in national, vocational, comprehensive and community schools receive their salaries directly from the state and their appointment by management boards is subject to ministerial approval. Teachers in secondary schools receive their incremental salaries from the state and a small basic salary from their employers, the secondary school authorities. The moves towards an all-graduate profession and the common salary scale have tended to unify the different branches of the profession and the individual teacher unions co-operate on many issues affecting teacher interests. Although a Registration Council exists for secondary teachers, as has been noted, no overall teacher council exists.

As is to be expected in the context of greater pupil participation, the largest increase in teacher numbers has been at second level. Here the teaching force went from about 6,800 in 1964 to 17,200 in 1979. As a result about one-third of the contemporary teaching force is under thirty years of age, and this has significant implications for future salary costs and promotional pressures. Women outnumber men in national and secondary schools; in national schools the ratio is about three to one and about six to five in secondary schools. The proportion of religious to lay teachers in the overall teaching force has greatly reduced.

Teaching has traditionally attracted students with a good academic record who have tended to make teaching their sole career in life. The closed career pattern has been somewhat modified in recent years by such things as the acceptance of mature students in national teacher training colleges and the giving of incremental credit for teaching overseas, particularly in underdeveloped countries. The more varied job opportunities as well as higher education grants have tended to divert some of the bright students from teaching and also encouraged more movement by teachers out of teaching to other careers. The reduction in the number of men, particularly in the national teaching force, is causing concern.

Although schemes for more posts with responsibility and vice-principalships have been introduced, promotional outlets within teaching are still limited and this affects professional morale. This is particularly the case in secondary schools where, except in a tiny minority of cases, principalships are not open to lay teachers. The system also suffers from a lack of job definition for many posts of responsibility, a fact which blurs both the power and the exercise of professional responsibility. The fact that seniority has played a large part in promotion causes frustration among younger teachers who, with recent expansion, now form a large proportion of the teaching force. Feeling that their salaries are depressed in relation to other professions, teachers have been pressing for payment for non-classroom activities such as parent teacher meetings, pastoral care duties and increased remuneration for the conduct of oral and written examinations.

The introduction of the 'new' curriculum in national schools undoubtedly increased the scope for the exercise of professionalism though the size of many classes has been a serious impediment. The implementation of the recommendations of the Intermediate Certificate committee's report of 1975 and those of the planning committee of the Teachers' Council in 1974 would further widen the involvement of teachers within the educational system. The introduction of a right for teachers to be released from the classroom for in-service or study purposes during one or more periods of their teaching careers would be very desirable, particularly in such a fast-changing educational milieu. Teachers have been slow to accept the idea of teacher assistants in classrooms fearing that such a trend might dilute the public's regard for teaching and be used by the authorities as a way of avoiding increasing the trained teacher supply. Teaching, particularly when based on an ideology of individual and small-group learning, is a highly labour intensive activity and salary increases cost the public purse a great deal, which has washback effects on public policy on education.

It remains to be seen to what extent technological advances can be used by teachers to improve their efficiency and also whether they can be used to develop schemes such as long distance learning and various forms of learning networks which may reduce the need of the physical presence of teachers. Although Ireland has not experienced the extremes of the 'back to basics' movement in the United States or aspects of 'the great education debate' in Britain, nevertheless, the re-emergence of a public climate seeking accountability and efficiency in the public services has implications for the education system. The optimism which surrounded education reform and expansion in a more buoyant economic period is less in evidence in the early 1980s. Those who looked to education as the great equaliser have been disappointed, and some others maintain that the expansion and changed ideology have led to a decline in standards. In any case, it is important that whatever resources are available for education are harnessed so as to make their full potential contribution.

Teachers have been increasingly vocal in their dissatisfaction with pay and conditions of employment and, yielding to pressure from the teacher unions, the Minister for Education set up a review body to examine these issues. The review body issued an interim report in September 1980. Among its recommendations were an increase in the common basic salary of about 7 per cent, the introduction of a series of long-service increment awards, the definition of teaching to include pastoral care and relations with parents, the raising of the points allowances for very large schools, the minimising of seniority as a promotional factor, the abolition of some posts of responsibility and the clearer definition of responsibility relating to other posts.[3] This report was rejected by the teacher unions who then entered into direct salary negotiations with the Minister for Education and relevant government departments.

As a result of these negotiations and the 1980 national wage agreement the teachers' common basic salary scale in June 1981 ranged from about £6,200 to £10,100 over a fourteen-year incremental span. Three further increments spread over eleven years brought the salary maximum to £11,800. Extra allowances are paid for qualifications which range from £300 for a pass degree to £1,200 for a doctorate and a Higher Diploma in Education with honours. Since 1969 posts of responsibility have operated whereby teachers allotted extra duties could qualify for special allowances. Posts of responsibility were categorised as A and B, commensurate with the level of responsibility involved. A teacher received £1,037 for an A post of responsibility and £460 for a B post of responsibility. The allowances for vice-principals range from £400 to £2,500 and for principals from £870 to £4,000 depending on the size of the school and the points ratings of the pupils. In a period of high inflation, of course, salary figures do not remain static for long and the above figures, while providing a guideline, are likely to change at frequent intervals.

The normal mechanism for processing teacher salary and allowance claims is through a scheme of conciliation and arbitration. The parties to the scheme are: (1) the Minister for the Public Service and the Minister for Education, (2) the INTO, ASTI, TUI, and (3) the managerial authorities of the schools. A conciliation council of twelve members representative of the three interests listed above considers claims relating to the general salary scale and allowances and claims relating to the principles governing the superannuation scheme. Where disagreement has been registered, or where an agreed recommendation of council has not been accepted by the Ministers, claims may then be referred to the arbitration board.

The arbitration board normally consists of fourteen persons, as follows: (1) a chairman, (2) two members of the Labour Court, (3) two officials nominated by the Minister for the Public Service and the Minister for Education, (4) two representatives of each of the teacher organisations, and (5) one representative of each of the managerial authorities. The chairman, after studying all submissions, decides whether a claim is arbitrable or not. The board's decision is in all cases the finding of the chairman, who submits a report to the Ministers. Within one month of the receipt of a report of the board, the Ministers present it to Dáil Éireann. The government may adopt one of the following courses: (1) within three months of receipt of the report, it may accept the findings of the board in full, (2) at the expiration of three months from receipt of the report the government may introduce a motion in the Dáil to reject the findings or to modify the findings or to propose the deferment of a final decision until the budget for the next financial year is being framed and indicate to what extent, if any, they propose to give effect to the findings in the interval.

Teachers participate in a contributory pension scheme. A teacher may retire voluntarily and be awarded a pension and gratuity provided he or she has given at least thirty-five completed years of pensionable service and has reached the age of fifty-five years. Teachers are not required to retire on pension until 31 August following their sixty-fifth birthday. Pension is calculated by multiplying 1/80th of the 'retiring salary' by the length of pensionable service to credit at the date of retirement up to a maximum of 40/80ths. Children's allowances are payable to teachers who were in the service prior to 31 December 1978.

Both lay and religious teachers who are not at the top of their incremental salary scales may get recognition for teaching service in other countries. The arrangements provide for the granting of up to four years' incremental credit for those undertaking teaching service abroad. From 1980, a maximum of five years' credit may be obtained for teaching overseas.

Categories and training of teachers
As variations exist in the employment regulations and training of various categories of teachers these are dealt with under separate headings.

National teachers
The teaching force in national schools is comprised almost totally of trained teachers (see Table 24). Two other trends which have become increasingly evident in recent years can also be observed in Table 24. These are the decline in the number of men teachers as a percentage of the total national school teaching body. Lay men teachers amount to about 26 per cent of the total teaching force. There has also been a decline in the proportion of religious teachers. Male and female religious teachers account for 12 per cent of the total teachers in national schools.

An assistant national teacher on taking up a first appointment is placed on probation for two years. For the successful completion of probation a teacher must complete two consecutive years of

Table 24: Number of trained and untrained national teachers
in service on 30 June 1979

National teachers	Trained	Untrained
Men		
Lay	4,701	3
Religious	352	2
Women		
Lay	11,596	64
Religious	1,627	42
Totals	18,276	111

Source: *Statistical Report of Department of Education 1978/79*
Table 22(6), p. 30

satisfactory service and obtain two consecutive satisfactory inspection reports. To be eligible for appointment as a principal teacher for schools with average enrolment of more than eighty pupils teachers must have at least five years' service. The points allocation per pupil for determining principals' and vice-principals' allowances are related to the age of the pupils, and they increase as the pupils advance through the school system.

   The state recognises six training colleges (or colleges of education) for national school teachers. They are St Patrick's College, Drumcondra, Dublin; Our Lady of Mercy College, Carysfort, Blackrock, Dublin; the College of Mary Immaculate, Limerick; Church of Ireland College, Rathmines, Dublin; St Mary's College, Marino, Dublin and Froebel College, Blackrock, Dublin. The colleges are privately owned and are under ecclesiastical control and management. The colleges are denominational, co-educational and are predominantly non-residential. They are heavily dependent on the state for capital and current costs. Academic staff salaries are paid by the state and the Minister for Education reserves the right to approve appointments. Public funding for the colleges comes through the Department of Education.

   As noted earlier St Patrick's, Our Lady of Mercy and Mary Immaculate Colleges have been recognised colleges of the National University of Ireland since 1974, with the two Dublin colleges linked to University College, Dublin, and the Limerick college linked to University College, Cork. As such the university has a voice in the appointment of university-recognised staff and the courses and examinations of the colleges are subject to monitoring by university personnel. The course of studies in the NUI recognised-colleges is a three-year BEd honours degree course. A satisfactory standard in the practice of teaching is a pre-requisite for the award of the degree. The Church of Ireland College, St Mary's, Marino, and Froebel College are associated with Trinity College. As well as general monitorship, some of the teaching is done by university staff and takes place both in the local colleges and in the university. Students associated with Trinity College pursue a fourth year if they want a BEd with honours.

The BEd is conceived as a professional degree in which educational and general academic studies are pursued concurrently. Education forms the predominant subject area and involves theoretical, methodological and practical elements. All students must achieve a level of competence to teach through the medium of Irish. At present the BEd for national teachers does not qualify for recognised teaching at post-primary level.

Some aspects of the administration of the colleges including the number of students to be admitted, their mode of selection and the level of student fees are subject to the approval of the Minister for Education. The number of students in the colleges increased from 1,108 in 1964 to 2,751 in 1978, an increase of 150 per cent. This involved considerable expansion in the colleges and the development of library and other facilities.

Entry requirements for students to training colleges are as follows:

1. All candidates must be at least seventeen years of age on 15 January following entry.
2. Entrance to the colleges is by way of an open competition based on the results of the Leaving Certificate examination in Irish, English, mathematics and three other subjects from the Leaving Certificate programme, together with an interview and tests in oral Irish and music.
3. All candidates must achieve at least Grade C on three higher course papers including Irish; Grade D in ordinary course mathematics; Grade C in ordinary course English or Grade D in higher course English; Grade D on ordinary Leaving Certificate or matriculation paper in Latin or a modern language.

4. Candidates may combine the results of the Leaving Certificate examination in the year in which they apply for entry to the colleges with the results of the Leaving Certificate examination in the immediately preceding year.
5. All candidates must pass an interview and an oral Irish examination and take a music test in the September preceding entrance to the colleges. The grades achieved in the interview and oral Irish and music tests are taken into account in compiling the merit list on the basis of which places in the colleges are finally allocated. A high level of proficiency in spoken Irish and a high standard in oral communication in English is required of all candidates.

A limited number of places are available for the category known as 'mature students'. These students must be at least twenty-one years of age on 15 January following entry to the colleges. From 1982 the minimum age will be raised to twenty-four years. Otherwise such students must satisfy the ordinary requirements for college entrance, or some alternatives at first arts level, and must pursue the same course as the main student body.

A one-year course exists for university graduates who may wish to qualify as national teachers. Such graduates must also have attained good grades in English, Irish and mathematics in the Leaving Certificate examination or some alternatives in first arts examination. The course for graduates lays a special emphasis on the methodology of primary school teaching.

Table 25: **Number of students in national teacher training colleges, 1978/9**

Lay		Religious		Total	
Men	423	Men	14	Men	437
Women	2,286	Women	28	Women	2,314
Total	2,709	Total	42	Total	2,751

Source: *Statistical Report of Department of Education 1978/9* Table 25, p. 32

It can be noted that female students outnumber males by more than five to one. The small number of religious students in training also reflects the reduced proportion of religious in the general national school teaching body. University graduates formed 17 per cent of the training college entrants in 1978/9.

Traditionally the state has subsidised student costs in training colleges at high levels. Accordingly, student fees which cover board and tuition have been maintained at a relatively low level, though recent years have seen significant fee increases. Grants are available to students who satisfy the Leaving Certificate requirements of the university grant scheme and whose family income is within the limits laid down by that scheme. Loans in the form of repayable advances of college fees in whole or in part are available to students whose family income is within the limits set out in the university grants scheme.

Secondary teachers

The number of teachers in secondary schools who received incremental salaries in 1978/9 was 10,830. Of these, 78 per cent were lay teachers and about 54 per cent of all teachers were women. There were also 362 full-time teachers who did not hold incremental posts and 2,056 who were part-time teachers. Secondary teachers receive their incremental salaries and any extra allowances for qualifications or posts of responsibility direct from the state. What is known as the 'basic salary', amounting to £400 per annum, is paid by the school authorities as employers. The number of incremental positions is based on the Department of Education's quota figure which, in 1980, authorised an incremental position on the ratio of 1:19 recognised pupils. In recent years secondary teachers have become very concerned about the threat of redundancies as religious orders decide to close some secondary schools.

Secondary teacher training for the most part is conducted within the universities and is based on the consecutive model, with the professional element succeeding the undergraduate course. The professional course is termed the Higher Diploma in Education and is a one year post-graduate course offered by each of the university colleges. The course covers a wide range of educational studies both theoretical and methodological. Students must also engage in teaching practice in approved schools and under authorised supervision. Normally students are responsible for making their own arrangements for teaching practice facilities in schools, though various schemes of block placement are arranged by the education departments. The Higher Diploma is awarded on an honours and a pass basis and satisfactory performance in teaching practice is an essential element for both grades of award. In recent years the number graduating with the Higher Diploma has exceeded the teaching vacancies available, causing considerable employment problems for holders of the Higher Diploma. Teacher training courses on the concurrent model exist for physical education teachers in Thomond College, for domestic science teachers in St Angela's College, Sligo, and for art teachers in the National College of Art and Design. The concurrent model blends educational/ professional studies with general academic study.

A Registration Council for secondary teachers was established in 1918 under the Intermediate Education (Ireland) Act of 1914 and now operates under the Registration Council (Constitution and Procedure) Rules, 1926. The Council normally consists of the following members: two appointed by the Minister for Education, eleven appointed by teacher and manager associations and one appointed by each of the governing bodies of UCD, UCC, UCG, TCD and Maynooth College. The Council, subject to the approval of the Minister for Education, makes regulations for admission of applicants to the Register. This is the only professional council for teachers. The council prescribes that all applicants for registration must:

1. (i) hold a degree of a university or other degree-awarding authority acceptable to the Council as suitable for registration and a teacher training qualification acceptable to the Council; or

   (ii) hold a diploma or certificate at the appropriate specialist level acceptable to the Council in one of the following subjects: art, home economics, physical education, music, religious education, woodwork or metalwork. The teacher training content of such a course must also be acceptable to the Council.

2. satisfactorily complete one year of full-time teaching experience in a recognised second-level school in Ireland,

3. produce satisfactory evidence of character as required by the Council, and

4. pass a test of competency in oral Irish. The test in oral Irish is given by an inspector of the Department of Education and consists of a short interview involving questions of a general conversational nature.

In 1980 the Registration Council submitted new draft regulations to the Minister for Education for his approval.

Vocational teachers

Vocational teachers fall into two major categories (1) teachers of general subjects who must be university graduates and (2) teachers of specialist subjects who must hold recognised teaching diplomas awarded as a result of their having successfully completed training courses in colleges of art, of domestic science, or of physical education, or in institutions where approved courses are provided for the training of teachers of woodwork and metalwork. More than half the vocational teachers are in category (2). Although not an essential requirement, a large number of vocational teachers in category (1) also hold the Higher Diploma in Education.

Thomond College of Education in Limerick offers a four-year BA degree course awarded by the NCEA for student teachers of physical education. Education studies form part of the course as well as another academic subject and the graduates may take up employment in all types of second-level schools. Thomond College has been designated as the centre for teacher-training courses in craft and applied subjects. Since 1979 student teachers of woodwork, metalwork and rural science have been admitted to courses in Thomond College and it is intended that these courses will be awarded degree status by the NCEA.

As with other teachers, vocational teachers are required to have qualifications which indicate proficiency in the Irish language. Courses and examinations are held annually for the awards of An Ceard Teastas Gaeilge and An Teastas i dTeagase na Gaeilge. An Ceard Teastas Gaeilge is a required qualification for the great majority of vocational school teachers. It consists of a written and oral test in Irish. Teachers of Irish require either a degree and An Teastas i dTeagasc na Gaeilge or a degree with Irish as a subject and the Higher Diploma in Education.

Previous relevant experience outside teaching may be taken into account in setting the incremental salary position of teachers of trade and woodwork subjects. In 1978/9 there were 4,457 full-time teachers in second-level vocational schools and a large number of part-time teachers made up an estimated equivalent of 645 full-time teachers. The ratio of male to female full-time staff is about 2:1 in favour of male teachers. Vocational schools have a smaller teacher pupil ratio than other post-primary schools at 1:16, because of the greater presence of technical and applied subjects which require small group guidance and supervision.

In-service training and teacher centres

In the rapidly changing educational milieu the importance of facilities for in-service education for teachers has been receiving increasing attention internationally.[4] The idea of a once-for-all initial training for a career that spans over forty years is generally regarded as outdated. As yet no contractual entitlement to release from full-time teaching to participate in in-service training exists for Irish teachers. Teacher unions have formed policies seeking such release and urging the formation of co-ordinated policies in the in-service area. Up to now in-service training has had a low profile in education estimates; for instance the estimates for 1981 allotted only the meagre sum of £185,000 for in-service teacher training. The Department of Education set up a special committee in 1980 with representatives of teacher unions, the inspectorate, colleges of education and universities on it to identify and make recommendations on priority areas on in-service training.

In the past various agencies have taken initiatives in organising in-service schemes which have been generally of a short-term and voluntary character. The courses have concentrated on the maintenance and development of the professional competence of teachers, updating on subject content and pedagogic techniques, including the use of audio-visual media. Teachers may be released for full-time attendance, usually of one year's duration, at diploma and Master of Education courses directed towards greater specialisation and personal development. In most instances they are expected to arrange for and pay substitutes during their term of absence from the school.

There are twenty-one teacher centres set up by the Department of Education on a regional basis. They are financed by the Department, administered by directors (four of whom are full-time) and managed by an elected committee of teachers. The centres are open to all teachers and they provide in-service courses, lectures, workshops, meetings, induction programmes and they also act as resource centres. The premises are made available to various educational groups such as subject associations and most of the activities occur outside teaching hours. Although recent decades have witnessed significant changes in pre-service training it is likely that the spotlight will shift to in-service training in the years ahead.

Teacher unions

There has been a growth in co-operation among teachers based on the common salary scale, the growth of an all-graduate profession, and the realisation of the common problems and concerns of teachers yet the teachers are represented by three separate teacher unions, all affiliated to the Irish Congress of Trade Unions.

The Irish National Teachers' Organisation (INTO) is the oldest and largest of the unions. It represents lay primary teachers in the Republic of Ireland and has approximately 15,500 members. In Northern Ireland it represents both primary and post-primary teachers and has a membership of about 5,500 there. The INTO was founded in 1868 and since then has been concerned with improvements in the status, salaries, pensions and conditions of work of teachers. It also concerns itself with matters of educational policy and seeks to promote improvements in the operation of the education system. The INTO is a thirty-two-county organisation with a head office at 35 Parnell Square, Dublin 1, and an office in Belfast at 23 College Gardens, Belfast. Branches exist at local level throughout the country. The organisation is organised into districts, each of which returns a representative to the central executive committee of the organisation. These, together with the president, vice-president, ex-president, general secretary, general treasurer and Northern secretary, manage the affairs of the organisation between the annual delegate congresses. Three sub-committees — the finance committee, the education committee and the Northern committee — help the central executive committee in its formulation and conduct of policy. The INTO's quarterly journal in the Republic is called *An Múinteoir Náisiúnta* and in Northern Ireland it publishes *The Northern Teacher*. Its newsletter is known as *Tuarasgáil*.

The Association of Secondary Teachers of Ireland (ASTI) was founded in 1909. Its membership is made up of lay teachers mainly from secondary schools. It has a membership of about 9,500 teachers and is the trade union for most secondary teachers. Other secondary teachers, particularly religious, belong to various professional groupings which have not formed themselves into trade unions. Lay teachers in comprehensive and community schools may be members of the ASTI, or of the Teachers Union of Ireland whose membership is mainly vocational teachers. The ASTI publishes a quarterly journal *The Secondary Teacher* as well as a newsletter called *Astir*. The ASTI head office is at 13 Highfield

Road, Rathgar, Dublin 6.

The Vocational Teachers Association was formed explicitly as a trade union in 1955, from earlier associations. In 1973 the association was renamed the Teachers Union of Ireland. It has a membership of over 6,000, mainly composed of teachers in vocational schools and colleges, personnel in the third-level colleges associated with vocational education committees and some teachers in community and comprehensive schools. Its executive committee is made up of the president, vice-president, general secretary, assistant general secretary, administrative officer and one representative from each of the regional areas into which the organisation is divided. The executive is assisted by sub-committees dealing with finance, community and comprehensive, conditions of service and education and organisation. As is the case with the other teacher organisations its annual delegate conference is held during the Easter vacation. Its journal is called *The TUI News* which includes articles on education as well as union affairs. TUI head office is at 73 Orwell Road, Rathgar, Dublin 6.

Apart from teacher unions there are many associations, councils and committees composed of teachers, managers, parents and interested persons which influence the education system in various ways and which represent the views of their members in relation to the system.

Chapter Fifteen

Third-level education

Developments in third-level education, 1960-80

Perhaps in no area have the changes in education since the mid-1960s been more dramatic than in third-level education. As a result the structure and emphasis of third-level education in the early 1980s is in marked contrast to the picture presented, say, in 1960. To understand the present-day system one needs to grasp the key developments which led to it and, as *Investment in Education* was a landmark document for the other two levels, the *Report of the Commission on Higher Education* also marks a watershed in third-level changes.

The need for an investigation of higher education provision was reflected in the establishment of a commission on higher education in 1960. It had wide terms of reference: 'to inquire and make recommendations in relation to university, professional, technological and higher education generally'. Despite the urgency of reform measures, the commission's voluminous report was not published until 1967.[1]

The report deplored the lack of a co-ordinating, planning agency for higher education and noted that 'higher education outside the universities has remained comparatively under-developed'. With regard to the university sector, it remarked 'increasing numbers of students, low entry standards, and inadequate staffing and accommodation have produced a highly unsatisfactory situation, in which academic standards are endangered despite the efforts of academic staff to keep them as high as possible'. The universities' performance in the areas of post-graduate studies and research was deemed to be less than satisfactory. The modes of university government and academic appointments were seen as requiring reforms. With regard to the future, it recognised that there would be a growing demand for third-level places and the report projected that student numbers would rise from 16,300 in 1964/5 to 26,000 in

1975/6. This increase was felt to be a 'startling figure' but, in the event, the projection fell far short and the real number in 1975/6 turned out to be 33,000 students.

The main recommendations of the commission's report were as follows. The NUI structure should be dissolved allowing UCD, UCC and UCG to become independent universities; the future status of Maynooth was left open by the commission. Trinity College should continue as an independent university. A permanent statutory commission on higher education should be established to act as an overall planning and budgetary authority. As a further aid to co-ordination and to help avoid unnecessary duplication, a council of Irish universities should be established representative of the different institutions. To cater for some of the increased demand for third-level education, institutions known as 'new colleges' should be set up initially in Dublin and Limerick but later in other places. These would have a more vocational bias than the universities and would pursue courses only to the pass degree level in humanistic, scientific and commercial studies. These new institutions would also foster the cultural life of the regions in which they were situated. Among other groups who would receive their basic degree qualification from the new colleges were the national teachers, a proposal which was strongly opposed by the involved parties. The colleges would also have functions in the training of secondary and vocational teachers. The report recommended the establishment of a technological authority to promote and assist technological training and research and recommended that the existing colleges of technology in Dublin should be expanded.

Other proposals were that the government of all third-level colleges should be modernised and made more democratic. The entry standards for university should be raised to a minimum of two honours obtained in the Leaving Certificate or its equivalent in the matriculation examination. A wide-ranging government grant scheme was proposed to promote greater participation among pupils from low-income families. More positive attitudes to the role of student organisations were encouraged. To improve teaching and teacher-student relationships, a reduction in the teacher-student ratio was seen to be essential. The expansion of teaching through Irish in the universities was urged, with a particular role for UCG.

The fortunes of the individual recommendations of the commission on higher education varied greatly. The situation had been changing considerably while the commission deliberated and some of its key proposals such as the new colleges were not seriously considered. More notice was taken of others such as the minimum entry standard, grants for students, expansion of the Dublin colleges of technology. Trinity College moved towards improving its governing structures and a council of Irish universities was established but this led to no effective steps on planning or co-ordination. A permanent planning and budgetary authority — the Higher Education Authority — was established on an ad hoc basis in 1968 receiving statutory powers in 1971. The proposals regarding the dissolution of NUI and the reform of governing structures were to witness peculiar gyrations of policy and the dissolution had not been implemented by mid-1981.

University developments

Shortly after the publication of the commission's report, the Minister for Education, Donogh O'Malley, went directly against the advice of the report on university re-organisation. He declared that it was the intention of the government to re-organise Trinity College and University College, Dublin, within a single university.[2] This 'merger' proposal gave rise to much controversy which made it clear that such a proposal would not be easily carried out. A more extensive statement of government policy on university re-organisation was made on 6 July 1968. The government announced that the NUI would be dissolved and Cork and Galway would be constituted as separate universities. With regard to University College, Dublin, and Trinity College, it was suggested that a restructured University of Dublin would be an indivisible corporate body with the two component colleges retaining their identity. Each college would have its own council which would be subject to the overall authority of a combined governing body. The government decided on the allocation of various faculties and departments between the two colleges in the interests of economic use of resources. The statement also announced government approval for a permanent authority to deal with finance and planning aspects of higher education (the HEA).

Much further discussion and disputation were to take place concerning the nature of the proposed university re-organisation. The Irish Federation of University Teachers was against a merger, favouring two cō-operating universities in Dublin. Indeed, academic opinion in general opposed the proposed merger. A working party representative of the NUI and Trinity College presented an alternative plan to the HEA on 7 April 1970. It urged the establishment of four independent universities with some modifications on the proposed division of faculties between the two Dublin universities. Meanwhile, the Irish hierarchy made decisions in these years which resulted in making the courses offered by Maynooth College available to lay as well as clerical students from 1966, and the removal of the ban on Catholic students attending Trinity College in 1970.

The Higher Education Authority presented its report on the 'Re-organisation of university education' in 1972.³ In general the HEA favoured the joint plan submitted by the NUI and Trinity College. Although remarking that a single Dublin university would be the simplest administrative arrangement, the HEA felt that circumstances had changed since 1967/8. They recommended two separate universities for Dublin, linked by a statutory conjoint board which would be an effective agency for the co-ordination of the courses offered by each university. Cork and Galway should be independent. The report called for 'a quick and lasting solution'.

On 16 December 1974 the Minister for Education in the Coalition Government, Richard Burke, announced a very different plan for higher education.⁴ He favoured a comprehensive rather than a binary third-level system whereby non-university, third-level institutions would be linked for degree-awarding purposes with the universities. University College, Cork and Galway were now to combine to form a newly-structured, federal National University of Ireland and the two Dublin colleges were to get independent status. These proposals also became very controversial and were not converted into legislative form. In July 1976 the government again changed its mind and came out in favour of independent status for Cork, Galway and Maynooth. The return of a Fianna Fáil administration in 1977 saw the re-assertion of the binary third-level policy. The government declared its intention of preparing legislation for four independent universities with reformed governing structures. The status of Maynooth College was not defined. In July 1977 the Royal College of Surgeons of Ireland became a recognised college of the National University of Ireland. It would seem that the early 1980s will see the long-delayed legislative re-organisation of Irish university education into five independent universities, with Maynooth offering a limited range of faculties.

Despite the absence of comprehensive university legislation, certain rationalisations in the allocation of faculties have occurred, notable examples being the co-ordination of veterinary medicine within University College, Dublin and dentistry and pharmacy in Trinity College. Student numbers in the universities have continued to increase, though as a proportion of all third-level students they have decreased. University College, Dublin, transferred almost all its faculties to its new campus in Belfield, a move which had been approved prior to 1960. Engineering, medicine and veterinary medicine await new buildings in the Belfield campus. Trinity College, Dublin, acquired new buildings, notably its new Berkeley Library and its new Arts and Social Sciences Building. University College, Galway, has partially completed a long-term expansion of its facilities and Cork and Maynooth have also acquired new buildings.

The introduction in 1968 of a student grant scheme for third-level education, linked to a means test, provided a valuable support to enable many students to avail themselves of third-level education. Despite the increase in student numbers, there has been little change in the imbalance in participation in university by different socio-economic groups since the mid-1960s.[5] Students under their overall union, the Union of Students in Ireland, became a much more vocal and active element in third-level affairs. Their activities, notably in 1968/9 contributed to improvements in the administrative structures and educational procedures within the universities. The expansion of careers and appointments offices in the universities has proved of great value to students.

University teaching has increasingly availed of the benefits of educational technology and computer facilities have been introduced in all universities. Expanded and modernised libraries are still proving inadequate for the demands made upon them. In an effort to streamline and co-ordinate student applications for university places, the Central Applications Office (CAO) was established. The proposal for this office was submitted to the HEA by the heads of the Irish universities in 1973. The HEA approved the plan and the CAO was founded in 1976. It supplements the course information services of the individual colleges and processes the various applications. The 1970s witnessed restrictions in admissions for several professional faculties. The operation of a points system based on success rates in the Leaving and matriculation examinations became the predominant factor and, in some colleges, the sole factor in discriminating among applicants for restricted faculties.

Third-level education outside the university

The last twenty years have seen a striking development of non-university, third-level education from an admittedly small base in 1960. Although a great deal of the work of the universities is, of course, technological and professional in character, yet a keynote in the development of other forms of third-level education was the desire to promote technological and applied studies. The investment in education report and the commission on higher education had drawn attention to the inadequacies of technological and technician education. The OECD report in 1963 on the training of technicians in Ireland also urged action to improve existing facilities. The Minister for Education, Patrick Hillery, in May 1963 had indicated the government's interest in setting up regional technical colleges and a Leaving Certificate with a technical bias. In September 1966 a steering committee on technical education was established 'to advise the Minister generally on technical education and, in particular, on behalf of the Minister, to provide the Department of Education's Building Consortium with a brief for the technical colleges'. The government had already decided to establish eight regional technical colleges in the following centres — Cork, Limerick, Waterford, Galway, Sligo, Dundalk, Athlone and Carlow — and were considering the siting of a college in Letterkenny.

To assist the design team with work in progress, a 'preliminary brief' was submitted to the Department in January 1967 and the final report of the committee was published in May 1969.[6] The committee noted that the education to be provided in regional colleges covered a very wide range, including senior cycle post-primary, apprentice and technician courses, and various types of adult education, and spanned a wide range of occupations in technical, scientific, commercial, catering and other fields of specialisation. The report stressed the need for a big expansion in technician education and urged the establishment of a national council for educational awards which would act as the validating and qualification awarding body for the regional colleges and for technological education generally.

The report urged a flexible building design which would facilitate the expansion of colleges when the projected demand made itself felt. Although seeing the colleges providing senior level post-primary education, it also saw them providing post-Leaving Certificate full-time, part-time or equivalent, courses over one or two years leading to higher technician awards. A few colleges would offer full professional courses. Many forms of technician and trade courses and adult education courses were to be provided. The report endorsed the eight sites selected by the government but felt that Letterkenny should have a local technical college pending expansion when it might be raised to regional status. The report made specific recommendations about buildings and equipment, the early recruitment of supervisory staff, the mode of college administration and the setting up of regional education councils which might be accountable for all education in each of the regions. The Higher Education Authority also advised the government in March 1969 to set up a council for national awards for third-level institutions outside the universities.

The first five regional technical colleges at Carlow, Waterford, Athlone, Dundalk, and Sligo opened in September 1969 to be followed later by others in Cork, Galway and Letterkenny. Tralee Technical College was raised to regional status in 1979. Once in operation, the colleges soon found themselves called upon to cater increasingly for third-level demand. At first they provided certificate and diploma awards but in 1974 the first proposal for a degree course was submitted. In 1972 the government set up the National Council for Educational Awards on an ad hoc basis to act as the academic authority for the college courses and awards as well as courses in future years in other non-university colleges. The number of students in Regional Technical Colleges grew from 1,214 in 1972/3 to 4,579 by 1979/80.[7]

Another form of third-level institution came into being in Limerick — the National Institute for Higher Education (NIHE). People in Limerick had been campaigning to have a university set up there but in March 1969 the HEA advised the government against this course of action, echoing the commission on higher education. The HEA urged instead the setting up of a college of higher education in Limerick whose work 'should be based primarily on a technological content, but with a significant element of the humanities'.[8] From this emerged the NIHE for which a campus of 120 acres was purchased near Limerick to be shared by the National College of Physical Education (Thomond College) set up in 1970. A director and planning board were appointed for NIHE in 1970 and the first students were admitted in 1972. The bill giving a statutory basis for the institute was passed in 1980.

In Dublin the pressures on the existing colleges of technology and the college of commerce had become very great. Growing demand and inadequate facilities urged the Dublin VEC to submit plans for a new technological/higher commercial college in Ballymun, a northern suburb of Dublin. The VEC planned to transfer to the proposed new college all the third-level educational activities then undertaken at the College of Commerce, Rathmines, and at the College of Technology, Bolton Street and some of the third-level courses at the College of Technology, Kevin Street. The HEA reported to the government in December 1970 endorsing the main aspects of the VEC plan, though it had some reservations as regards the Ballymun site.[9] The new college with an orientation towards the more practical aspects of education for industrial, commercial and technological vocations was to be approved by the government as a Dublin institute for higher education, but not under the control of the VEC.

The decision by the Coalition government in 1974 to withdraw degree-awarding powers from the NCEA caused considerable confusion and dissatisfaction in the non-university third-level sector. Arrangements were made by which Thomond College came under the aegis of University College, Cork and NIHE Limerick, under University College, Galway, and Trinity College arranged with the Dublin VEC to award degrees to some of the graduates from their technological colleges. The return of Fianna Fáil to office saw the NCEA resuming its degree-awarding function in November 1977. It became the body responsible for validating courses and awarding certificates, diplomas and degrees to NIHE, Thomond College, the Dublin College of Commerce and the colleges of technology as well as the regional colleges. The bill giving statutory status to the NCEA was approved by the Oireachtas in 1979, thereby enshrining the binary system of third-level education.

In Dublin the six higher-level colleges under the VEC were reorganised in 1978 as the Dublin Institute of Technology (DIT). Arrangements went ahead for the establishment of a NIHE, Dublin, situated in the Ballymun complex. The Dublin NIHE received its first students in November 1980. The huge growth in population in the greater Dublin area, an increase of 66 per cent between 1971 and 1979 in the Dublin County districts, and the increased educational demand led the HEA to undertake the planning studies which would point the way for appropriate decisions. One of these studies was published by the HEA in October 1979. It recommended the building of four new colleges in the greater Dublin region sited in areas where demographic trends indicated future demand. The colleges would be largely based on the regional colleges model with greater scope for the humanities and social sciences and with more specific provision for recurrent education.[10]

Thus, over fifteen years which saw considerable planning, pressures, trauma and some confusion Ireland evolved its present highly developed third-level structure. The formal dissolution of NUI is the main issue to be resolved. New institutions have come into being, new co-ordinating and award-giving agencies, new courses and, overall, a more dynamic third-level system. The young men and women of Ireland were not slow to make use of the expanded opportunities, and in the period from 1964/5 to 1978/9 the increase of full-time student enrolment was 128 per cent, from 16,327 to 37,156.[11]

Third-level education today

Having traced the pattern of events through which the present structure evolved during the period 1960-80, this section gives an account of the various components of the third-level system today. There are two bodies placed between the government and the third-level institutions which exercise important powers. These are the Higher Education Authority and the National Council for Educational Awards. The former has powers and responsibilities ranging over the whole of third-level and the latter relates to much of the non-university sector, where it is the course-validating and award-giving body. The third-level sector has evolved along a binary pattern, to which the legislation of the 1970s, giving statutory recognition to new institutions, has given a secure base. The structure is now likely to be unchanged for a considerable period. The *White paper on educational development* (Chapter X) has indicated that the government intends to assume a strong steering influence on third-level developments and has clearly signalled that its priorities lie in the promotion of technological and applied studies which have a direct relationship with manpower requirements.

The Higher Education Authority (HEA)
The Higher Education Authority is a body corporate comprising a

chairman and no't more than eighteen members, all of whom are appointed by the government on the recommendation of the Minister for Education. At least seven of the ordinary members are academic members and at least seven are other than academic members. The chairman of the Authority is appointed by the Minister for Education on a whole-time basis. The HEA has set up sub-committees such as the finance committee, physical development committee, education and research committee and a liaison committee.

The HEA is the funding agency for universities and other designated third-level institutions from funds provided by the state. The designated third-level institutions, other than universities, include the Royal College of Surgeons in Ireland, the National Institutes for Higher Education at Limerick and Dublin, the National College of Art and Design, the National Council for Educational Awards and the Royal Irish Academy. It is envisaged that other third-level institutions will come under the authority of the HEA in the years ahead. Any request by a designated institution of higher education for state subvention has to be submitted for examination and recommendation to the HEA. The HEA advises the Minister on third-level education. This is planned in relation to the development of second-level education, economic development and manpower policy. Among the general functions of the Authority are:

— furthering the development of higher education
— assisting in the co-ordination of state investments in higher education and preparing proposals for such investment
— promoting an appreciation of the value of higher education and research
— promoting the attainment of equality of opportunity in higher education
— promoting the democratisation of the structure of higher education.

In meeting its responsibilities the HEA can institute and conduct research studies and publish reports on such studies. In the course of its work it has advised the government on such major issues as the establishment of the NCEA, the founding of the NIHEs, the re-organisation of the universities, teacher training. It has published reports on topics such as student performance in university, future enrolments and demands in third-level education. It publishes annual reports setting out its financial accounts and student statistics in the designated institutions. Normally expansion plans of institutions and the development of new courses where they involve extra expenditure have to be submitted for the approval of the HEA. The HEA also exercises control over the numbers of staff which may be appointed and on the internal promotion patterns of the institutions. The range of its influence on third-level education is considerable, though it does not impinge on purely academic issues or the academic freedom of the personnel employed.

The National Council for Educational Awards (NCEA)
The National Council for Educational Awards Act, 1980, has given a statutory base to the NCEA. Under the legislation the NCEA has as its general function: to encourage, facilitate, promote, co-ordinate and develop technical, industrial, scientific, technological and commercial education, and education in art or design, provided outside the universities, whether professional, vocational or technical, and to encourage and promote liberal education. The Council has the power to confer degrees, diplomas, certificates or other educational awards on persons who the Council is satisfied have attended or otherwise pursued courses of study conducted by, or provided under the supervision of, an institution to which the Act applies, that is a 'designated institution'. Such courses must for the time being stand approved by the Council, as must research assignments. The NCEA acts as the validating and award-giving body for many non-university institutions of higher education. It assesses the standards of courses in designated institutions and overseas transferability arrangements of students between the courses of different designated institutions.

The members of the Council are a chairman, a director and twenty-three other members. The Minister appoints nine ordinary members representative of industrial, commercial and agricultural interests. NIHE Dublin, NIHE Limerick and Thomond College all have two representatives each and the National College of Art and Design has one representative. University institutions have four representatives and there are three representatives of governing bodies, staff or students of any institution to which the Act applies. The government appoints the chairman who acts in a part-time capacity. The Council appoints a full-time director subject to the approval of the Minister, and the director acts as the chief officer of the Council. The Council may engage consultants, examiners, assessors or advisers to assist it in its functions.

The Council has a number of committees and boards of studies with advisory panels to assist it in implementing its functions.

The NCEA publishes annual reports and occasional discussion documents in its area of concern. Because the NCEA is so closely involved in the academic development of the relatively new non-university sector it is charged with the heavy responsibility of ensuring that standards of courses and awards are such that they will be acceptable and receive endorsement in Ireland and internationally. To help ensure this the Council makes use of a wide panel of experts and external examiners in the various fields of study. The categories of award currently conferred by the NCEA are one-year certificates, national certificates, national diplomas, degrees and graduate diplomas. During the period 1972-9 the Council awarded 1,075 one-year certificates, 6,100 national certificates and 2,457 national diplomas and it conferred 410 degrees. Engineering, science and design accounted for about two-thirds of all NCEA awards. The work of the Council is expanding rapidly as many new courses are being presented for its approval by different institutions. A recent development is the offering of degree courses jointly by a regional college and a national institute of higher education.

The university sector
As the third-level sector is now a complicated system Table 26 may help to distinguish the various institutional components. Up to recent years the universities held almost sole sway in third-level education. By 1978, however, despite great expansion they catered for only about 60 per cent of third-level students. There are two universities in the Republic of Ireland – the National University of Ireland (NUI) and Dublin University. Both universities are autonomous institutions but they derive about 85 per cent of their income from state funds. Trinity College is the sole constituent college of Dublin University. The NUI is a federal university with a central office in Dublin. The NUI itself does not teach or undertake research, these functions being left to its constituent or recognised colleges; it is, however, the authority for appointing professors and lecturers to the university, for conducting entry and degree examinations, for maintaining the standards of courses and examinations and for awarding degrees and diplomas. The authorities of the NUI are: the Chancellor, who is the head and chief officer of the university; the Vice-Chancellor

Table 26: Third-Level Education Institutions

Type of Institute		Other

Under Statutory Governing Body	*Universities*
	1. University of Dublin
	 Trinity College
	2. National University of Ireland
	 Constituent Colleges: UCD
	         UCC
	         UCG
	
	Recognised Colleges
	 Maynooth
	 St. Patrick's College of Education
	 Our Lady of Mercy College of Education
	 Mary Immaculate College of Education
	 St. Angela's College of Domestic Science
	 Royal College of Surgeons
		NIHE Limerick
		NIHE Dublin
		Thomond College
		Nat. College of Art & Design

Under Voc. Education Auth.	Dublin Inst. of Technology Regional Tech. Colleges (RTCs)	
Private Management	Colleges of Education for Primary Teachers St. Patrick's Our Lady of Mercy Mary Immaculate St. Mary's, Marino Church of Ireland Froebel St. Angela's College of Domestic Science	

who is the chief executive officer; the Pro-Vice-Chancellors; the Senate; the General Board of Studies; Faculties and Convocation. Dublin University authorities include the Chancellor; Pro-Chancellors; the Provost; the Board of Trinity College; the University Council; and the faculties.

The NUI has three constituent colleges – University College, Dublin (UCD), University College, Cork (UCC) and University College, Galway (UCG). It also has six recognised colleges – St Patrick's College, Maynooth (1910); St Patrick's College of Education, Dublin; Our Lady of Mercy College of Education, Dublin; Mary Immaculate College of Education, Limerick (all three of which were accorded recognised status in 1974); the Royal College of Surgeons, Dublin (1977); and St Angela's College, Sligo (1978). The constituent colleges lay down their own programme and carry out their own examinations subject to the overall authority of the NUI. The recognised colleges plan their programmes and examinations with the advice of academic personnel in the constituent college to which they are linked. John Wilson, the Minister for Education, announced his government's intention of bringing in legislation in 1981 which will dissolve the NUI federal structure giving independent status to the colleges in Dublin, Cork, Galway and Maynooth, with the other recognised colleges linked to one or other of the new universities.

The universities, as long established institutions, have won international recognition for their graduate and post-graduate awards. In recent years there has been greater involvement by university personnel in international academic affairs, conferences and research programmes. Staff exchange schemes, sabbatical leave and involvement as extern examiners to universities abroad have helped to widen staff experience. Irish universities have also provided consultants and advisory staff to institutions in underdeveloped countries on an increasing scale.

All the university colleges have benefited from new buildings and plans for expansion to cater for larger student numbers and to provide up-dated facilities and equipment for teaching and research. The most striking development in this regard is the building of a wholly new university campus for UCD at Belfield, which is not yet complete. Post-graduate work and research have become more pronounced features of the universities' activities. The universities continue to suffer from high staff-student ratios compared with the experience in other developed countries, though the problem is most acute in the arts and commerce faculties. Many of the staff recruited to cope with the expansion in student numbers tend to be young and the younger age groups now form a large proportion of the overall staff. The HEA has decreed that a 4 : 6 ratio shall obtain between senior and junior staff positions.

The mode of government and administration within the universities has gradually evolved along democratic lines, though many junior staff and students seek further development. It is expected that the new legislation affecting the NUI colleges will include governing structures consonant with contemporary views on the exercise of authority within academic institutions. This is likely to have most significant effect on Maynooth College where hitherto the final authority rested with a Board of Trustees drawn solely from among the Catholic bishops. With the increasing acceptance of economic targets as society's goals and the accelerated pace of technological change, the universities have not escaped charges of irrelevance and the divorce of their concerns from the apparent current needs of Irish society. A closer scrutiny would reveal that the universities have developed many areas of studies which have a strongly applied thrust and that many of the professional faculties are the most favourably endowed financially and have the lowest teacher-student ratios. The operation of the points selection system has tended to siphon off some of the brightest students from arts faculties. Further, arts faculties have been subjected to political criticisms in a time of recession because of their alleged lack of alignment with economic priorities. The development of the non-university third-level sector may have been prompted by the need for more flexible course arrangements and the promotion of some subject areas which do not easily fit into the university tradition of education anywhere. Personnel from the universities participate on the Council of the NCEA and on its boards of studies.

Some reports in the 1970s urged a re-appraisal of the financial support for students in third-level education, allowing fees to float to levels reflective of the actual costs and devising a scheme of re-payable loans and graduated fee schemes for students.[12] The government has not adopted these proposals but a policy of fee increases linked to annual inflation levels has been promoted. Owing to a cut-back in state grants, the universities in 1981 experienced severe financial problems which may lead to particularly large fee increases in 1981/2. The generally lower level of fees and the range of shorter courses with closer links to employment may have attracted more students of poorer socio-economic circumstances to the newer institutions of the non-university third-level sector.

As is the case with many universities internationally, Irish universities have introduced limits to the number of students admitted to the various courses at under-graduate level, except for those in the arts faculties. Most courses are over-subscribed and a system of selection is operated to discriminate among matriculated students. What is known as a 'points' system has been introduced whereby a certain number of points are allotted to different levels of performance in subjects taken at the Leaving and/or matriculation examinations. The points scheme operated by NUI colleges is based solely on the results of the examinations, but Trinity College takes other factors into account. A special weighting in favour of subjects cognate to the courses for which entry is sought is operated by Trinity College and UCG. The points schemes vary between different colleges and the number of points required to gain access to faculties can fluctuate from year to year. UCD, UCC, UCG and Trinity College all offer courses in arts, science, law, business studies, engineering, medicine and social science. As well as this UCD offers agriculture, architecture, veterinary medicine and physiotherapy. UCC offers dairy science and Trinity College offers dentistry and pharmacy. Maynooth College, as a recognised college, offers courses in three faculties, arts, philosophy and science. Courses taken in UCG may be studied through the medium of Irish. The various university institutions issue calendars and information booklets annually which detail entry requirements, courses offered, points systems, information on registration, fees etc.

Applications for university places and for places in Thomond College and NIHE Limerick are processed through the Central Applications Office (CAO) which has its central office in Galway. The CAO is a company limited by guarantee and was founded in January 1976 to provide information for intending students and process applications for entry to undergraduate degree and diploma courses. It is envisaged that it will in the future perform such a function for other institutions of higher education. In the CAO scheme it is necessary for an applicant to complete only one application form in order to apply for entry to courses in all the colleges affiliated to it. A total of ten courses may be chosen in order of preference and in any combination of colleges. Application literature is distributed in an organised manner to all post-primary schools in the Republic of Ireland and Northern Ireland. The normal closing date for applications is 15 March for the following academic year, though provision is made for late applications. Places are allocated in late August following receipt of the current year's examination results. Each applicant is given a place in the highest of his course preferences which his merit rating will allow. It is intended that the CAO will provide expanded services on maintaining continuing student records and compiling statistical information within its ambit of concern.

The non-university third-level sector
The institutions involved in the non-university sector are the national institutes of higher education at Limerick and Dublin, the regional technical colleges, the third-level colleges under VECs which, in Dublin, have grouped as the Dublin Institute of Technology (DIT), Thomond College in Limerick and the National College of Art and Design in Dublin. These institutions cater for about 10,000 students but development plans indicate that this number will greatly increase in the years ahead. The courses offered are varied and range in duration from one-year certificate courses to four-year degree courses. Efforts have been made to design the courses with a flexible structure; at times they include work experience and transition between different courses and institutions is also facilitated. The course fees for the non-university sector tend to be low and are heavily subsidised by the state. Many of the new institutions have been well equipped. The NCEA acts as the overall academic validating and award-giving agency for this sector of third level. As the various institutions differ in their origins, functions and mode of administration an outline description is given of each type of institution.

National Institute for Higher Education, Limerick (NIHE Limerick)
The government appointed a planning board for NIHE, Limerick in 1970 and the Institute received its first students in 1972. During 1976 and 1977 the Institute operated as a recognised college of the NUI. In 1978 the NCEA became the degree-awarding body. A bill was introduced in 1980 to give statutory existence to NIHE, Limerick. This bill defined the academic functions of the Institute

as follows:

1. To provide degree, diploma and certificate level courses and, with the approval of the Minister for Education, such other courses in education as may seem appropriate to the governing body;
2. to engage in research in such areas as may seem appropriate to the governing body.

The governing body is to consist of a chairman, the director and twenty-three ordinary members. The government appoints the chairman and the governing body appoints the director, subject to the approval of the Minister. Every ordinary member of the governing body is to be appointed by the government on the recommendation of the Minister. The bill provides for the setting up of an academic board which, subject to the governing body, will concern itself with many facets of the academic and educational work of the Institute. During the debate on the bill in the Dáil, commentators criticised the high level of control the Minister for Education and his Department could have over the work of the Institute.

The NIHE, Limerick provides national and regional education oriented towards applied science and practical business methods. It works on the credit-module rather than on the traditional course system. Programmes of study to degree level are offered in business studies, computer systems, European studies, electronic engineering, industrial and management mathematical science, industrial chemistry, mechanical engineering, materials and production engineering. At present the college has about 1,000 students but with the completion of its second phase of development, it expects to offer places to a student population of 3,250.

National Institute for Higher Education, Dublin (NIHE, Dublin)
The government set up the National Institute for Higher Education, Dublin in 1975 and its governing body held its first meeting in June of that year. Planning for the Institute has been going ahead and it admitted the first students, 300 in number, in November 1980 at its site in Ballymun, Dublin. It is intended that the Institute will discharge a national and local role in relation to the operation of programmes leading to certificate, diploma, degree, professional and post-graduate awards through whole-time and part-time study, with the addition of various courses not leading to formal qualification. It is planned that the Institute will develop to cater for

5,000 students. The first courses offered by the Institute are as follows: engineering and design, computer studies, science and paramedical studies, business studies and communicating studies. It is planned to extend its range of courses as the Institute expands its student intake and distance learning pilot programmes are planned for 1981/82.

Regional technical colleges   The function of regional technical colleges (RTCs) is to educate for trade and industry over a broad spectrum of occupations, ranging from craft to professional level, notably in engineering and science but also in commercial, linguistic and other specialities. The programmes for the colleges include:

1. Junior and senior trade certificate courses, on day or block release for local apprentices, and on block release for apprentices from a wider area.
2. Courses for hotel and catering at all levels.
3. Part-time day, block release and full-time courses for technical qualifications at various levels, e.g. draftsman, laboratory assistant, agricultural technician, telecommunications technician, etc.
4. Post-Leaving Certificate or post-senior trade certificate:
   — Courses of one year's duration for receptionists, and courses in secretarial studies, in computer programming, etc.
   — Courses of two year's duration leading to the award of a National Technician Certificate
   — Courses of one year's duration, subsequent to the award of an appropriate National Technician Certificate, leading to the award of a National Technician Diploma
   — Courses of three years' duration leading to the award of a National Technician Diploma
   — Courses of more than three years' duration leading to a professional or degree-level award
5. Adult education courses, including re-training courses

Certain colleges specialise in certain subject areas and detailed information on the particular courses available is obtainable from the individual colleges. Provision exists for transfer of students between various courses on the basis of satisfactory standards of achievement on lower-level courses. National Certificates and Diplomas as well as some degrees are awarded to students of these colleges who successfully complete third-level courses under the validation of the National Council for Educational Awards.

Regional technical colleges are administered by boards of management. Each college has a board of management which operates as a sub-committee of the local vocational education committee. Originally the board was comprised of seven members — one representative each of agricultural, employer and trade union interests, one representative of the Department of Education, one representative of the VEC, the chief executive officer of the VEC, and the college principal. Boards have now been increased to twelve members to allow for more representation from VECs in the region or from industrial interests. For the decisions of the boards of management to be legally valid, they must be ratified by the local vocational education committee. The boards propose the annual programmes both educational and financial, sanction all expenditure, select and appoint staff (other than the college principal) and receive reports on progress generally. The principal, under the direction of the board, is responsible for the administration of policy within the college. There is also a college council, broadly representative of education, industrial, agricultural and general developmental interests within the region as a whole.

The regional technical colleges are funded through the vocational education committees by the Department of Education. In 1978/9 the running costs of regional technical colleges were £6,275,900 and capital expenditure amounted to £2,260,661. In 1978/9 there were 3,753 students enrolled in full-time third-level courses in the regional colleges, and they had a full-time teaching staff of 710 with a further full-time equivalent of part-time teachers amounting to 83 teachers. It is envisaged that four new colleges on the regional technical college model will be built during the 1980s to cater for the increased population in the greater Dublin area.[13]

The National College of Art and Design, Dublin In 1971 the National College of Art was reconstituted as the National College of Art and Design and a governing board was appointed by the government. Some of the functions previously exercised by the Department of Education in relation to the college have been transferred to this board. In 1976 the college was designated as an institution of higher education under the Higher Education Act, 1971.

The College offers three-year diploma courses in fine art, visual communications, fashion and textiles, craft design and a four-year course in industrial design. The faculty of education in the college offers a one-year principles of teaching art for diploma holders as well as a four-year diploma in art and design education for those who intend to specialise in art teaching. The college offers a wide range of evening courses. The college's work in art and design education is to be co-ordinated under the aegis of the NCEA, and it is expected that the college will be able to offer degrees.

Third-level colleges of the vocational education authorities

The Dublin Institute of Technology (DIT)   The DIT comprises six colleges under the Dublin vocational education committee structure, which provide degree-level, professional, technician, apprentice and other courses. The colleges are the College of Technology, Bolton Street (1911), College of Technology, Kevin Street (1886), College of Commerce, Rathmines (1902), College of Music, Chatham Row (1905), College of Marketing and Design, Parnell Square (1906) and the College of Catering, Cathal Brugha Street (1941). The DIT was established by the City of Dublin Vocational Education Committee in 1978.

The Institute serves the needs of approximately 3,000 whole-time students, 7,000 part-time students and 5,500 craft apprentices in its wide range of courses. It has a full-time staff of about 500 and almost as many acting in a part-time capacity. Individual colleges specialise in certain subject areas and many of the courses have enjoyed a high reputation for many years. Graduates of the following professional courses of DIT are eligible for the award of degrees of the University of Dublin: applied sciences; architecture; business studies; construction economics; mechanical/production engineering; electrical engineering; structural engineering; environmental economics; hotel and catering management; marketing. DIT offers its own diploma and certificate awards and also provides courses leading to awards by the NCEA and institutions such as the London City and Guilds.

The directorate comprises the principals of the six colleges involved. There is a governing body and an inter-college academic council. The DIT is funded through the Dublin VEC by the Department of Education. Course enquiries and applications go to the individual colleges.

Limerick Technical College   The college operates under the City of Limerick Vocational Education Committee but does not have RTC status. It has three constituent schools — the School of Art and Design, the School of Engineering and the School of Professional and Management Studies. The School of Engineering includes departments of building and civil engineering, electrical and electronic engineering, mechanical and automobile engineering and marine radio and radar.

Crawford Municipal School of Art and Cork School of Music   The School of Art founded in 1885 is housed in the same building as the art gallery. Both of these schools are run under the auspices of the Cork VEC and provide a wide range of courses in the arts.

The School of Art, Dun Laoghaire, Dublin   The School of Art in Dun Laoghaire has some of its courses recognised for third-level purposes, and is operated by the VEC.

The financing of third-level education
The mode of financing third-level institutions varies and reflects somewhat their historical development. The Higher Education Authority acts as the main agency through which the government finances university and other designated institutions. The five university colleges, the College of the Pharmaceutical Society of Ireland, the Royal College of Surgeons in Ireland, NIHE, Limerick and NIHE, Dublin, the National College of Art and Design, Thomond College, the National Council for Educational Awards and the Central Applications Office all receive their state grants through the agency of the HEA. On the other hand regional colleges and technological colleges and training colleges under the VEC receive their state grants through the VEC. These latter are now largely replaced by Thomond College. National teacher training colleges are financed directly from the Department of Education.

The government estimates for expenditure on third-level education for 1980 included £45 million for non-capital grants and £6 million for building and capital grants to be disbursed through the HEA to the universities and other designated institutions. The running costs of the regional technical colleges were estimated for 1980 as £13 million with a further £2 million for building grants and capital grants to regional and some other colleges. The running

costs of the national teacher training colleges were put at about
£4½ million with a further million for capital costs, to be disbursed from the Department of Education.[14] The estimated costs
from public funds per full-time equivalent student in 1979 in the
various institutions was as follows: regional technical colleges
£1,170; technological colleges £1,260; universities £1,375;
NIHE Limerick £1,490 and colleges of education £1,710.[15]
However, such raw figures mask important cost differences and
need to be used with caution.

Participation in third-level education — some student statistics

Recent years have seen a significant increase in the number of
students in full-time third-level education. Numbers rose from
23,100 in 1968/9 to 37,156 in 1978/9, representing an increase of
60 per cent during the decade. Yet the percentage of the age cohort
twenty to twenty-four years participating in third level at about
11 per cent is low, particularly when seen in relation to most
other EEC countries where it was more than 20 per cent, even in
the early 1970s. (It is true, of course, that many Irish students
enter and graduate from third level earlier than their European
counterparts.)

With increasing numbers of pupils completing the senior cycle of
second-level education, educational authorities and demographers
are concerned about future provision at third level. One recent
study conducted for the HEA attempted to project the number of
places required given a number of policy assumptions. These projections are set out in Table 27 and provisions that may have to
be made, depending on which policy options are adopted, are
dicussed.

Maintaining the 11 per cent participation is obviously feasible
but most commentators suggest that this is an unrealistic option
and that there will be gathering momentum which will require
considerable expansion in the years ahead. The *White paper on
educational development* in 1980 estimated an increase of about
12,000 in third-level students between 1980 and 1990, leading to
a student body of 51,000.[16] However, its projections seem to be
based more on the supply of places which will be made rather than
on the demand which will be in evidence and many commentators
regard the projections as too low.

A striking aspect of the recent participation rates in third-level
education is the increased enrolment in non-university colleges.

Table 27: **Projections of third-level enrolments 1976-91, based on a number of policy options**

Basis for projection	1976 (actual)	1981	1986	1991
Maintaining 11% participation rate	33,003	36,800	37,700	40,400
Assuming certain percentages of senior-cycle second-level students obtain third-level places	33,003	38,700	17% 42,700	46,700
	33,003	50,100	22% 55,200	63,000
	33,003	73,000	32% 80,000	88,500
Estimates in white paper 'national development 1977/80'	33,003	44,400	46,500	47,900
Participation rates in other EEC countries (assuming that Ireland achieves certain rates by 1991)	33,003	49,400	10% 53,600	54,300
	33,003	49,400	12% 58,900	65,200
	33,003	49,400	14% 64,300	76,100

Source: John Sheehan *Future enrolments in third-level education* (HEA, 1978), p. 7

For instance, in 1968/9 university students accounted for 17,500 of the full-time third-level student body of 23,100, or 76 per cent of the total. In 1978/9 university students formed 61 per cent of the total full-time, third-level students. This trend is expected to continue and, of the 12,000 new places projected in the white paper for 1990, only 3,000 are planned for the five universities. Such a pattern would establish about a 50:50 ratio between students in universities and in other third-level institutions.

A continuing point of concern is the imbalance in the represen- tation of socio-economic classes in third-level education but particularly in the university sector. The *Investment in Education Report* showed that 85 per cent of university entrants in 1963 were from the social groups A, B and C (farmers, professionals, clerks etc) and only 15 per cent were from the groups D, E, F and G (skilled, semi-skilled, unskilled and unemployed), though these latter groups formed the majority of the general population. Despite calls for greater equality of educational opportunity and the introduction of the higher education grants scheme in 1968, the basic imbalance has altered little except for an increase of boys from families where the father's occupation is skilled manual worker. Of the 6,143 full-time undergraduate students who entered the universities and NIHE, Limerick for the first time in 1978/9 and whose socio-economic background was classified, only 574 or 9 per cent were from the skilled manual, semi-skilled and unskilled categories.[17]

Table 28 sets out the number of full-time students and the types of third-level institution attended by them in 1978/9 and Table 29 indicates the number of full-time students by field of study in the individual colleges designated under the HEA Act. It can be seen that arts, commerce, law and social/economic students account for about 60 per cent of the full-time university students. Science and engineering students comprise a further 24 per cent. About 13 per cent are in the professional faculties of medicine, veterinary, dentistry and architecture while 3 per cent are in agricultural studies. Arts continues to dominate in the fields of study but it is worth noting that in the five-year period 1973/4 to 1978/9 the increased number of students taking science and engineering was greater than the increase in the arts and commerce areas.[18] In line with manpower needs in the economy in recent years some graduate conversion courses have been operating to make more skilled personnel available in science and engineering.

Higher education grants and scholarships
A higher education grants scheme is in existence for university and some other third-level students. Overall the grants benefit about 30 per cent of higher education students but only about 22 per cent of university students receive grants. The grants are set so as to cover fees and a basic subsistence level of maintenance. Grants are awarded on a combined means/merit/location basis. The highest grant that any student can currently receive is £1,000 per annum plus fees and this applies to both grants under the

Table 28: Number of full-time students in the various types of third-level institutions, 1978/9

Type of institution	Male	Female	Total	Percentage of total third-level students
Universities	12,846	10,039	22,885	61.6
NIHE, Limerick	698	218	916	2.5
National College of Art and Design	148	230	378	1.0
College of Pharmacy (pharmaceutical assistants' course)	1	46	47	.1
Royal College of Surgeons in Ireland	558	176	734	1.9
Teacher training				
— national	480	2,021	2,501	
— vocational	173	11	184	8.2
— domestic science	—	177	177	
— physical education	88	88	176	
Vocational technological	2,397	968	3,365	20.6
Regional technical colleges	3,023	1,251	4,275	
Other aided institutions	37	76	113	
Other non-aided institutions	991	415	1,406	4.1
Total	21,440	15,716	37,156	100.0

Source: *HEA Accounts and Student Statistics Report 1978/9*, p. 13

Table 29: Full-time students (undergraduate and postgraduate) by field of study and college at 1 March 1979, (colleges designated under HEA Act)

Field of study	UCD	UCC	UCG	TCD	MAY	NIHEL	NCAD	RCSI	Totals
Arts	3,188	1,719	1,525	1,894	1,023	0	43	0	9,392
Art and design	0	0	0	0	0	24	335	0	359
Economic and social studies	0	0	0	760	0	0	0	0	760
European studies	0	0	0	0	0	135	0	0	135
Social science	293	103	0	0	0	0	0	0	396
Commerce	869	478	422	0	0	375	0	0	2,144
Law	471	194	62	230	0	0	0	0	957
Science	1,051	641	802	854	158	0	0	0	3,506
Engineering	772	459	291	553	0	382	0	0	2,457
Architecture	215	0	0	0	0	0	0	0	215
Medicine	1,076	448	430	636	0	0	0	734	3,324
Dentistry	0	111	0	212	0	0	0	0	323
Veterinary medicine	326	0	0	1	0	0	0	0	327
Agricultural science and forestry	436	0	76	0	0	0	0	0	512
Dairy science	0	141	0	0	0	0	0	0	141
Totals	8,697	4,294	3,608	5,140	1,181	916	378	734	24,948

Source: *Accounts and Student Statistics of HEA*, 1978/79, Table 1, p. 30

Higher Education Grants Scheme and to scholarships under the Vocational Education Scheme. The academic requirements for qualifying for a university grant are higher than the minimum entry standard.

Grants are funded partly from the Department of Education and in part from local authorities. Applications for these grants are directed to the local authorities. University scholarship schemes also exist for Gaeltacht students and for students whose second-level education was conducted through the medium of Irish. In addition seven scholarships to attend university are awarded by the state in commemoration of the signatories of the 1916 Proclamation. Initially, when introduced in 1968 the grants were mainly intended for university education but since 1974 students enrolled for certain courses in the colleges of technology, the NIHE, the National College of Art and Design and the regional technical colleges may also benefit. Grants and loans to trainee teachers are funded by the state through the Department of Education vote. Scholarships are awarded by the VECs to regional technical colleges and RTCs may benefit also from general grants schemes. Overall the expenditure on these various grant and scholarship schemes for the year 1978/9 amounted to about £5½ million, benefiting 10,698 students.[19] In all about 30 per cent of third-level students benefit from grants. In 1980 the Union of Students of Ireland calculated that the average cost of maintaining a student in third-level education, exclusive of fees, was about £1,600.

Unions at third level

The Union of Students of Ireland (USI) The Union of Students of Ireland represents over 70,000 students, organised in constituent student unions in sixty different third-level colleges in the Republic of Ireland and Northern Ireland. It acts as a student trade union and campaigns for increased expenditure on education, improved grants schemes and various reforms in the education system. It conducts research, organises seminars and publishes booklets on educational issues. The policy of USI is decided by the annual congress and the national council and its three full-time officers carry out the day-to-day business of the Union. At national and local level USI provides many facilities and services to students including travel and insurance services.

The Irish Federation of University Teachers (IFUT)   The Irish Federation of University Teachers is the trade union to which most university and professional training college staff belong. Local staff associations in the colleges elect representatives to the council and to the executive of the IFUT. As well as pressing for improved salaries and conditions of employment for its members, the IFUT carries out research, holds seminars and issues publications on aspects of Irish education policy, particularly policy pertaining to third-level education.

Apart from the IFUT, third-level academic staff belong to other trade unions such as the Teachers' Union of Ireland (TUI), the Workers Union of Ireland (WUI) and the Association of Scientific, Technical and Managerial Staffs (ASTMS).

Chapter Sixteen

Adult Education

Internationally the definition and role of adult education in society have been undergoing fundamental re-appraisal. Terms such as permanent education, recurrent education, continuing education have made their way into educational discourse and indicate a significant new direction. Education is being seen more as a life-long process rather than an experience undergone by the young in preparation for adulthood or the world of work. The new emphasis seeks to maximise the opportunities for people to participate in courses and avail of the resources of formal and non-formal educational provision at different stages throughout their lifetimes. Indeed, many commentators believe that up till now formal education has been the poorer because of the limited experience of life and work held by most of its clientele.

Ireland has shared in the new debate on adult education and has been affected by many of the influences underlying the increased emphasis on it. The pace of technological change has made it imperative for many adults to participate in education and re-training courses to meet the needs of their work and careers. With the rise of educational standards generally, many of these who for one reason or another experienced little formal education feel the need or the desire to improve their standard of education. In Ireland half the adult population over twenty-five years of age left formal schooling before the age of fifteen years of age and so there is the considerable matter of social justice involved in catering for their needs. The great amount of leisure time experienced in contemporary society owing to shorter working weeks, earlier retiring ages, longer life expectancy and sometimes, alas, unemployment, allows opportunity for the development of personal interests through forms of educational services.

Adult education has been provided in a variety of forms by many agencies for a long period in Ireland. However, in line with an

273

increasing ·amount of change in many aspects of educational provision, the late 1960s experienced developments in adult education auguring a more concerned and co-ordinated approach to the issue. In 1969 a national association for adult education, Aontas, was founded. It was an advisory and consultative body for the promotion and development of adult education as well as a general reference and promotional agency in the field of adult education. In the same year the government took the initiative of setting up an advisory committee on adult education. Its terms of reference were 'to report on the needs of the Community in the matters of Adult Education, and to indicate the type of permanent organisation to be set up in order to serve those needs.'[1]

In a wide-ranging report presented to the government in November 1973, the committee endorsed new conceptions of adult education variously termed permanent, continuing and recurrent education and urged that adult education provision should not be a peripheral area of concern. Among its recommendations were the establishment of a special section in the Department of Education with a specific budget to service adult education, the establishment of regional and county education committees who would employ specialist officers to cater for adult education in their areas, the establishment of an inter-departmental committee concerned with adult education, and the recognition of Aontas as the national advisory body on adult education. Universities and other institutes of higher education were urged to take steps to provide training courses for adult and community education officers. The report urged that there should be improved information about, and communication between, the available agencies and facilities for adult education.

Although the organisational structures recommended by the adult education report have not been implemented, a greater sense of direction exists within adult education generally. Aontas, the National Association of Adult Education, has been accepted as the main advisory and consultative body as well as a general reference agency for all those involved in adult education. The government has indicated its intention of ratifying a convention of the International Labour Organisation which would entitle workers to paid educational leave as of right. Public demand for and awareness of the importance of adult education have greatly increased. Maynooth College has established a Department of Adult Education which offers a diploma course in adult education. Other universities have adult or extra-mural education officers with responsibility for fostering adult and community-oriented courses. In 1979 the Minister for Education allowed the VECs to make fifty new appointments of adult education officers. A ministerial committee is examining the potential for Irish circumstances of forms of 'distance-learning'. Some people feel that changing technology and reproduction equipment will allow greater flexibility in the use of prepared broadcast material in the years ahead.

The concept of permanent or continuing education has not become a reality. However, the idea gave rise to a working party of the NCEA to examine the feasibility of a more embracing concept, that of recurrent education. The NCEA published a discussion document on an NCEA award structure for recurrent education in May 1978.[2] It defined recurrent education as a distribution of education in a recurring way over the life-span of the individual. This would mean a break with the present practice of a long, uninterrupted pre-work period of full-time schooling which has been described as a 'front-end model'. It also implies the alternation of education with other activities of which the principal would be work, but which might also include leisure and retirement. Thus, what is envisaged is a dramatic change from age-old conceptions of schooling completed in childhood and youth as a preparation for adult life to availing of formal education periodically throughout a life-span.

The discussion document suggested the establishment of a new award in recurrent education, termed the foundation certificate, based on a modular course structure and using a wide range of teaching methods. Many existing courses could be incorporated within the scheme and a system of accreditation for work experience would be devised. Provision for the foundation certificate has been made by the NCEA. The NCEA's normal certificate and national diploma courses can be taken subsequent to the foundation certificate. It seems likely that future years will see significant developments in this area of adult education.

The *White paper on educational development* in 1980 endorsed the general educational guidelines of the report on adult education and identified as priority areas for provision of recurrent education the disadvantaged, the illiterate and those wishing to avail of second-chance education.[3] The vocational education committees were seen as having an important role in the development of comprehensive adult education services attuned to local needs.

The range of institutions and agencies providing adult education is very wide indeed. The VEC schools and colleges continue their impressive contribution by providing a vast range of courses in a variety of forms to suit participants. The community and comprehensive schools as well as some secondary schools do not confine their attentions to young people during daytime, but are frequently ablaze with light at night as many adults avail of special courses and facilities. The regional colleges and NIHEs have a strong commitment to adult education. They show considerable flexibility in their admission requirements and their formal courses can lead to professional qualifications. The universities offer extra-mural courses for the general public on campus and, in some instances, on a regional basis, and a number of diploma and degree courses which can be taken part-time at evenings and weekends. Maynooth College offers a diploma course in adult and community education. Voluntary bodies such as Macra na Feirme and the Irish Countrywomen's Association provide many courses, and Radio Telefís Éireann provide a range of adult education programmes.

There are a number of institutions specially devoted to adult education. These include the Dublin Institute of Adult Education which offers over seventy courses and which is funded jointly by the Department of Education and the Catholic archdiocese of Dublin. The National Adult Literacy Agency promotes a range of adult literacy programmes. The Irish Congress of Trade Unions operates the People's College and the Jesuit Order run the College of Industrial Relations, both in Dublin. All the agencies mentioned publish brochures about the courses they provide. Some of them place notices in the public press and during adult education week in September much publicity is given to the facilities available. In 1980 Aontas published its first edition of *National directory of adult and community education agencies* which provides valuable information, sources of information and contact personnel in the various agencies.

The whole area of youth employment training has assumed greater importance and has greatly expanded in recent years. The rising youth population, the effects on employment of economic recession and the changing job patterns and work practices have emphasised the need for training and re-training programmes. Ireland benefits from some EEC grants for such training schemes and an account of some of the main agencies involved — AnCO, CERT, agriculture training groups — is given in Appendix Three.

Short accounts are also included in Appendix Four on some of the training and research institutes which have grown up largely since the 1960s and outside the traditional educational framework.

As well as formal education courses there has been a considerable development of leisure and outward-bound activities of an educational character geared towards young adults. Groups such as the National Sports Council — Cospóir, the National Youth Council, Foróige and various sports organisations benefit from Department of Education grants to promote activities involving physical, health and environmental education.

Appendix One

The Structure of the
Irish Education System

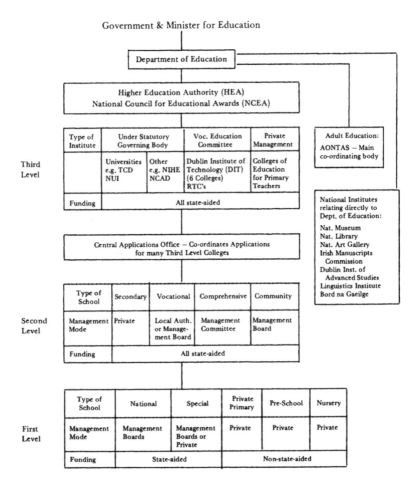

Government & Minister for Education

Department of Education

Higher Education Authority (HEA)
National Council for Educational Awards (NCEA)

Third Level

Type of Institute	Under Statutory Governing Body		Voc. Education Committee	Private Management
	Universities e.g. TCD NUI	Other e.g. NIHE NCAD	Dublin Institute of Technology (DIT) (6 Colleges) RTC's	Colleges of Education for Primary Teachers
Funding	All state-aided			

Adult Education:

AONTAS — Main co-ordinating body

National Institutes relating directly to Dept. of Education:

Nat. Museum
Nat. Library
Nat. Art Gallery
Irish Manuscripts Commission
Dublin Inst. of Advanced Studies
Linguistics Institute
Bord na Gaeilge

Central Applications Office — Co-ordinates Applications for many Third Level Colleges

Second Level

Type of School	Secondary	Vocational	Comprehensive	Community
Management Mode	Private	Local Auth. or Management Board	Management Committee	Management Board
Funding	All state-aided			

First Level

Type of School	National	Special	Private Primary	Pre-School	Nursery
Management Mode	Management Boards	Management Boards or Private	Private	Private	Private
Funding	State-aided		Non-state-aided		

278

Appendix Two

Some Specialist Schools and Educational Resources

1. There are a number of colleges of music, the following being the main ones:

> Royal Irish Academy of Music, Dublin (RIAM)
> Dublin College of Music
> Cork Municipal School of Music
> Limerick Municipal School of Music

The Royal Irish Academy of Music is the senior institute for the teaching of music in all its forms. It is an autonomous institution which gets some funds from the Department of Education. It has more than 3,000 students enrolled at various levels. Diplomas of associate in teaching and licentiate in teaching or performing may be obtained by examinations in schools and other centres throughout Ireland. Approximately 18,000 students are examined each year.

The Dublin College of Music and the Cork and Limerick Schools of Music are funded and run by the vocational education committees. They offer a wide range of courses and prepare students for internal college diplomas as well as external awards.

2. The Department of Education funds the National Film Institute which provides educational films for schools as well as promoting media education. Its education officer liaises with schools.

3. The Arts Council with the help of its education officer offers a range of facilities to schools in the arts area including a subsidised writers in schools scheme as well as loan and purchase facilities for works of art. The Arts Council is one of the agencies which fund TEAM — a theatre group specialising in educational and young peoples' theatre.

4. National cultural institutions such as the National Gallery of Art, the National Museum and the National Library have education officers who liaise with schools and help promote these institutions as educational resources. These institutions and societies preserved and collected much that is central to the cultural heritage of the nation. The National Museum contains the national collections pertaining to the antiquities, fine arts (exclusive of painting and sculpture) and the natural history of Ireland. The main collections are situated in Kildare Street and Merrion Street, Dublin and they are open free to the public at set hours on six days a week. Visits by school pupils are encouraged. It also provides slides and photographs of its most notable exhibits. The National Gallery of Art is situated in Merrion Square, Dublin and it too is open free to the public on six days a week. Public lecture series are held throughout the year and guided tours for school parties are arranged by the education officer. The Gallery is the main repository for painting and sculpture with over 2,000 oil paintings of all Western European Schools, about 4,000 drawings and watercolours, engravings and sculptures. The National Library in Kildare Street, Dublin houses a vast collection of manuscript and printed material by Irishmen or relating to Ireland and is the recognised Irish bibliographical centre. The Library also holds collections of prints, drawings, photographs, maps and newspapers. Readers' tickets are required to use the library and these are made available mainly to recommended adult readers, and sometimes to students. The National Library publishes a series of packs of facsimile documents on historical themes or personalities which assist the teaching of history in schools, and also organises special exhibitions. The National Museum, Gallery and Library are all funded by the Department of Education but benefit from donations and subscriptions from individuals and groups of patrons. It is intended that these institutions will come under the care of the proposed National Heritage Council.

5. Radio Telefís Éireann (RTE) provides some educational services. The potential contribution of RTE to the educational system has never been satisfactorily tapped. It has suffered from a lack of long-term planning in the context of divided authority between the Department of Education and RTE, and also from the inadequate financial resources to provide sustained high-level

service. In 1977 only 1.82 per cent of the total output of radio broadcasting was devoted to educational broadcasting and only 5.7 per cent of television broadcasting was devoted to adult and school/pre-school education categories. The report of a special advisory body in 1979 considered that school broadcasting had reached a point of crisis.*

Telefís Scoile was initiated in February 1964 and produced programmes linked to the post-primary examination syllabuses. A cut-back in funding in 1975 has meant severe curtailment of any new material for this series. A pilot programme, Radio Scoile, was introduced for Gaeltacht schools in April 1975 but did not lead to the establishment of a general schools' radio service. A short pre-school programme on both radio and television is in operation. A number of interesting and valuable programmes have been broadcast on both radio and television in the area of formal adult education but the demands, needs and scope of adult education call for a much more thorough response from RTE. A weekly radio programme on educational affairs is transmitted at present.

Among its recommendations for improvement the advisory committee in 1979 urged the setting up of a schools broadcasting council and a council for adult education broadcasting. It also urged the setting up of a radio service for primary schools, extending the radio provision for post-primary schools as well as providing new material for school television. For pre-school children daily programmes on radio and television were recommended with some attention to helping adults in assisting early childhood education. Adult education on a wider scale, including industrial education and education for the disadvantaged, was advocated by the committee. In the context of the developments in information and media technology, it seems likely that the potential of radio and television both in the range of materials that could be provided and the flexibility of their use will come to play a more central role within educational provision and resources in the decades ahead. In 1980 the Minister for Education convened a representative committee on educational broadcasting to advise him on future policy. A committee was also

*Report of Advisory Committee on Educational Broadcasting, (Dublin: Radio Telefís Éireann, 1979), p. 12

established in 1980 to explore the possibilities of distance-learning, with the aid of the broadcasting media.

Appendix Three

Employment Training Institutions

There are several agencies charged with the responsibility of training and education relating to particular types of employment. The whole area of training and, indeed, re-training for employment has become a growth area in Irish society. The following gives an outline of the main training agencies and their various functions.

Industrial and Apprentice Training (AnCO)
The Apprenticeship Act of 1959 which had set up An Céard Comhairle (The Apprenticeship Board) was repealed by the Industrial Training Act, 1967. This set up An Comhairle Oiliúna (The Industrial Training Authority), popularly known as AnCO. AnCO subsumed the functions of the earlier apprenticeship board. AnCO was given wide responsibilities for training at every level in industry and commerce throughout the country. It has given priority to the training needs of industry and co-operates with firms and educational bodies which have functions in this field. AnCO depends on two main sources for its funding, grants-in-aid from the Irish government and grants from the European Social Fund. The grants from these two sources amounted to £21,760,606 in 1978. In 1980 a total of about 16,000 people were trained by AnCO on its various courses.

AnCO's industrial training policy operates under three headings (1) training within industry, (2) training centres, and (3) apprentice training. With regard to (1) AnCO provides support in a number of ways to companies undertaking training programmes. A levy/grant scheme exists through which firms pay a percentage of their payroll (variable according to firm size) into a fund. The levy may be paid back in grants if firms follow training requirements laid down by AnCO. Under a technical assistance grants scheme AnCO pays up to 50 per cent of the cost of attendance at courses by managers and supervisors as well as trade union officials. Special support exists for training courses in new industries. AnCO has a team of training advisers to assist in the planning of all such courses. With regard to (2), training centres, AnCO has established fifteen permanent training centres in the following places: Athlone, Millfield — Cork, Douglas — Cork, Ballyfermot, Beresford Place — Dublin, Cabra, Tallaght, Dundalk, Galway, Gweedore, Limerick, Sligo, Shannon, Tralee and Waterford. It services other locations by means of AnCO mobile units. The centres offer a wide range of courses for young people and adults of both sexes. With regard to (3), statutory apprenticeship schemes are administered by AnCO, and in 1980, 21,498 apprentices were registered with that body. Since 1976 the total period of apprenticeship has been reduced from five to four years. Apprentices who achieved Grade D in four Leaving Certificate subjects may be allowed to complete their apprenticeship in three years. All apprentices receive a period of 'off the job' training in their first year which is provided in centres approved by AnCO and run by AnCO, the VECs or industry. Applicants must be at least fifteen years of age and have obtained Grade D in any three subjects of the Group or Intermediate Certificate. All apprentices are required to attend appropriate day or block release courses in vocational educational establishments during their first three years. It is the responsibility of the prospective apprentices to get in touch with suitable employers and then inquire about vacancies. When the apprenticeship has been obtained, AnCO, which must be satisfied that the firm is suitable for providing a proper apprenticeship, will register the apprentice and issue a card. The apprentice carries out his on-the-job training in the approved employment workplace. At the end of the course a compulsory test and certification occur. The Department of Education operates the junior and senior trade certificates. Some apprentices also take the London City and Guilds examinations.

The National Manpower Service (NMS)

The NMS, operating under the Department of Labour, assists job seekers to find suitable jobs and employers to recruit workers. The Service, which is organised on a regional basis, collects information on the labour market. It provides occupational guidance and advises workers about alternative employment and training facilities. A careers information service is also provided.

Training for the hotel and tourism industry (CERT)

The Council for Education, Recruitment and Training for the Hotel Industry (CERT) was set up in 1963. It is the national body responsible for co-ordinating the education, recruitment and training of staff for the hotel, catering and tourism industries. The chairman and council of CERT are appointed by the Minister for Labour and are representative of appropriate interests in the hotel and tourism fields. CERT's income revenue in 1980 amounted to £1,567,000, 98 per cent of which came from the Department of Labour and the European Social Fund.

CERT holds a national recruitment campaign each year, aimed at boys and girls of Intermediate and Group Certificate standard. In May and June 1980, 2,569 boys and girls applied and 563 places were allocated at eight training centres. Formal training is provided in management, reception, housekeeping, cookery, food service, bar and tourist-guiding. In conjunction with the VECs CERT co-ordinates this training at thirteen locations and in 1980 a total of 1,738 people received formal training. Trainees are provided with free accommodation, transport, uniforms and equipment as well as a weekly training grant. Trainees are placed in industry for a period of supervised work experience, during which CERT makes a financial contribution towards their wage costs. CERT also offers in-service courses of varying duration to meet specific needs of existing staff in the industries. In 1980 a total of 3,669 staff were trained by CERT on in-service courses. Industry-based training is assisted by training advisers and eight-man teams of training services. CERT's training centre at Roebuck, Dublin provides training courses for unemployed people as well as some specialised courses to meet the needs of the industry.

Agricultural and other training

Since its establishment in 1980 ACOT (The Council for Development in Agriculture) has assumed responsibility for most of the advisory services and educational courses in agriculture. It operates the advisory and training schemes designed to develop agriculture and horticulture and to benefit rural districts formerly conducted by the County Committees of Agriculture. Winter agricultural classes and winter farm schools are conducted throughout the country. Courses in poultry-keeping and farm home management are available for females. Eleven agricultural colleges and six home-economics colleges provide basic training in farm management and related subjects. Most of the colleges are under the control of ACOT and others, under private management, are state-aided. Standard syllabuses are followed in the colleges and certificates are awarded upon successful completion of courses. A third form of agricultural training is that provided by the Farm Apprenticeship Board which provides practical training for young people who, having spent one year in an agricultural college, intend to make a career in farming. The apprenticeship course lasts for up to four years and leads to a qualification in farm management, the Farm Apprenticeship Certificate. The Munster Institute, which was founded in 1853, as well as offering short courses in poultry management also offers a three-year residential course in (1) poultry keeping and dairying, and (2) farm home management. The Department of Dairy Science in UCC offers a two-year diploma course which qualifies students for careers as creamery managers. It is likely that agricultural education will expand considerably in the years ahead under the influence of ACOT.

A number of other government Departments run institutions which provide various forms of apprenticeship and training. The Department of Fisheries and Forestry operates a number of forestry schools which provide theoretical and practical training for trainee foresters. The Department of Defence is responsible for the Air Corps apprentice training school and the army school of music. Institutions for the training of marine radio officers are conducted under the aegis of the Department of Posts and Telegraphs.

Appendix Four

Some Research and Training Institutes

There has been a considerable growth and expansion of research and training institutes in recent decades, outside the formal third-level education structures. Many of the long established societies such as the Royal Dublin Society, the Royal Irish Academy, the Royal Society of Antiquaries of Ireland continue to operate, promoting knowledge, skill and interest relating to various facets of Irish culture. As was the case with higher education and education generally in the early 1960s, a survey team was also set up to examine the research situation in 1963, jointly by the Minister for Industry and Commerce and the OECD. It was asked to assess scientific and technological research activities performed in Ireland with a view to formulating recommendations for the balanced development of national research effort over the following fifteen years, in relation to economic growth. In their report the survey team expressed concern about the danger of too many, separate research institutes being established and urged that a careful look should be taken when planning further initiatives to see if they could best be furthered in the universities or existing institutes. The report urged the establishment of a national science council which inter alia would have the function of advising the government generally on appropriate national policies for research, development and technology. It also called for a national policy for research, development and technology and for a national authority that would co-ordinate research. In the event, succeeding years have seen the expansion of existing, and the setting up of many new, research and training institutes, some state-sponsored and others largely owing to private initiatives.

This appendix describes briefly some of these institutes and the role they perform in Irish society today. There are many other professional and voluntary societies, spanning a very wide range of activities and interests, whose work could be termed educational.

287

However, the very number of such societies, the fact that their training work is mainly professional and that information on them is available elsewhere urge a selective rather than comprehensive inclusion of institutes or societies for the present purposes.

Royal Dublin Society (RDS)

The Royal Dublin Society was founded in 1731 to promote agriculture, industry, science and arts. It got its royal charter in 1750. It was involved in the foundation of a number of national institutions such as the Botanic Gardens, the National Museum, the National Library, the College of Science and the Veterinary College. The Society publishes two research journals — the *Journal of earth sciences* and the *Journal of life sciences*. It promotes interest in agriculture, science and the humanities by means of lectures, exhibitions, recitals, competitions, short special courses and its extensive library. The RDS promotes major international events such as the Spring Show, the Horse Show, the Industries Fair and the Winter Fair. Its current membership stands at 13,500.

Royal Irish Academy

The Royal Irish Academy was founded in 1785 and incorporated by royal charter in 1786. The Academy is a society for the advancement of science and learning, or as its charter puts it for 'promoting the study of science, polite literature, and antiquities'. It has about 250 members elected on grounds of academic distinction. The Academy is governed by a president and a council of twenty-one members elected annually. It is financed by a government grant-in-aid, the income from trust funds and the sale of publications, including *Proceedings of the Royal Irish Academy*. Further state grants are received for specific projects of a large-scale character relating to Irish culture, such as *The new history of Ireland* and the *National atlas of Ireland*. The Academy's library, as well as holding important collections of books and pamphlets relating to Irish society, also contains many of Ireland's most precious ancient manuscripts.

Irish Manuscripts Commission

The Commission was established by the government in 1928 and is run by a chairman and board appointed by the government on the proposal of the Minister for Education. Its terms of reference include the following: to report and advise on collections, manuscripts and other papers of historical significance to Ireland; to prepare after consultation with universities and other learned bodies, programmes of work to be undertaken; editing, preparation and publication of calendars and catalogues of manuscripts and papers, unpublished texts and manuscripts.

Dublin Institute of Advanced Studies

This Institute was founded by act of parliament in 1940. It has three schools – Celtic studies, theoretical physics and cosmic physics. The Institute is operated under the aegis of the Department of Education and it is financed wholly out of state funds. Each school is under the management of a governing board. The general government of the Institute and the administration of its affairs are vested in the council of the Institute. It is specified in the establishment order of each school that one of its functions is 'the training of advanced students in methods of original research'. This is done each year by the award of a limited number of research scholarships, the normal qualification for candidates being a PhD degree, or its equivalent, in an appropriate subject. Scholars are required to be in full-time attendance in the schools. There is no formal teaching or lecturing in the Institute but seminars, summer courses and symposia are held from time to time and are attended by professors and scholars from Ireland and abroad.

The Linguistics Institute of Ireland

The Linguistics Institute was established to carry out research and experimentation on various aspects of language study including the teaching and learning of language, with particular reference to the Irish language. The members of the Institute's council, all part-time, are appointed by the Minister for Education. There is a permanent director whose appointment has to be approved by the Minister.

The National Board for Science and Technology

The National Board for Science and Technology was established in 1978 under the terms of the National Board for Science and Technology Act, 1977. The Board is the chief adviser to the government on policy and planning in the field of science and technology in Ireland and is the central organisation for promotion and co-ordination in this area. The Board must prepare and review a national programme for science and technology. Further, the

Board is required to co-ordinate activities related to science and technology and to promote the co-ordination of public investment with private investment in these areas. It prepares a science budget based on the proposals of all institutions engaged wholly or partly in science and technology, and who are in receipt of state monies. In addition the Board has promotional functions relating to research, science and technology and to the application of science and technology to economic and social development and the development of national resources. The Board also liaises with many international agencies related to its field of concern. The Board for Science and Technology operates under the aegis of the Department of the Taoiseach.

The Institute of Public Administration (IPA)

The Institute of Public Administration was founded in 1957 by a group of public servants working in the civil service, local government and the state-sponsored bodies sectors. Its aim is to promote the study and improve the standard of public administration. A voluntary body, the Institute in 1963 became a company limited by guarantee. It is open to individual and corporate membership. It derives its income from fees and from an annual government grant-in-aid.

The Institute provides a wide variety of services, mainly educational. It offers short-term courses on specialised subjects to the public service; it provides a one-year whole-time course in public administration at graduate level as well as a one-year part-time course. The Institute also offers a diploma in administrative science after a four-year course of study. Diploma holders can attend Trinity College for one year's further study leading to an honours degree in public administration. The Institute undertakes administrative research projects, engages in training of administrative students from developing countries and publishes books and periodicals dealing with Irish government and public affairs, in particular *Young Citizen*, the social education magazine for schools.

The Economic and Social Research Institute (ESRI)

The Economic Research Institute was founded in 1960 to undertake applied economic research in Ireland. It was renamed the Economic and Social Research Institute in 1966 when the state took over the major financing of the Institute. It is an independent, non-profit-making body whose research is designed to increase knowledge of the social and economic conditions in Ireland and to help provide relevant data for policy-makers. The main disciplines pursued by the Institute are economics, sociology, social psychology and statistics. The council of the Institute is representative of Irish universities both north and south, and of employers' organisations, trade unions, banking and government departments. The Institute has about seventy staff members including forty researchers. The Institute provides research facilities for university staff as well as post-graduate training in the social sciences by means of fellowships, research assistantships and by lectures and seminars. As well as producing registers and commentaries on social affairs the Institute has published up to 100 reports in its general research series.

There are many other state-sponsored agencies which conduct research and training activities relating to specific spheres of responsibility including the following:

— The Agricultural Institute (An Foras Talúntais) is the national agricultural research organisation and it organises many conferences for the dissemination of research findings.

— The National Institute for Physical Planning and Construction Research (An Foras Forbartha) provides research, training and advisory services in relation to the physical environment.

— The Institute for Industrial Research and Standards (IIRS) engages in many applied research programmes and acts as the Irish national standards organisation responsible for drawing up standard specifications.

— The Medico-Social Research Board carries out studies into the incidence of human disease and the operation of the health services and advises the Minister for Health on such matters.

— The National Economic and Social Council (NESC) promotes studies on many facets of Irish economic and social life and acts as an advisory body to the government.

— The Irish Management Institute (IMI) is an independent agency which benefits from state grants. It is concerned mainly with management development and training in finance, marketing, production and personnel.

Information details on these and other organisations involved in research and training may be obtained in the *Administration Yearbook and Diary* published annually by the Institute of Public Administration, and from the agencies themselves.

Notes to Chapters

Chapter One

1. See Corcoran *State policy in Irish education*; Corcoran *Education systems in Ireland*; Jones *Charity school movement*
2. See Dowling *Hedge schools of Ireland*; Brenan *Schools of Kildare and Leighlin*; O'Connell *Schools and scholars of Breifne*
3. See O'Boyle *Irish colleges on the continent*
4. See Bowen *Protestant crusade* pp. 61-82, 195-258
5. See Corish (ed.) 'The church since emancipation: Catholic education'
6. See Balfour *Educational systems of Great Britain and Ireland* p. 79
7. See Akenson *Irish education experiment*. This specialised study of the national system in the nineteenth century is very helpful on the background to the emergence of the system.
8. See *Copy of Report of Commissioners of Irish education enquiry* (1791)
9. See *Fourteenth report of the commissioners of the board of education in Ireland* (1812-13)
10. See Moore *An unwritten chapter in the history of education*; Lynch 'The Kildare Place Society, 1811-1831' (MA thesis)
11. See *Ninth report of the commissioners of Irish education inquiry* (1826-27)
12. See *Report from the select committee to whom the reports on the subject of education in Ireland were referred* (1828)
13. See *Copy of letter from the Chief Secretary of Ireland to the Duke of Leinster, on the formation of a board of commissioners for education in Ireland* (1831-2)
14. See McDowell *The Irish administration*
15. See Ó Raifeartaigh 'Mixed education and the synod of Ulster, 1831-40'; McIvor *Popular education in the Irish Presbyterian church*
16. See Kelly 'Education', and *Census of Ireland* (1902) CXXIX, p. 81
17. See Fitzpatrick *The life, times and correspondence of Dr. Doyle*
18. See Costello *John MacHale, Archbishop of Tuam*; for the effects on schools in Connaught see Kelly 'National system of education in Connaught 1831-70' (MA thesis), and Fahy *Education in the diocese of Kilmacduagh*
19. *Rescript of Pope Gregory XVI to the four Archbishops of Ireland*
20. See Hayes 'The educational ideas of Paul Cardinal Cullen'
21. See Vidler *The church in an age of revolution* pp. 146-156
22. Kavanagh *Mixed education* gives an interesting, if partisan, contemporary account of controversies in these years.
23. Norman *The Catholic Church and Ireland in the age of rebellion*
24. Daly 'The development of the national school system 1831-40'

gives an interesting account of events at local level in the early years of the national school system.

25. See McNeill *Vere Foster* pp. 101-180
26. See Goldstrom *The social content of education*
27. See Wall 'The decline of the Irish language'; de Fréine *The great silence* pp. 66-74 passim
28. See Kaestle *Joseph Lancaster and the monitorial school movement*
29. For an interesting contemporary perspective see Sullivan *Lectures and letters on popular education*
30. See Ó hEideáin *National school inspection in Ireland*
31. See Burke 'Agricultural education in Ireland under the national board 1831-70' (MEd thesis)
32. See *Royal commission of inquiry into primary education (Ireland)* Vol. 1, pt. 1: *Report of the commissioners* (C6), H.C. 1870, XXVIII, Pt 1. Vol. II, as well as the seven other volumes of material relating to the report in H.C. 1870, XXVIII parts ii to v.
33. See *Report of the commissioners* p. 293
34. See Coolahan 'The ideological framework of the payment by results policy in nineteenth-century education'
35. See *Annual reports of the commissioners of national education* for the years in question.
36. See Coolahan 'The payment by results policy in the national and intermediate schools of Ireland' (MEd thesis)
37. The regulations and duties of teachers can be found in Appendix A of any of the annual reports of the commissioners of national education.
38. See O'Connell *The story of the INTO* pp. 7-10 passim
39. See *Fiftieth report of the commissioners of national education*, (1884) pp. 15-18; Parkes 'The

founding of a denominational training college – the Church of Ireland College, 1878-84'
40. See Selleck *The new education*
41. See *Royal commission on manual and practical instruction in primary schools: final report* (1898)
42. See *Revised programme of instruction in national schools*, published in appendix of annual reports of commissioners 1900-1921
43. See INTO Executive Committee's statement in *The Irish Teacher's Journal* XXXIV/37 (27 October 1900) 4-6
44. See Starkie *Recent reforms in Irish education*; O'Riordan *A reply to Dr. Starkie's attack on the managers of national schools*; and Curry *Dr Starkie and the catholic school managers of Ireland*
45. See *Report of Mr. F.H. Dale on primary education in Ireland* (1904)
46. See Mac Aodha 'Was this a social revolution?'
47. See *Dale Report* (1904) pp. 1020-1026
48. Pastoral letter of the Catholic hierarchy, quoted in *The Teacher's Journal* XXXIV (6 October 1900) 4
49. See *Freeman's Journal* 19 April 1904; Miller *Church, state and nation in Ireland 1898-1921* pp. 113-138
50. See *Report of the vice-regal committee of inquiry into primary education 1918* (Killanin) (1919)
51. See Coolahan 'A study of curricular policy for the primary and secondary schools of Ireland, 1900-35' (PhD thesis) pp. 145-254
52. See National Programme Conference *National programme of primary instruction* p. 3
53. See *Report of the Department of Education* (1924-25) p. 21
54. Quoted in *The Irish School Weekly* 11 February 1922, p. 127

55. See National Programme Conference *Report and Programme* (1926)

56. Department of Education *Revised Programme of Primary Instruction* (1934)

57. See *Annual reports of the Department of Education for 1931*, pp. 39, 51

58. See *Report of committee on inspection of primary schools* (1927) pp. 16-18; *Report of commission on technical instruction* (1927) p. 37

59. See *Dáil Éireann Proceedings* vol. 83, col. 1097, 27 May 1941

60. See Irish National Teachers' Organisation *Report of committee of enquiry into Irish as a teaching medium*

61. *Report of commission on vocational organisation* (1944)

62. See Irish National Teachers' Organisation *A plan for education*

63. See *Report of the council of education on (1) the function of the primary school, (2) the curriculum in the primary school* (1954)

64. *Irish Times* 5 January 1923

65. McNeill, 'A view of the state in relation to education'. For a later example see General Mulcahy's (Minister for Education) address to the Council of Education in *Terms of reference of the council of education* (1950). See also Mescal *Religion in the Irish system of education* pp. 56, 100

66. *Report of the national programme conference* (1926) p. 16

67. Quoted in Rev. E. Cahill *The framework of a christian state* p. 374

68. See *Dáil Éireann Proceedings* vol. XVI, cols. 463, 464, 7 June 1926

69. See O'Connell *The story of the INTO* pp. 440-446

70. See *Investment in Education* (1966) par. 9.72, p. 259; par. 9.75, p. 260

71. See *Report of the Department of Education* (1924-25) p. 41

72. See *Report of committee on inspection of primary schools* (1927) p. 7

73. See O'Connell *The story of the INTO* pp. 213-234

Chapter Two

1. See MS 2455, pcc/52 and pcc/64, in Lord St. Aldwyn MSS (Hicks-Beach's Papers)

2. See Lee *The modernisation of Irish society, 1848-1918* pp. 16-19

3. See Council of Education *Report on the curriculum of the secondary school* (1962)

4. See Sexton 'The lay teachers' struggle for status in catholic secondary schools in Ireland, 1878-1937' (MEd thesis)

5. See *Report of Messrs. Dale and Stephens on intermediate education in Ireland* (1905) p. 61

6. See *Copy of report of the commissioners of Irish education enquiry* (1791) p. 364

7. See *Report from the select committee on foundation schools and education in Ireland* (1837-8); see also Wyse *Education reform*

8. See *Report of the commissioners appointed to enquire into the endowments, funds and actual condition of all schools endowed for the purpose of education in Ireland* (1857-8) p. 269

9. See *Census of Ireland, 1871* (1876); see also Committee of Irish Catholics *Intermediate education*

10. See Birch *St. Kieran's College, Kilkenny*; Corcoran *The Clongowes Record, 1814-1932*; and various centenary volumes of the older, established colleges

11. See Monsell MS 8317, Keenan and Sullivan to Emly, July 1875

12. See *Census of Ireland, 1871* (1876) Pt. III, p. 163

13. See, for instance, Shaw 'How to improve school education in

Ireland'

14. See Diligite Justitiam (ed. Howley?) *Inner history of the intermediate act*; Farragher, series of articles on the background to the Intermediate Act in *Blackrock College Annuals*, (1957-60 and 1978); Edwards 'The beginning of the Irish Intermediate Education system'; *The Secondary Teacher* 8/1,2 (1978) special feature on centenary of 1878 Intermediate Act

15. See Monsell MS 8317, Keenan to Emly, 2 December 1876

16. See *Intermediate Education (Ireland) Act*, 1878 (41, 42 Vict. c.66)

17. For details of the operation of the system see Coolahan 'Payment by results in national and intermediate schools' (MEd thesis); Byrne 'The Irish Intermediate Education Act, 1878 — before and after' pp. 126-144

18. See *Census of Ireland, 1901* (1902) p. 83

19. See *Commission on Intermediate Education (Ireland) 1898* First Report with Appendix (c. 9116, c. 9117), H.C. 1899, XXii; *Final Report* (c. 9511), H.C. 1899, XXii; *Evidence* (c. 9512), H.C. 1899, XXiii; Pt. II of *Appendix to Final Report* (c. 9513), H.C. 1899, XXIV

20. See *Dale and Stephens report* (1905)

21. See Ó Buachalla (ed.) *A significant Irish educationist*

22. See Hubard 'Intermediate education in Ireland'

23. See Starkie *History of primary and secondary education during the last decade* p. 3.

24. See *Dale and Stephens report* (1905) p. 756

25. See Sexton 'The lay teachers' struggle for status in Catholic secondary schools in Ireland 1878-1937' (MEd thesis); Riordan 'The association of secondary teachers, Ireland, 1909-68' (MEd thesis)

26. See *Intermediate Education (Ireland) Act* 1914 (4,5 Geo. V.c.41)

27. For a valuable study of this and other issues see McElligott *Secondary education in Ireland, 1870-1921*

28. See *Report of the vice-regal committee on the conditions of service of teachers in intermediate schools, and on the distribution of grants from public funds for intermediate education* (1919) p. 661

29. *ibid.*, p. 679

30. *ibid.*, p. 677 ff.

31. See Coolahan 'The Education Bill of 1919 — problems of educational reform'

32. See *Report of the Intermediate Education Board for 1919* (1920) p. viii

33. See Whyte *Church and state in modern Ireland 1923-70* p. 21 ff

34. See *Report of the Department of Education for 1924-25* (1926) p. 7

35. See *The School Weekly* LXX (October 1921) 104

36. Original reports in Office of Minister for Education

37. See *Irish Times* 8 November 1926; *Times Educational Supplement* 27 November 1927

38. See Report of the Survey Team *Investment in education* (1966) p. 280, par. 10.26

39. See *Investment in education, annexes and appendices* (1966) p. 310, Table v, c. 4

40. See *Report of Investment in education team* p. 61, Table 4.3

41. See Council of Education *The curriculum of the secondary school* (1962) p. 18, par. 163

Chapter Three

1. See Byrne, 'Mechanics institutes in Ireland, 1825-50'

2. See Keating 'Sir Robert Kane and the Museum of Irish industry'

3. See *Technical Instruction Act* 1889 (52, 53 Vict. c. 41)

4. See *Report of the Recess committee on the establishment of a department of agriculture and industries for Ireland* (1896)

5. See *The Agriculture and Technical Instruction (Ireland) Act* 1899 (62 and 63 Vict. c. 50)

6. See Clune 'Horace Plunkett' (MEd thesis)

7. See O'Donovan 'A study of the influence of Archbishop W.J. Walsh on primary and post-primary education in Ireland, 1890-1901' (MEd thesis) pp. 70-91

8. See *Report of the Department of Agriculture and Technical Instruction* (DATI) for the year 1901-02 p. 881

9. See *Report of DATI* for 1919-20 p. 92

10. See *Report of the Department Committee of Inquiry into the Provisions of the Agriculture and Technical Instruction Act, 1899* (1907) p. 905

11. See *Report of DATI* for 1919-20, p. 99

12. See *Report of DATI* for 1918-19, p. 171

13. See *Report of the commission on technical education* (1927) p. 12

14. *ibid.*, p. 31

15. See *Report of the Department of Education for 1930-31* p. 167

16. See *Report of commission on technical education* (1927) p. vii

17. *ibid.*, p. 18

18. See *Vocational Education Act* 1930 (No.29) in public statutes of the Oireachtas (1930) pp. 601 ff

19. *ibid.*, p. 601

20. See Letter from J.M. O'Sullivan, Minister for Education, to Most Rev. Dr Keane, Bishop of Limerick, 31 October 1930

21. See Department of Education *Vocational continuation schools and classes, memorandum for the information of committees* (1931)

22. See Department of Education *Organisation of whole-time continuation courses, memorandum V40* (1942)

23. See O'Riordan 'Technical/vocational education'

24. See *Report of the Department of Education for 1959-60* p. 89

25. See *Report of the Department of Education for 1937-38* p. 74

26. See *Report of commission on vocational organisation* (1944) pp. 217, 220

27. See *Report of Department of Education for 1959-60* pp. 118, 121

28. For changing conceptions of the system see Dolan 'The origins of the vocational education system and changing conceptions of it, 1930-1978' (MEd thesis)

Chapter Four

1. See Moody 'The Irish university question of the nineteenth century'; O'Rahilly 'The Irish university question'

2. See Sanderson (ed.) *The universities in the nineteenth century*

3. See Maxwell *A history of Trinity* p. 5

4. See Kearney *Scholars and gentlemen* pp. 56-70, 172

5. See Maxwell *A history of Trinity* p. 148

6. *ibid.*, p. 211, and *Report of the commissioners appointed to inquire into the state, discipline, studies and revenues of the university of Dublin* (1852-3)

7. See O'Boyle *The Irish colleges on the continent*

8. See Ó Fiaich *Ma Nuad* p. 21 & 32; Healy *Maynooth College*

9. See *Report from the select committee on foundation schools and education in Ireland* (1837-38) vii, p. 345

10. See *Bill to enable Her Majesty to endow new colleges for the advancement of learning in Ireland* (1845)

11. Quoted in Moody and Beckett *Queen's, Belfast* vol. 1, p. 1

12. See Gwynn O'*Connell, Davis and the Colleges' Bill*
13. Rescripts printed in Battersby *Catholic directory, almanac and registry for 1851* pp. 130-134
14. See *ibid.*, p. 189, and Whyte 'Political problems 1850-60' p. 8
15. See Sir Robert Kane *The Queen's University and the Queen's Colleges*
16. See *Charter, statutes etc. of Royal University of Ireland*, (Dublin: HMSO, 1882)
17. See *Final report of the commissioners on university education (Ireland)* (1903) p. 25
18. *ibid.*, p. 9
19. For a detailed analysis of Newman's experiment see McGrath *Newman's university*
20. For facets of the Catholic University's history see Tierney (ed.) *Struggle with fortune*
21. See McKenna 'The Catholic University of Ireland' p. 370
22. See Fathers of the Society of Jesus *A page of Irish history*
23. See Holmes *Magee 1865-1965* p. 70
24. College of Science Association *The College of Science for Ireland* pp. 13, 14
25. Norman *The Catholic church and Ireland in the age of rebellion* pp. 446-454
26. See Larkin *The Roman Catholic Church and the plan of campaign, 1886-88* pp. 29-31
27. See Walsh *The Irish university question*
28. See *Final report of the commissioners on university education* (1903) (Robertson Commission)
29. See *Final report of the royal commission on Trinity College, Dublin, and the University of Dublin* (1907) (Fry Commission)
30. See *Irish Universities Act* 1908 (8 Edw. 7) in *Public General Acts* 1908 (ch. 38)
31. *ibid.*, third schedule of the Act
32. See *Report of the royal commission on the University of Dublin* (1920)
33. See Bailey *A history of Trinity* p. 41
34. See de Brún 'Iolsolaíocht trí Gaeilge'. The jubilee issue 1908-58 of *The University Review* II/3 & 4 (1958) has some interesting articles on the development of education within the national university colleges.
35. For details of foreign students in Irish universities (1940-65) see *Commission on Higher Education* (1967) vol. 2, chap. 30, pp. 789-809
36. *ibid.*, vol. 1, p. 31, table 12
37. *ibid.*
38. *ibid.*, vol. 2, p. 733

Chapter Five

1. See *Second programme for economic expansion* Part 1 (1963), par. 14
2. See *Dáil Éireann Proceedings* vol. 177, cols. 470-471, 28 October 1959
3. See National Economic and Social Council *Educational expenditure in Ireland* (1975) p. 38

Chapter Six

1. See *White paper on educational development* (1980)
2. See Economic and Social Research Institute *Irish educational expenditures* (1978) (Tussing Report) pp. 96, 97
3. See Sheehan *Future enrolments in third-level education* pp. 6, 7, 8; Irish Federation of University Teachers *University financing in Ireland* pp. 2, 3
4. See *White paper on educational development* (1980) pp. 8, 75, 76
5. See Hyland Associates *Report on Department of Education school transport scheme* (1979) and *White paper on educational development* (1980) p. 89
6. See Higher Education Authority (Clancy and Benson) *Higher education in Dublin* (1979) p. 16

7. See *Dáil Eireann Proceedings* vol. 326, col. 1005, 4 February 1981 (unrevised) and Tussing 'Accountability, rationalisation and the white paper on educational development' p. 13
8. See National Economic and Social Council *Educational expenditure in Ireland* (1975) p. 14
9. *ibid.*, p. 16
10. See ESRI *Educational expenditures* (1978) p. 175. In this context see also Sheehan & Barlow *Financing education.*
11. See *Programme for national development 1978/81* (1979) p. 86
12. See *White paper on educational development* (1980) p. 79
13. See *Adult education in Ireland* (1973) p. 15
14. See *Census of population, 1971* vol. XII
15. See Arts Council Working Party (Ciaran Benson) *The place of the arts in Irish education* (1979)

Chapter Seven

1. For reference to this and other cases see Osborough 'Education in the Irish law and constitution'
2. See *Rules for national schools* (1965) (most recent edition) p. 8
3. For an account of this pilot plan see *Dalkey School Project* available from 20 Burdett Avenue, Sandycove, County Dublin
4. See *Rules for national schools* (1965) Rule 68, p. 38

Chapter Nine

1. See *Investment in education* (1966) and *Investment in education – annexes and appendices* (1966)
2. See *Dáil Éireann Proceedings* vol. 225, col. 1854, 6 December 1966
3. See O'Connor 'Post-primary education: now and in the future' p. 233

Chapter Ten

1. See *Investment in education* (1966) Table 9.22, p. 226, and *Statistical report of Department of Education for 1978/79* Table 5, p. 18
2. See *Primary school curriculum: teachers' handbook* vols. 1 and 2 (1971)
3. See *Statistical report of Department of Education for 1974/75* Tables 10.1 and 11.1, pp. 22, 23, and also *Statistical report of Department of Education for 1978/79* Tables 12 and 13, pp. 22, 23
4. See *Dáil Éireann Proceedings* vol. 326, cols. 738, 740, 3 February 1981 (unrevised report)
5. See *White paper on educational development* (1980) Table 2, p. 3
6. See *Investment in Education* (1966) Table 1.2, p. 4, and *Statistical report of the Department of Education for 1978/79* Table 6, p. 18
7. See *Primary school curriculum: teachers' handbook* (1971) Part 1, p. 12
8. See Irish National Teachers' Organisation *Primary school curriculum: questionnaire analysis*; Conference of Convent Primary Schools *Evaluation of the new curriculum for primary schools* and Educational Research Centre (Fontes and Kellaghan) *The new primary school curriculum: its implementation and effects*
9. See McGee 'An examination of trends in reading achievement in Dublin over a ten-year period'
10. For this and other statistics relating to 1978/9 see *Statistical report of Department of Education for 1978/9*

Chapter Eleven

1. See *Report of commission of inquiry on mental handicap* (1965)
2. See *Statistical report of the*

Department of Education for 1970/71, and figures made available by the Department of Education for 1980.

3. See *Report of committee on the education of children who are handicapped by impaired hearing* (1972)
4. See Holland *The Rutland Street Project*
5. See Department of Education report on educational facilities for the children of itinerants (1970) pp. 44-53
6. See Robins *The Lost Children* p. 305
7. See *Statistical report of the Department of Education for 1968/9-1971/2* Table 1, p. 74
8. See *Report on the reformatory and industrial school systems* (1970)
9. See *Task force on child care services – final report* (1980) pp. 193, 272

Chapter Twelve

1. Speech delivered by Dr Hillery at a press conference on 20 May 1963.
2. See Circular from Minister for Education, George Colley, to the authorities of secondary and vocational schools, January 1966 p. 3
3. See *Report of Department of Education 1960-61*, p. 136 and *Statistical report of Department of Education for 1966-67* p. 50
4. Speech by Donogh O'Malley to the National Union of Journalists in Dun Laoghaire, 10 September 1966
5. See *Statistical reports of the Department of Education from 1966 to 1975*
6. See Circular issued by the Department of Education on community schools, October 1970. Reprinted in *Studies* LIX/236 (Winter 1970) 341-345
7. See Educational Research Centre

(Madaus and McNamara) *Public examinations: a study of the Irish Leaving Certificate* (1970)
8. See Coolahan (ed.) *University entrance requirements*
9. See *The Intermediate Certificate examination report (ICE)* (1975)
10. See Heywood, McGuinness, & Murphy *Final report of the public examinations evaluation project*
11. See Raven *Education, values and society*; Mulcahy *Curriculum and policy in Irish post-primary education*
12. See AIM Group *Education is everybody's business*
13. See Arts Council Working Party (Benson) *The place of the arts in Irish education* (1979)
14. See *White paper on educational development* (1980), Par. 6.19, p. 48
15. *ibid*., par. 10.34, pp. 78, 79
16. See *Dáil Éireann Proceedings* vol. 326, No. 4, col. 735, 3 February 1981

Chapter Thirteen

1. See *Government white paper on the restoration of the Irish language* (1965) pp. 98-140
2. See *Report of the Department of Education for 1958/59* Appendix II, p. 56
3. See *Statistical report of the Department of Education for 1978/79* Table 18, p. 28
4. See *Statistical report for 1958/59* Appendix III, p. 79
5. See *Statistical report for 1978/79* Table 3a, p. 65
6. *ibid.*
7. See Comhairle na Gaeilge *Irish in Education* (1974)
8. See *The white paper on educational development* (1980) pp. 13-23

Chapter Fourteen

1. See *Investment in education* (1966) Table 1.1, p. 4, and *Statistical report for 1978/79*

pp. 30, 66, 72, 78

2. See *Report on the establishment of An Chomhairle Mhúinteoireachta* (1974)

3. See *Interim report of review body on teachers' pay* (1980)

4. See Belbenoit *In-service education and the training of teachers in the European Community*

Chapter Fifteen

1. See Commission on Higher Education *Report* vols. I and II (1967)

2. See *The Irish Times* 18 April 1967

3. See Higher Education Authority *Report on university re-organisation* (1972)

4. See *Irish Independent* 17 December 1974

5. See Higher Education Authority (Clancy and Benson) *Higher education in Dublin* (1979) pp. 13, 16

6. See Steering Committee on Technical Education *Report on regional technical colleges* (1967)

7. See *White paper on educational development* (1980) Table 8, p. 73

8. See Higher Education Authority *A council for national awards and a college of higher education at Limerick* (1969)

9. See Higher Education Authority *Report on Ballymun project* (1970)

10. See Higher Education Authority (Clancy and Benson) *Higher education in Dublin* (1979)

11. See *Commission on Higher Education Report* (1967) Vol. 1, Table 8, p. 26, and *Statistical report for 1978/79* Table 1, p. 2

12. See, for instance, National Economic and Social Council *Educational expenditure in Ireland* (1975) p. 24, and Economic and Social Research Institute (Tussing) *Irish educational expenditures* p. 177

13. See *White paper on educational development* (1980) p. 76

14. See *Estimates for the public services* (1980) p. 48

15. See *Dáil Éireann Proceedings* 1979, vol. 320, cols. 103-104

16. See *White paper on educational development* (1980) pp. 8, 9

17. See Higher Education Authority *Accounts 1978 and student statistics 1978/79* Series No. 7, Table 38, p. 69

18. *ibid.*, p. 16

19. See *Statistical report of the Department of Education for 1978/79* pp. 96, 97

Chapter Sixteen

1. See Report of Advisory Committee *Adult education in Ireland* (1974)

2. See National Council for Educational Awards *Discussion document on an award structure for recurrent education* (1978)

3. See *White paper on educational development* (1980) p. 91

Bibliography

This bibliography contains items cited in the text and a limited number of other important sources for the study of modern Irish education. It is arranged as follows:

1. Manuscript sources
2. Official publications of United Kingdom government prior to Irish independence
   (a) Bills and Acts (chronological order)
   (b) Reports of commissions and committees on Irish education (chronological order)
   (c) Annual reports of the Commissioners of National Education, of the Intermediate Education Board for Ireland and of the Department of Agriculture and Technical Instruction
3. Official publications of the Irish Free State and the Irish Republic relating to education
   (a) Bills and Acts (chronological order)
   (b) Official reports etc. on the education system (chronological order)
   (c) Annual reports of the Department of Education
4. Some official reports on areas cognate to education and reports of various other agencies on education
5. Newspapers and magazines
6. Unpublished theses
7. Books and pamphlets
8. Articles
9. Helpful reference guides for research students on modern Irish education

1. Manuscript sources

Minutes of the meetings of the Commissioners of National Education 1831-1900 (manuscript); 1900-1921 (printed) (National Library of Ireland)

Minutes of the meetings of the Commissioners of Intermediate Education 1878-1900 (manuscript); 1900-1920 (printed) (Department of Education, Dublin)

Larcom Papers, MSS 7652-7655, National Library of Ireland

Monsell Papers, MS 8317, National Library of Ireland

Mayo Papers, MS 11,217

Bonaparte-Wyse Papers, unsorted and uncatalogued, National Library of Ireland

Doyle Papers, MS 8466, National Library of Ireland

Lord St. Aldwyn Papers, MSS 2455 et al., Record Office, County Hall, Gloucester.

2.   Official Publications of United Kingdom Government prior to Irish independence

(a)   Bills and Acts (chronological order)

Bill to enable Her Majesty to endow new colleges for the advancement of learning in Ireland H.C. 1845 (299) I

Charter of incorporation lately granted by Her Majesty to the board of national education in Ireland H.C. 1846 (193) XLII, 191

Bill for the extension of university education in Ireland H.C. 1873 (55) VI, 329

Bill to provide for additional payments to teachers in national schools in Ireland H.C. 1875 (223) IV, 407

Intermediate Education (Ireland) Act H.C. 1878 (275) III, 543

Bill intituled, an Act to promote the advance of learning and to extend the benefits connected with university education in Ireland H.C. 1878-79 (283) VII, 599

Bill for improving the position of teachers in national schools in Ireland H.C. 1878-79 (246) IV, 555

Bill intituled, an Act to reorganise the educational endowments of Ireland H.C. 1884-85 (176) I, 445

Bill to enable councils of counties and municipal boroughs to provide technical schools and classes H.C. 1889 (211) VII, 223

Bill for the distribution and application of certain duties of customs and excise: and for other purposes connected therewith H.C. 1890 (404) VI, 437

Bill to improve national education in Ireland H.C. 1892 (420) IV, 645

Agriculture and technical instruction Act H.C. 1899 (280) I, 73

Bill to amend the law relating to intermediate education in Ireland H.C. 1900 (315) II, 515

Bill to provide for the establishment and function of an administrative council in Ireland and for other purposes connected therewith H.C. 1907 (182) II, 481

The Irish Universities Act H.C. 1908 (358) II, 1097

Bill to amend the law relating to intermediate education in Ireland H.C. 1913 (322) III, 205

Bill to amend the law relating to secondary education in Ireland H.C. 1914 (161) III, 477

Bill to make further provision with respect to education in Ireland and for other purposes connected therewith H.C. 1919 (214) I, 407

2. (b) Reports of commissions and committees on Irish education (chronological order)

Copy of report of the commissioners of Irish education enquiry (1791), in report of the commissioners appointed to inquire into the endowments, funds and actual conditions of all schools endowed for the purpose of education in Ireland Vol. II, H.C. 1857-58 (2336-1) XXII, Pt. III, pp. 341-79

Fourteenth report of the Commissioners of the Board of Education in Ireland H.C. 1812-13 (21) V, 221

Ninth report of the Commissioners of Irish Education inquiry H.C. 1826-27 (516) XIII

Report from the select committee to whom the reports on the subject of education in Ireland were referred H.C. 1828 (341) IV

Copy of the letter from the Chief Secretary of Ireland to the Duke of Leinster, on the formation of a board of commissioners for education in Ireland H.C. 1831-2 (196) XXIX

Report of the select committee appointed to inquire into the progress and operation of the new plan of education in Ireland H.C. 1837 (485) IX, 1

Report from the select committee on foundation schools and education in Ireland H.C. 1837 (701) VII, 345

Report of the commissioners appointed to inquire into the state, discipline, studies and revenues of the University of Dublin H.C. 1852-3 (1637) XLV, 1

Report from the select committee of the House of Lords appointed to inquire into the practical working of the system of national education in Ireland, with minutes of evidence Part 1, H.C. 1854 (525) XV, Pt. II,1; Part II, H.C. 1854 (525) XV, Pt. II,1

Report of Her Majesty's Commissioners appointed to inquire into the endowment, funds and actual condition of all schools endowed for the purposes of education in Ireland H.C. 1857-58 (2336-1) XXII, Pt. I,1

Report of the commissioners appointed to inquire into the nature and extent of the instruction afforded by the several institutions in Ireland for the purpose of elementary or primary education; also into the practical working of the system of national education in Ireland Vol. 1, Part I, H.C. 1870 (C.6) XXVIII, 1; Part II, Vols. 1-V111, H.C. 1870, XXV111, Pts. II-V

Census of Ireland 1871, Pt. 111, H.C. 1876 (C. 1377) LXXXI

Census of Ireland 1901, Pt. 11, H.C. 1902 (Cd. 1190) CXXIX

Royal commission on manual and practical instruction in primary schools under the Board of National Education in Ireland — final report H.C. 1898 (C. 8923) XLIV, 1. Further reports, evidence and appendix in H.C. 1897, XLIII and H.C. 1898, xliv

Report of the Commissioners on Intermediate Education (Ireland) — final report H.C. 1899 (C. 9511) XXII, 629. First report, appendices and evidence in H.C. 1899 XXII, XXIII, XXIV

Report of the Commissioners on University Education (Ireland) — final report H.C. 1903 (Cd. 1483-4) XXXII, 1. First, second and third reports in H.C. 1902, XXXI, XXXII

Report of Mr. F.H. Dale, His Majesty's inspector of schools, Board of Education, on primary education in Ireland H.C. 1904 (Cd. 1981) XX, 947

Report of Messrs. F.H. Dale and T.A. Stephens, His Majesty's inspectors, Board of Education, on intermediate education in Ireland H.C. 1905 (Cd. 2546) XXVIII, 709

Report of the royal commission on Trinity College, Dublin, and the University of Dublin — final report H.C. 1907 (Cd. 3311-12) XLI,1. First report H.C. 1906 (Cd. 3174, 3176) LVL, 601

Report of the departmental committee of inquiry into the provisions of the agricultural and technical instruction act, 1899 H.C. 1907 (Cd. 3572) XVII, 799. Evidence and appendix in H.C.'1907, XVIII

Report of vice-regal committee of inquiry into primary education (Ireland) 1913 – final report H.C. 1914 (Cd. 7235) XXVIII, 1081. Other reports and appendixes H.C. 1913, XXII; H.C. 1914, XXVIII

Report of vice-regal committee of inquiry into primary education (Ireland) 1918 – final report H.C. 1919 (Cmd. 60) XXI, 741. Evidence, memoranda etc. in H.C. 1919 (Cmd. 178) XXI

Report of the vice-regal committee on the condition of service and remuneration of teachers in intermediate schools and on the distribution of grants from public funds for intermediate education in Ireland H.C. 1919 (Cmd. 66) XXI, 645

Report of the royal commission on the University of Dublin H.C. 1920 (Cmd. 1678) XIII, 1189

2. (c) Annual reports

The annual reports of the Commissioners of National Education (1834-1921), of the Commissioners of the Intermediate Education Board for Ireland (1879-1920) and of the Department of Agriculture and Technical Instruction (1901-1920) contain vital data on the development of their respective branches of education. It is important to note that the appendixes to the annual reports contain such material as statistics, programmes of instruction, rules and regulations, correspondence, inspectors' reports. The following list relates only to annual reports specifically referred to in the text.

Report of the Recess committee on the establishment of a department of agriculture and industries for Ireland (Dublin: Browne and Nolan, 1896). Although not a government report, this report was very influential in the area of technical education.

Fiftieth report of the commissioners of national education for the year 1883 H.C. 1884 (4053)

Report of the department of agriculture and technical instruction for the year 1901-02 H.C. 1902 (Cd. 1314) XX

Report of the intermediate education board for the year 1919 H.C. 1920 (Cd. 904) XV

Report of the department of agriculture and technical instruction for 1918-19 H.C. 1920 (Cmd. 929) IX

Report of the department of agriculture and technical instruction for the year 1919-20 Dublin: H.M.S.O., 1921

3. **Official Publications of the Irish Free State and the Irish Republic relating to education**

(a) **Bills and Acts (chronological order)**

Intermediate Education (Amendment) Act 1924 No 47 in public statutes of the Oireachtas

School Attendance Act, 1926 No 17 in public statutes of the Oireachtas

Vocational Education Act, 1930 No. 29 in public statutes of the Oireachtas

Apprenticeship Act, 1959 No 39 in public statutes of the Oireachtas

Vocational Education (Amendment) Act, 1970 No 15 in public statutes of the Oireachtas

Higher Education Authority Act, 1971 No 22 in public statutes of the Oireachtas

National Council for Educational Awards Act, 1979 No 30 in public statutes of the Oireachtas

(b) **Official reports on the education system (in chronological order**

National Programme Conference *National programme of primary instruction* Dublin: Browne and Nolan, 1922

Department of Education *Programme for students in training 1924-25* Dublin: Alex Thom, 1924

Department of Education *Rules and programmes for secondary schools 1924-25*

National Programme Conference *Report and programme* Dublin: Stationery Office, 1926

Committee on inspection of primary schools *Report* Dublin: Stationery Office, 1927

Commission on Technical Education *Report* Dublin: Stationery Office, 1928

Department of Education *Vocational continuation schools and classes, memorandum for the information of committees* 1931

Department of Education *Notes for teachers* (in various national school subjects), Dublin: Stationery Office, 1933-34

Department of Education *Revised programme of primary instruction* Dublin: Stationery Office, 1934

Inter-departmental committee on the raising of the school leaving age *Report* Dublin: Stationery Office, 1936 (P. 2086)

Department of Education *Organisation of whole-time continuation courses, memorandum V 40* 1942

Department of Education *Terms of reference to the Council of Education and inaugural addresses* Dublin: Stationery Office, 1950

Department of Education *Report of the council of education on (1) the function of the primary school, (2) the curriculum to be pursued in the primary school* Dublin: Stationery Office, 1954 (Pr. 2583)

Report of the council of education on the curriculum of the secondary school Dublin: Stationery Office, 1962 (Pr. 5996)

Commission on the restoration of the Irish language *Summary of the final report* Dublin: Stationery Office, 1963 (Pr. 7256)

Department of Education *Rules for national schools* Dublin: Stationery Office, 1965 edition

Government white paper on the restoration of the Irish language Dublin: Stationery Office, 1965 (Pr. 8061)

Investment in education — report of the survey team Dublin: Stationery Office, 1966 (Pr. 8311)

Investment in education — annexes and appendices Dublin: Stationery Office, 1966 (Pr. 8527)

Commission on Higher Education 1960-67 *Presentation and summary of report* vol. I (Pr. 9326); *Report* chapters 1-9, vol. II (Pr. 9389); *Report* chapters 20-32, vol. III (Pr. 9588) Dublin: Stationery Office, 1967

Steering committee on technical education *Report to the Minister for Education on regional technical colleges* Dublin: Stationery Office, 1967 (Prl. 371)

Tribunal on teacher salaries *Report presented to the Minister for Education* Dublin: Stationery Office, 1969 (Prl. 87)

Department of Education report on educational facilities for the children of itinerants in *Oideas* 5 (Autumn, 1970) pp. 44-53

Reformatory and industrial schools systems *Report* Dublin: Stationery Office, 1970 (Prl. 1342)

Department of Education *Curaclam na Bunscoile — Primary School Curriculum — Teacher's Handbook, Parts 1 and 2,* Dublin: Browne and Nolan, 1971

Report of committee on *The education of children who are handicapped by impaired hearing* Dublin: Stationery Office, 1972

Comhairle na Gaeilge *Irish in education* Dublin: Stationery Office, 1974

Planning Committee *Report on the establishment of An Chomhairle Mhúinteoireachta* 1974, limited circulation

Report of advisory committee *Adult education in Ireland* Dublin: Stationery Office, 1973 (Prl. 3465)

Committee on the form and function of the Intermediate Certificate Examination *Final report* (ICE) Dublin: Stationery Office, 1975 (Prl. 4429)

Department of Education *White paper on educational development* Dublin: Stationery Office, 1980 (Prl. 9373)

Review body on teachers' salaries *Interim report* Dublin: Stationery Office, 1980 (Prl. 9232)

Department of Education *Rules and programmes for secondary schools* Dublin: Stationery Office, published annually

3. (c) Annual reports of the Department of Education

The annual reports of the Department of Education 1924-25 to 1963-64.

Department of Education *Tuarascáil Tablaí Staitistic* (Statistical Report) 1964-65 to 1978-79.

The reports specifically referred to in the text are as follows:

Report of the Department of Education for the school year 1924-25 and the financial and administrative years, 1924-25-26 (Dublin: Stationery Office, 1926)

Report of the Department of Education 1930-31 (P. 733); 1937-38 (P. 3588); 1938-39 (P. 4281); 1958-59 (Pr. 5905); 1959-60 (Pr. 6218); 1960-61 (P. 6718);

Department of Education Tablaí Staitistic (Statistical Report) 1966-67 (Prl. 1121); 1968-69 —; 1971-72 (Prl. 3041); 1974-75 (Pr. 6223); 1978-79 (Pr. 8704)

4. Some official reports on areas cognate to education and reports of various other agencies on education (in chronological order)

Coimisiún na Gaeltachta *Report* Dublin: Stationery Office, 1926

Statement of government policy on the recommendations of Coimisiún na Gaeltachta Dublin: Stationery Office, 1928

Commission on vocational organisation *Report* Dublin: Stationery Office, 1944 (P. 6743)

Second programme for economic expansion Dublin: Stationery Office, 1963 (Pr. 7669)

Commission of inquiry on mental handicap *Report* Dublin:

Stationery Office, 1965 (Pr. 8234)

National Industrial Economic Council (NIEC) *Comments on 'Investment in Education'* Dublin: Stationery Office, 1966 (P. 8886)

Central Statistics Office *Census of population, 1966* vol. VII: 'Education', Dublin: Stationery Office (Prl. 1195)

Central Statistics Office *Census of population, 1971* vol. XII, Dublin: Stationery Office (Prl. 7415)

OECD *Reviews of national policies for education in Ireland* Paris: OECD, 1968

Higher Education Authority *First report, 1968-69* Dublin: Stationery Office, 1969 E/66

Higher Education Authority *A council for national awards and a college of higher education at Limerick* Dublin: Stationery Office, 1969 (Prl. 586)

Educational Research Centre (G. Madaus and J. McNamara) *Public examination: a study of the Irish Leaving Certificate* Dublin: Educational Research Centre, 1970

Higher Education Authority *Report on teacher education* Dublin: Stationery Office, 1970 E/67

Higher Education Authority *Report on university re-organisation* Dublin: Stationery Office 1972 (P. 2276)

Higher Education Authority *Report on Ballymun project* Dublin: Stationery Office, 1972 E/74

Higher Education Authority *Accounts and student statistics each year from 1972/73 up to 1978/79* Dublin: Higher Education Authority, Accounts Series Nos. 1-7

National Council for Educational Awards *Annual reports, 1972-73 to 1978-79* Dublin: National Council for Educational Awards

Higher Education Authority *Progress report, 1974* Dublin: Higher Education Authority, 1974

Higher Education Authority (Monica Nevin) *School performance and university achievement* Dublin: Higher Education Authority, 1974

National Council for Educational Awards *Art and design education* Dublin: NCEA, 1974

National Council for Educational Awards *Curriculum development in third-level education* Dublin: NCEA, 1974

National Council for Educational Awards *The planning and co-ordinating role of the NCEA* Dublin: NCEA, 1974

Government of Ireland *Bunreacht na hÉireann (Constitution of*

Ireland) Dublin: Stationery Office, 1975 edition

The National Council for Educational Awards *The NCEA in higher education* Dublin: NCEA, 1975

National and Economic Social Council (NESC) *Educational expenditure in Ireland* Report No 12, Dublin: Stationery Office, 1975 (Prl. 4730)

Conference of Convent Primary Schools *Evaluation of the new curriculum for primary schools* Dublin: 1975

National Council for Educational Awards *Student assessment in third-level education* Dublin: NCEA, 1976

National Economic and Social Council *Population projections 1971-86: the implications for education* Report No 18, Dublin: Stationery Office, 1976

Educational Research Centre (Patricia Fontes and Thomas Kellaghan) *The new primary school curriculum: its implementation and effects* Dublin: Educational Research Centre, 1977

Economic and Social Research Institute (ESRI) (Dale Tussing) *Irish educational expenditures – past, present and future* Paper No 92 Dublin: ESRI, 1978

Higher Education Authority (John Sheehan) *Future enrolments in third-level education* Dublin: Higher Education Authority, 1978

National Council for Educational Awards *Discussion document on an award structure for recurrent education* Dublin: NCEA, 1978

National Council for Educational Awards (J.P. Hennessy) *Higher technological education: employment needs and educational capacity in the 1980s* Dublin: NCEA, 1978

Higher Education Authority (Patrick Clancy and Ciaran Benson) *Higher education in Dublin: a study of some emerging needs* Dublin: Higher Education Authority, 1979

Radio Telefís Éireann *Report of Advisory Committee on Educational Broadcasting* Dublin: RTE, 1979

Arts Council's Working Party (Ciaran Benson) *The place of the arts in Irish education* Dublin: The Arts Council, 1979

Hyland Associates *Report on Department of Education school transport scheme* Dublin: Stationery Office, 1979 (Prl. 7837)

Estimates for public services, 1980 Dublin: Stationery Office, 1980 (Prl. 8699)

Public capital programme 1980 (Prl. 8363)

Task Force on child care services – final report Dublin: Stationery

Office, 1980 (Prl. 9345)

Heywood, J., McGuinness, S. and Murphy, D. *Final report of the public examinations evaluation project* Dublin: School of Education, Trinity College, 1980

5. Newspapers and magazines
Education Times
Fraser's Magazine
Freeman's Journal
Irish Independent
Irish Times
Irish Ecclesiastical Review
Irish School Weekly
Irish Teachers Journal
Nineteenth Century
Oideas
Secondary Teacher
Studies
University Review

Collections of newspapers cuttings on education in Public Record Office, Dublin (1899-1922)

6. Unpublished theses
Burke, Matthew. 'Agricultural education in Ireland under the national board, 1831-70' MEd thesis, University College, Dublin, 1979

Byrne, Mary M. 'The origins and development of services for the mentally handicapped in Ireland 1700-1960 with special reference to educational provision' MA thesis, University College, Dublin, 1979

Clune, Michael. 'Horace Plunkett and the origins and development of the department of agriculture and technical instruction 1895-1907' MEd thesis, Trinity College, Dublin, 1978

Coolahan, John. 'The payment by results policy in the national and intermediate schools of Ireland' MEd thesis, Trinity College, Dublin, 1975

'Curricular policy for the primary and secondary schools of Ireland 1900-35' PhD thesis, Trinity College, Dublin, 1973

Donovan, Patrick F. 'A study of the influence of Archbishop W.J. Walsh on primary and post-primary education in Ireland,

1890-1901' MEd thesis, University College, Dublin, 1979

Dolan, Paul. 'The origins of the vocational education system and changing conceptions of it, 1930-1978' MEd thesis, University College, Dublin, 1979

Kelly, P.J. 'The national system of education in Connaught, 1831-70' MA thesis, University College, Dublin, 1975

Lynch, Michael A. 'The Kildare Place Society, 1811-31' MA thesis, University College, Cork, 1958

Riordan, Patrick. 'The Association of Secondary Teachers, Ireland, 1909-68' MEd thesis, University College, Cork, 1975

Sexton, Peter. 'The lay teachers' struggle for status in Catholic secondary schools in Ireland 1878-1937' MEd thesis, University of Birmingham, 1972

7. Books and pamphlets

AIM Group. *Education is everybody's business* Dublin: Kincora Press, 1979

Akenson, Donald H. *The Irish education experiment: the national system of education in the nineteenth century* London: Routledge and Kegan Paul, 1970

A mirror to Kathleen's face: education in independent Ireland, 1922-60 Montreal and London: McGill — Queen's University Press, 1975

Atkinson, Norman. *Irish education: a history of educational institutions* Dublin: Allen Figgis, 1969

Aughmuty, J.J. *Irish education, a historical survey* Dublin: Hodges Figgis, 1937

Bailey, Kenneth C. *A history of Trinity College, Dublin 1892-1945* Dublin: Dublin University Press, 1947

Balfour, Graham. *The educational system of Great Britain and Ireland* Oxford: Clarendon Press, 1903

Batterberry, R. *Oideachas in Éirinn, 1500-1946* Dublin: Stationery Office, 1955

Battersby, W.J. *Catholic directory, almanac and registry for 1851* Dublin: Battersby, 1851

Belbenoit, G. *In-service education and the training of teachers in the European Community* Brussels: Commission of the European Communities, 1979

Birch, Rev. Peter. *St. Kieran's College, Kilkenny,* Dublin: Gill, 1951

Bowen, Desmond. *The Protestant crusade in Ireland, 1800-70*

Dublin: Gill and Macmillan, 1978

Brenan, Martin. *Schools of Kildare and Leighlin, 1775-1835* Dublin: Gill, 1935

Butt, Isaac. *The problem of Irish education* London: Longmans Green, 1875

College of Science Association *The College of Science for Ireland, its origins and development* Dublin: Dublin University Press, 1923

Committee of Irish Catholics *Intermediate education* Dublin: Kelly, 1872

Coolahan, John, (ed.). *University entrance requirements and their effect on second-level curricula* Dublin: Irish Federation of University Teachers, 1979

Corcoran, Timothy. *State policy in Irish education* Dublin: Fallon, 1916

Education systems in Ireland from the close of the middle ages Dublin: University College Dublin, 1928

The Clongowes Record, 1814-1932 Dublin: Browne and Nolan, 1932

Cahill, Rev. Edward. *The framework of a christian state* Dublin: Gill, 1932

Corish, Patrick J. (ed.). 'The Church since emancipation: Catholic education', vol. V in *A history of Irish catholicism* Dublin: Gill and Macmillan, 1971

Costello, Nuala. *John MacHale, Archbishop of Tuam* Dublin: Talbot Press, 1939

Curry, Rev. John. *Dr Starkie and the Catholic school managers of Ireland* Dublin: Browne and Nolan, 1903

De Fréine, Seán. *The great silence* Cork: Mercier, 1978

Diligite, Justitiam. (Ed. Howley) *Inner history of the Intermediate Act* Dublin, 1886

Dill, Sir Samuel. *Secondary education after the war* Dublin: Educational Company, 1916(?)

Dowling, P.J. *The hedge schools of Ireland* Cork: Mercier, 1968 edition

A history of Irish education: a study of conflicting loyalties Cork: Mercier, 1971

Duffy, P.J. *The lay teacher in Ireland* Dublin: Fallon, 1967

Durcan, Thomas J. *History of Irish education* (with special reference to manual instruction) North Wales: Dragon Books, 1972

Fahy, Sr.Mary de Lourdes. *Education in the diocese of Kilmacduagh in the nineteenth century* Gort: Convent of Mercy, 1972

Fathers of the Society of Jesus. *A page of Irish history: the story of University College, Dublin 1883-1909* Dublin: Talbot Press 1930

Fitzpatrick, J. *The life, times and correspondence of Dr Doyle* Dublin: Duffy, 1880

Federation of Irish Secondary Schools *Investment in education in the Republic of Ireland, with some comparative statistics* Dublin: Federation of Irish Secondary Schools, 1962

Gaelic League *Special pamphlets on education* Nos. 1-27 Dublin: Gaelic League, 1900-02

Goldstrom, J.M. *The social content of education 1808-70: a study of Irish school textbooks* Shannon: Irish University Press, 1972

Gwynn, Denis. *O'Connell, Davis and the Colleges' Bill* Cork: Cork University Press, 1948

Healy, John. *Maynooth College: its centenary history* Dublin: Browne and Nolan, 1895

Hillery, Patrick J. *Statement of Dr P.J. Hillery, Minister for Education, in regard to education* Dublin: mimeo, 1963

Hine, Maurice. *An apology for the intermediate* Dublin: McGee, 1899

The efficiency of Irish schools Dublin, 1889

Holmes, R.F.G. *Magee 1865-1965* Belfast, BMC Printing, Co., 1965

Holland, Seamus. *The Rutland Street project* London: Pergamon, 1979

Howley, Edward. *The universities and secondary schools of Ireland, with prospects for their improvement* Dublin: Kelly, 1871

Irish Federation of University Teachers *University financing in Ireland* Dublin: Irish Federation of University Teachers, 1975

Irish National Teachers Organisation *A plan for education* Dublin: INTO, 1947

Report of committee of enquiry into Irish as a teaching medium Dublin: INTO, 1941

Primary school curriculum questionnaire analysis Dublin: INTO, 1976

Inservice education and the training of teachers Dublin: INTO, 1979

The administration of national schools: a proposal for growth

Dublin: INTO, 1980

Jones, M.G. *The charity school movement* Cambridge: Cambridge University Press, 1938

Joyce, P.W. *A handbook of school management and methods of teaching* Dublin: Gill, 1892 edition

Kaestle, Carl F. *Joseph Lancaster and the monitorial school movement: a documentary history* New York and London: Teachers College Press, 1973

Kane, Sir Robert. *The Queen's University and the Queen's Colleges: their progress and present state* Dublin: 1856

Kearney, Hugh. *Scholars and gentlemen: universities in pre-industrial Britain* London: Faber and Faber, 1970

Kavanagh, James. *Mixed education, the Catholic case stated* Dublin and London: 1859

Larkin, Emmet. *The Roman Catholic Church and the plan of campaign, 1886-88* Cork: Cork University Press, 1978

Lee, Joseph. *The modernisation of Irish society, 1848-1918* Dublin: Gill and Macmillan, 1973

Lyons, F.S.L. *Ireland since the famine* London: Collins/Fontana, 1973 edition

McDowell, R.B. *The Irish administration, 1801-1914* London and Toronto: Routledge and Kegan Paul, 1964

McElligott, T.J. *Education in Ireland* Dublin: Institute of Public Administration, 1966

Secondary education in Ireland 1870-1922 Dublin: Irish Academic Press, 1981

McGrath, Fergal. *Newman's university — idea and reality* Dublin: Browne and Nolan, 1951

McGréil, M. *Educational opportunity in Dublin* Dublin: Catholic Communications Institute, 1974

McHugh, Stan. *The school survival kit* Dublin: Wolfhound Press, 1980

McIvor, John A. *Popular education in the Irish Presbyterian church* Dublin: Scepter, 1969

McNamara, John. *Bilingualism in primary education: a story of Irish experience* Edinburgh: University Press, 1966

McNeill, Mary. *Vere Foster 1819-1900, an Irish benefactor* Newton Abbot: David and Charles, 1971

McQuaid, Most Rev. John C. *Catholic education, its function and scope* Dublin: Catholic Truth Society, 1942

Higher education for Catholics Dublin: Gill, 1961

Maxwell, Constantia. *A history of Trinity College Dublin, 1591-1892* Dublin: Dublin University Press, 1946

Mescal, John. *Religion in the Irish system of education* London and Dublin: Clonmore and Reynolds, 1957

Miller, David W. *Church, state and nation in Ireland, 1898-1921* Dublin: Gill and Macmillan, 1973

Moody. T.W. and Beckett J.C. *Queen's, Belfast, 1845-1949: the history of a university* 2 vols., London: Faber and Faber, 1959

Moore, H. Kingsmill. *An unwritten chapter on the history of education being the history of the society for the education of the poor of Ireland generally known as the Kildare Place Society* London: Macmillan, 1904

Murphy, Michael W. *Education in Ireland — 1, 2, 3* Cork: Mercier, 1970, 71, 72

Mulcahy, Donal G. *Curriculum and Policy in Irish Post-Primary Education* Dublin: Institute of Public Administration, 1981

Murphy, Christina. *School report* Dublin: Ward River Press, 1980

Norman, E.R. *The Catholic church and Ireland in the age of rebellion 1859-73* London: Longmans, 1965

Ó Buachalla, Seamas. (ed.). *A significant Irish educationist: the educational writings of P.H. Pearse* Cork: Mercier, 1980

Ó Catháin, Seán S.J. *Secondary education in Ireland* Dublin: Talbot Press, 1958

O'Boyle, J. *The Irish colleges on the continent, their origin and history* Dublin: Browne and Nolan, 1935

O'Connell, Philip. *The schools and scholars of Breifne* Dublin: Browne and Nolan, 1942

O'Connell, T.J. *History of the Irish National Teachers' Organisation, 1868-1968* Dublin: INTO, 1969

Ó Cuiv, Brian (ed.). *A view of the Irish language* Dublin: Stationery Office, 1969

Ó Fiaich, Tomás. *Ma Nuad* Ma Nuad: An Sagart, 1972

Ó hEideáin, Eustás. *National school inspection in Ireland: the beginnings* Dublin: Scepter, 1967

O'Meara, John. *Reform in education* Dublin: Mount Salus Press, 1958

O'Riordan, Michael. *A reply to Dr. Starkie's attack on the managers of national schools* Dublin: Gill, 1903

Randles, Eileen. *Post-primary education in Ireland 1957-70* Dublin: Veritas, 1975

Raven, John. *Education, values and society: the objectives of education and the nature and development of competence* London: H.K. Lewis, 1977

Robins, Joseph. *The lost children: a study of charity children in Ireland 1700-1900* Dublin: Institute of Public Administration, 1980

Rescript of Pope Gregory XVI to the four archbishops of Ireland Dublin: 1841

Sanderson, Michael (ed.). *The universities in the nineteenth century* London: Routledge and Kegan Paul, 1975

Selleck, R.J.W. *The new education: the English background, 1870-1914* Melbourne: Pitman, 1968

Sheehan, J. and Barlow, A.C. *Financing education* Cork: Department of Adult Education, University College, Cork, 1981

Starkie, W.J.M. *Recent reforms in Irish education* Dublin: Blackie, 1902

  History of primary and secondary education during the last decade Dublin, 1911

Sullivan, Robert. *Lectures and letters on popular education* Dublin: Curry, 1842

Swan, T. Desmond. *Reading standards in Irish Schools* Dublin: Educational Company, 1978

Tierney, Michael. *Education in a free Ireland* Dublin: Martin Lester, 1919(?)

  (ed.) *Struggle with fortune* Dublin: Browne and Nolan, 1954

Tuairim. *Irish education* Surrey: Stonecot Printing Co., 1961(?)

Vidler, Alec R. *The Church in an age of revolution* Middlesex: Penguin, 1974 edition

Walsh, Most Rev. W.J. *Statement of the chief grievances of Irish Catholics* Dublin: Browne and Nolan, 1890

  The Irish university question: the Catholic case Dublin: Browne and Nolan, 1897

Whyte, John H. *Church and state in modern Ireland 1923-70* Dublin: Gill and Macmillan, 1971 edition

Windle, Sir Bertram. *The prospects for education in Ireland today* Athlone, 1917

Wyse, Thomas. *Education reform* London, 1836

8. Articles

Brenan, Rev. Martin. 'The vocational schools' in *Irish Ecclesiastical Record* 5th Ser., LVII (February, 1941) 13-27

Breathnach, R.A. 'Revival or survival: an examination of the Irish language policy of the State' in *Studies* XLV (1956) 129-145

Byrne, Kieran. 'Mechanics institutes in Ireland, 1825-50' in *Proceedings of the Educational Studies Association* (1979) 32-47

Byrne, Rev. P. 'The Irish Intermediate Education Act, 1878 – before and after' in *Irish Ecclesiastical Record* 5th Ser. (January 1915) 16, 17; (February, 1915) 126-44

Coolahan, John. 'The ideological framework of the payment by results policy in nineteenth-century education' in *Proceedings of the Educational Studies Association* (1977) 166-172

'The Education Bill of 1919 – problems of educational reform' in *Proceedings of the Educational Studies Association* (1979) 11-31

Crooks, Tony. 'Research and Development in curriculum and examinations at second level in Ireland' in *Compass* 6/2 (1977) 26-46

Daly, Mary. 'The development of the national school system, 1831-40' in A. Cosgrave and D. MacCartney (eds.) *Studies in Irish history* Dublin: University College Dublin, 1979, 151-63

de Brún, Mons. Pádraig. 'Iolscholaíocht trí Ghaeilge' in *University Review* 1/7 (1955) 24-33

(ed.) 'Community Schools' in *Studies* LIX (Winter 1970) 341-76

Edwards, R. Dudley. 'The beginnings of the Irish intermediate education system' in *Catholic university centenary book* Dublin: Catholic University School, 1967, 47-58

Farragher, Rev. S. 'Blackrock and the Intermediate Act' in *Blackrock College Annual* (1958) 11-20

'Centenary education – intermediate education' in *Blackrock College Annual* (1960) 66-73

'Intermediate education 1878-1978' in *Blackrock College Annual* (1978) 6-16

Finlay, Rev. Tom S.J. 'Practical education in our schools' in *Journal of the Statistical and Social Inquiry Society of Ireland* XI (1905) 351-362

Hayes, Charles. 'The educational ideas of Paul Cardinal Cullen' in *Proceedings of the Educational Studies Association* (1979) 1-10

Hubard, W.G. 'Intermediate education in Ireland' in *Fraser's*

Magazine 97 (March, 1878) 378-79

Joint Committee of Heads of Secondary Schools. 'Statement of Ireland's claim for exchequer grants in aid of secondary schools' in *Irish Educational Review* III/10 (July 1910) 633-37

Keating, Patrick. 'Sir Robert Kane and the museum of Irish industry' in *Proceedings of the Educational Studies Association* (1980) 276-286

Kelly, Timothy F. 'Education' in M. Hurley (ed.) *Irish Anglicanism 1869-1969* (Dublin: Figgis, 1970) 51-64

Mac Aodha, Brendán S. 'Was this a social revolution?' in Seán Ó Tuama (ed.) *The Gaelic League idea* Cork: Mercier, 1972, 11-30

MacCartney, Donal. 'Education and language 1938-51' in K.B. Nowlan, T.D. Williams (eds.) *Ireland in the war years and after, 1939-51* Dublin: Gill and Macmillan, 1969, 80-93

McDonagh, Kevin. 'The way the money goes — educational expenditure patterns' in *Oideas* 17 (1977) 5-96

McGee, Patrick. 'An examination of trends in reading achievement in Dublin over a ten-year period' in V. Greaney (ed.) *Aspects of reading* Dublin: Educational Company, 1977, 27-35

McKenna, Rev. L.S.J. 'The Catholic University of Ireland' in *The Irish Ecclesiastical Record* 5th Ser., XXXI (1928) 351-71

'State rights in Irish education' in *Studies* XVI (June, 1927) 115-130

MacNeill, Eoin. 'A view of the state in relation to education' in *The Irish Review* I/1 (October 1922) 3,4; I/3 (November, 1922) 28, 29

Mahaffy, J.P. 'How to circumvent cramming in Irish secondary schools' in *Nineteenth century* 44 (August, 1898) 867-880

Molloy, Rev. Gerard. 'Secondary education in Ireland' in *Irish Ecclesiastical Record* IV (1898) 481-503

Moody, T.W. 'The Irish university question of the nineteenth century' in *History* 43/148 (1958) 90-109

Ó Catháin, Rev. Seán. 'Education in the new Ireland' in F. Mac-Manus (ed.) *The years of the great test 1926-39* Cork: Mercier, 1969, 104-114

O'Connor, Seán. 'Post-primary education: now and in the future' in *Studies* LVII (Autumn, 1968) 233-49

Ó Cuiv, Brian. 'Education and language' in T.D. Williams (ed.) *The Irish struggle 1916-26* London: Routledge and Kegan Paul, 1960, 133-166

O'Rahilly, Alfred. 'The Irish university question' in *Studies* L (Autumn, 1961) 225-70; L (Winter, 1961) 353-70

Ó Raifeartaigh, T. 'Mixed education and the synod of Ulster 1831-40' in *Irish Historical Studies* IX (March, 1955) 281-99
'Changes and trends in our education system since 1922' in *Journal of the Statistical and Social Inquiry Society* XX (1957-58) 42-51

O'Riordan, Muiris. 'Technical vocational education, 1922-52: the cultural emphasis' in *Proceedings of the Educational Studies Association* (1977) 194-200

Osborough, N.W. 'Education in the Irish law and constitution' in *The Irish Jurist*, XII, new series (1978) 145-180

Parkes, Susan. 'The founding of a denominational training college — the Church of Ireland College, 1878-84' in *Proceedings of the Educational Studies Association* (1980) 74-84

Shaw, George F. 'How to improve school education in Ireland' in *Journal of the Statistical and Social Inquiry Society of Ireland* III (1863) 368-75

Tussing, A. Dale. 'Accountability, rationalisation and the white paper on educational development'. Script of paper delivered at the Statistical and Social Inquiry Society of Ireland, Cork, 13 March 1981

Wall, Maureen. 'The decline of the Irish language' in Brian Ó Cuiv (ed.) *A view of the Irish language* Dublin: Stationery Office, 1969, 81-90

Whyte, John H. 'Political problems, 1850-60' in P.J. Corish (ed.) *A history of Irish catholicism* Vol. V, Dublin: Gill, 1967, 1-39

9. Helpful references/guides for research students on modern Irish education

Hayes, Richard (ed.). *Sources for the history of Irish civilisation: articles in Irish periodicals*
Sources for the history of Irish civilisation: manuscript sources Boston: G.K. Hall, 1970

Maltby, Arthur and McKenna, Brian. *Ireland in the nineteenth century: a breviate of official publications.* Guides to official publications, vol. 4 Oxford: Pergamon Press, 1979 (Education, pp. 163-190)

A guide to Irish official publications with a breviate of reports, 1922-72. Guides to official publications, vol. 7, Oxford: Pergamon Press, 1980

Parkes, Susan. *Irish education in the British parliamentary papers in the nineteenth century and after 1801-1922* Cork: History of Education Society and Cork University Press, 1978

Educational Studies Association of Ireland. *Register of theses on educational topics in universities in Ireland* Galway: Officina Typographica, 1980

On-going publications specialising in articles of educational interest:

Curriculum Development Association. *Compass*

Department of Education. *Oideas*

Educational Research Centre. *Irish Journal of Education*

Educational Studies Association of Ireland. *Annual Proceedings* (from 1981 to be called *Irish Educational Studies*)

Reading Association of Ireland. *Annual Proceedings.*

Index